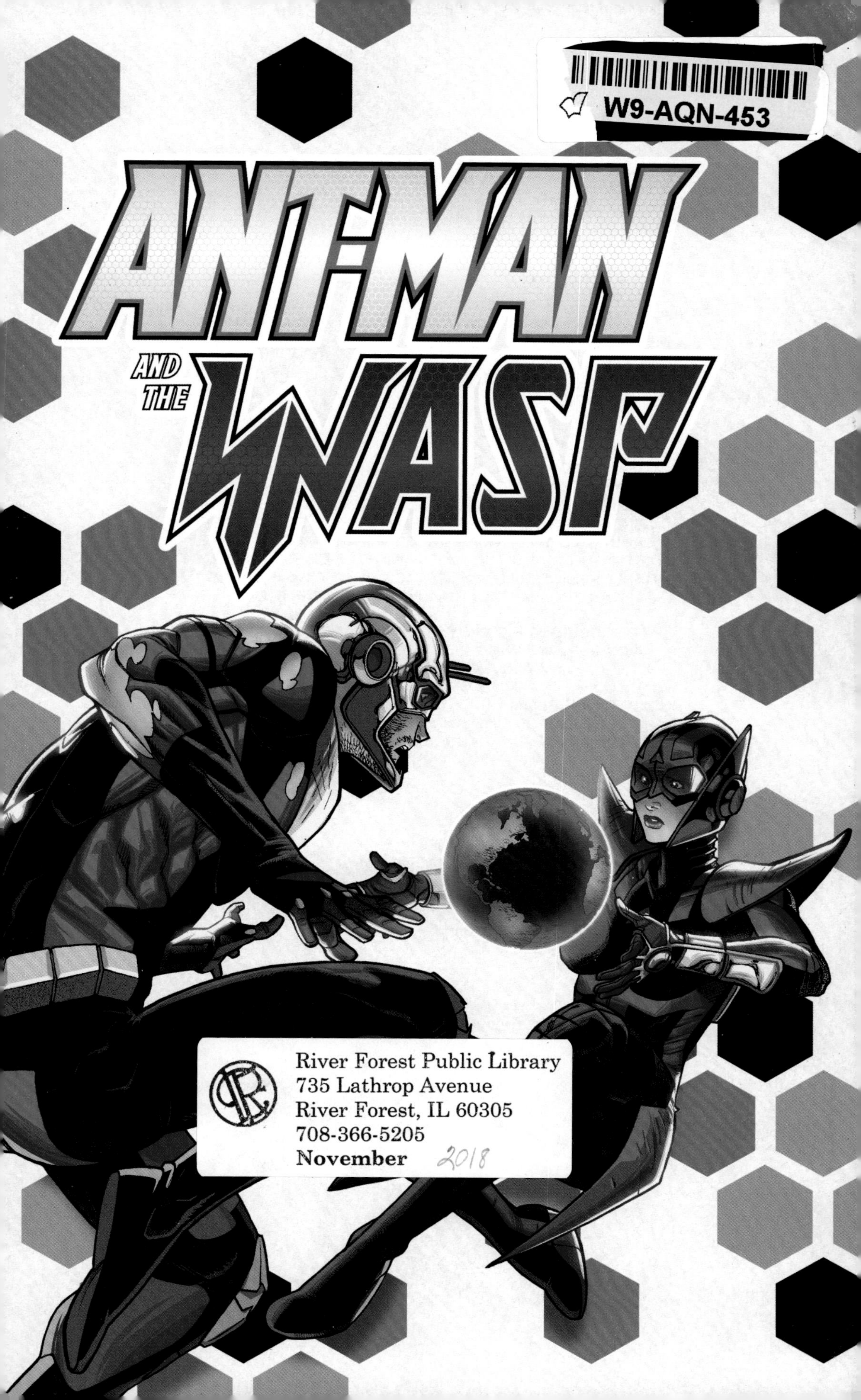
ANT-MAN
AND THE WASP

WHEN THE ORIGINAL ANT-MAN, HANK PYM, RETIRED FROM THE JOB, ELECTRONICS TECHNICIAN/BURGLAR SCOTT LANG STOLE THE COSTUME TO SAVE HIS DAUGHTER. BUT WHEN TRUE VILLAINY REARED ITS HEAD, SCOTT ROSE/SHRUNK TO THE OCCASION, PROVING HIMSELF WORTHY OF THE TECH AND THE NAME. WITH HIS CHECKERED PAST MOSTLY BEHIND HIM, SCOTT TOOK ON THE SIZE-CHANGING, ANT-COMMUNICATING ABILITIES OF ANT-MAN!

TEEN SCIENCE PRODIGY NADIA ESCAPED THE RUSSIAN ASSASSIN-TRAINING RED ROOM TO SEARCH FOR HER FATHER, HANK PYM, IN THE UNITED STATES. HIS FORMER WIFE, JANET VAN DYNE, BECAME NADIA'S STEPMOTHER AND HELPED HER CLAIM HER TRUE INHERITANCE: HER FATHER'S SHRINKING TECHNOLOGY AND HEROISM. IN JANET'S HONOR, NADIA WEARS THE MANTLE OF THE WASP!

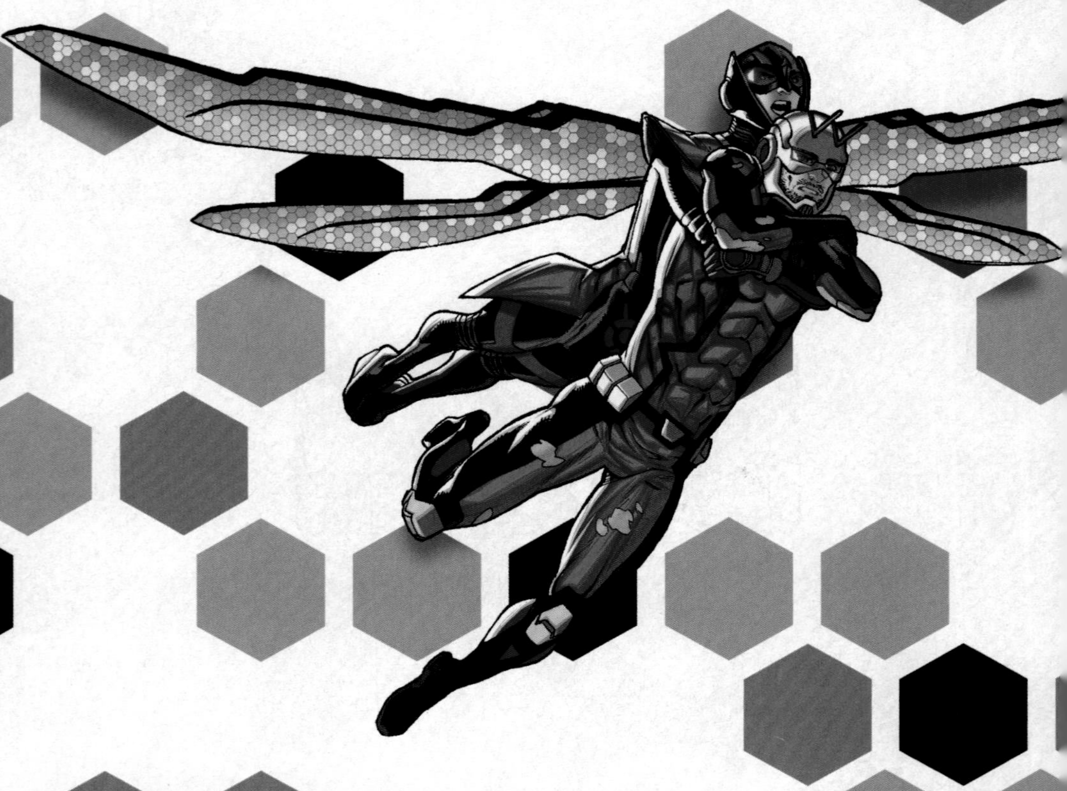

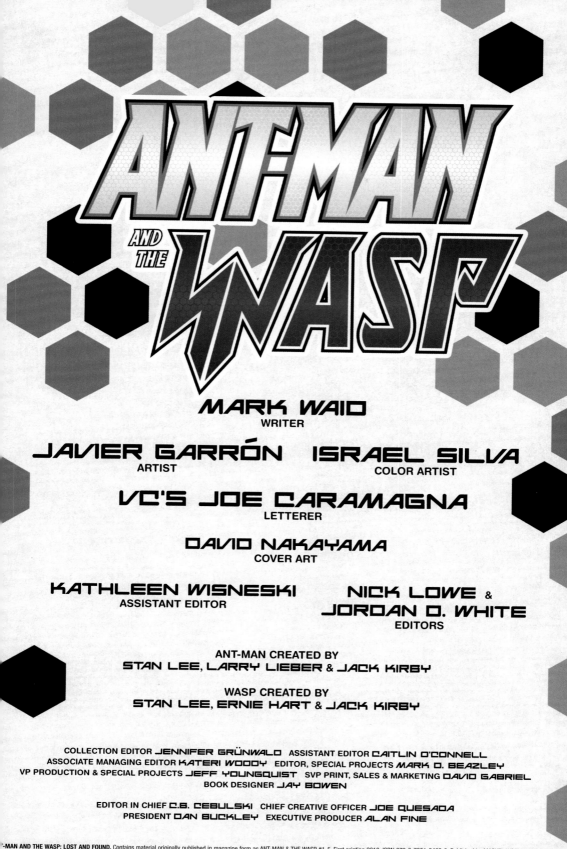

ANT-MAN AND THE WASP

MARK WAID
WRITER

JAVIER GARRÓN
ARTIST

ISRAEL SILVA
COLOR ARTIST

VC'S JOE CARAMAGNA
LETTERER

DAVID NAKAYAMA
COVER ART

KATHLEEN WISNESKI
ASSISTANT EDITOR

NICK LOWE &
JORDAN D. WHITE
EDITORS

ANT-MAN CREATED BY
STAN LEE, LARRY LIEBER & JACK KIRBY

WASP CREATED BY
STAN LEE, ERNIE HART & JACK KIRBY

COLLECTION EDITOR JENNIFER GRÜNWALD ASSISTANT EDITOR CAITLIN O'CONNELL
ASSOCIATE MANAGING EDITOR KATERI WOODY EDITOR, SPECIAL PROJECTS MARK D. BEAZLEY
VP PRODUCTION & SPECIAL PROJECTS JEFF YOUNGQUIST SVP PRINT, SALES & MARKETING DAVID GABRIEL
BOOK DESIGNER JAY BOWEN

EDITOR IN CHIEF C.B. CEBULSKI CHIEF CREATIVE OFFICER JOE QUESADA
PRESIDENT DAN BUCKLEY EXECUTIVE PRODUCER ALAN FINE

-MAN AND THE WASP: LOST AND FOUND. Contains material originally published in magazine form as ANT-MAN & THE WASP #1-5. First printing 2018. ISBN 978-0-7851-9462-0. Published by MARVEL WORLDWIDE, INC., a sidiary of MARVEL ENTERTAINMENT, LLC. OFFICE OF PUBLICATION: 135 West 50th Street, New York, NY 10020. Copyright © 2018 MARVEL No similarity between any of the names, characters, persons, and/or institutions in this azine with those of any living or dead person or institution is intended, and any such similarity which may exist is purely coincidental. **Printed in Canada.** DAN BUCKLEY, President, Marvel Entertainment; JOHN NEE, Publisher; QUESADA, Chief Creative Officer; TOM BREVOORT, SVP of Publishing; DAVID BOGART, SVP of Business Affairs & Operations, Publishing & Partnership; DAVID GABRIEL, SVP of Sales & Marketing, Publishing; JEFF YOUNGQUIST, VP of uction & Special Projects; DAN CARR, Executive Director of Publishing Technology; ALEX MORALES, Director of Publishing Operations; DAN EDINGTON, Managing Editor; SUSAN CRESPI, Production Manager; STAN LEE, Chairman ritus. For information regarding advertising in Marvel Comics or on Marvel.com, please contact Vit DeBellis, Custom Solutions & Integrated Advertising Manager, at vdebellis@marvel.com. For Marvel subscription inquiries, please 888-511-5480. **Manufactured between 9/14/2018 and 10/16/2018 by SOLISCO PRINTERS, SCOTT, QC, CANADA.**

87654321

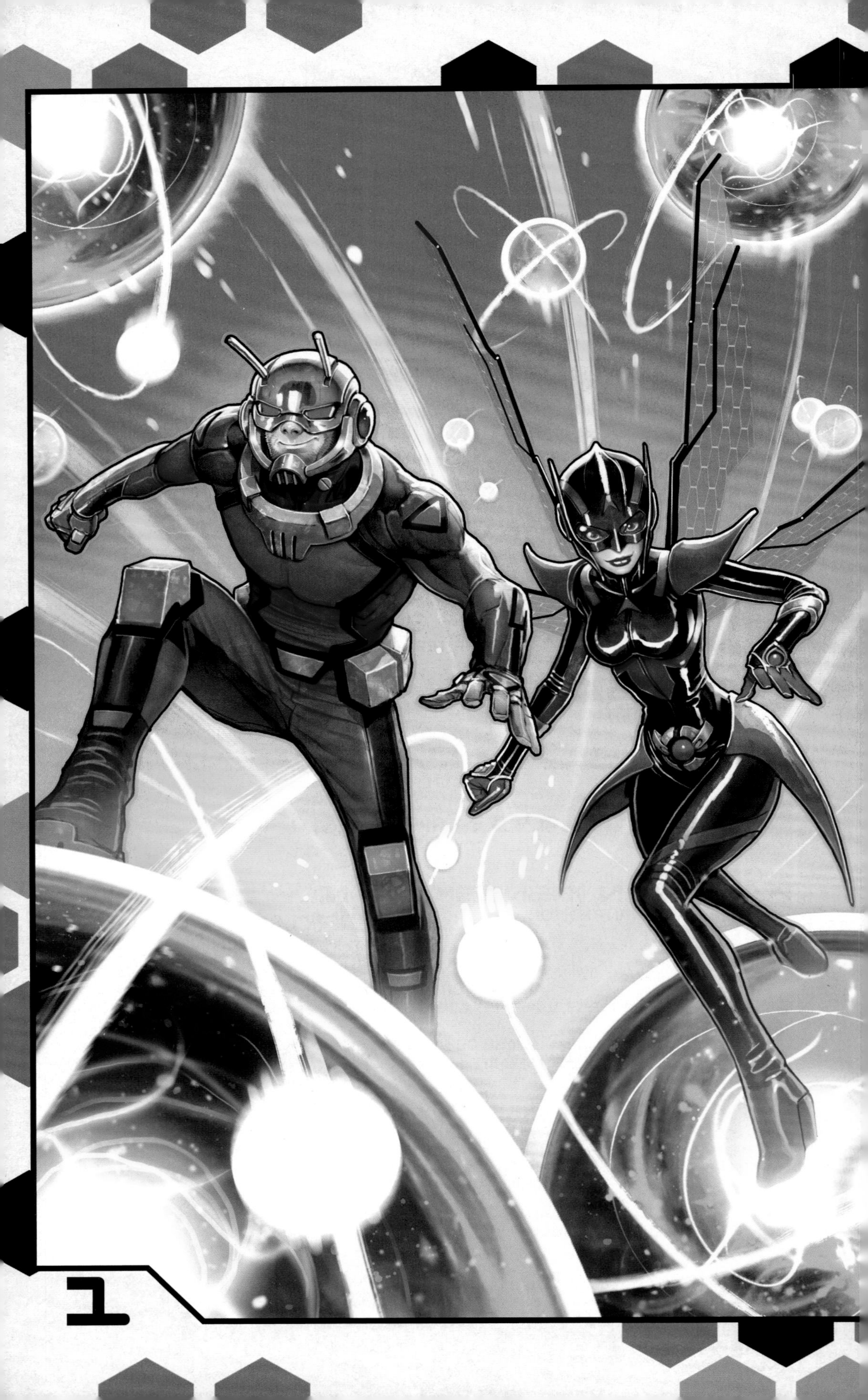
1

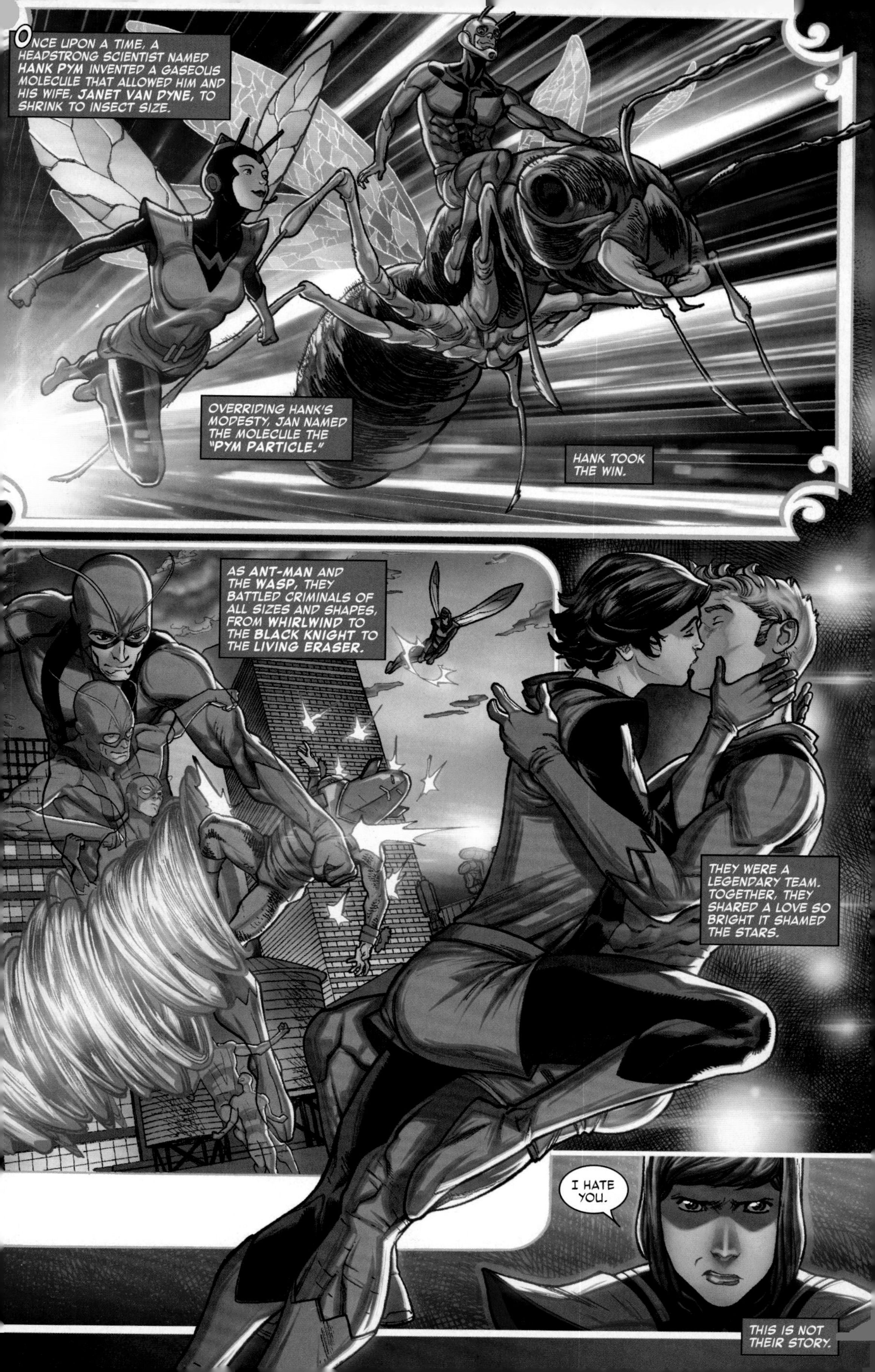
ONCE UPON A TIME, A HEADSTRONG SCIENTIST NAMED HANK PYM INVENTED A GASEOUS MOLECULE THAT ALLOWED HIM AND HIS WIFE, JANET VAN DYNE, TO SHRINK TO INSECT SIZE.
OVERRIDING HANK'S MODESTY, JAN NAMED THE MOLECULE THE "PYM PARTICLE."
HANK TOOK THE WIN.
AS ANT-MAN AND THE WASP, THEY BATTLED CRIMINALS OF ALL SIZES AND SHAPES, FROM WHIRLWIND TO THE BLACK KNIGHT TO THE LIVING ERASER.
THEY WERE A LEGENDARY TEAM. TOGETHER, THEY SHARED A LOVE SO BRIGHT IT SHAMED THE STARS.
I HATE YOU.
THIS IS NOT THEIR STORY.

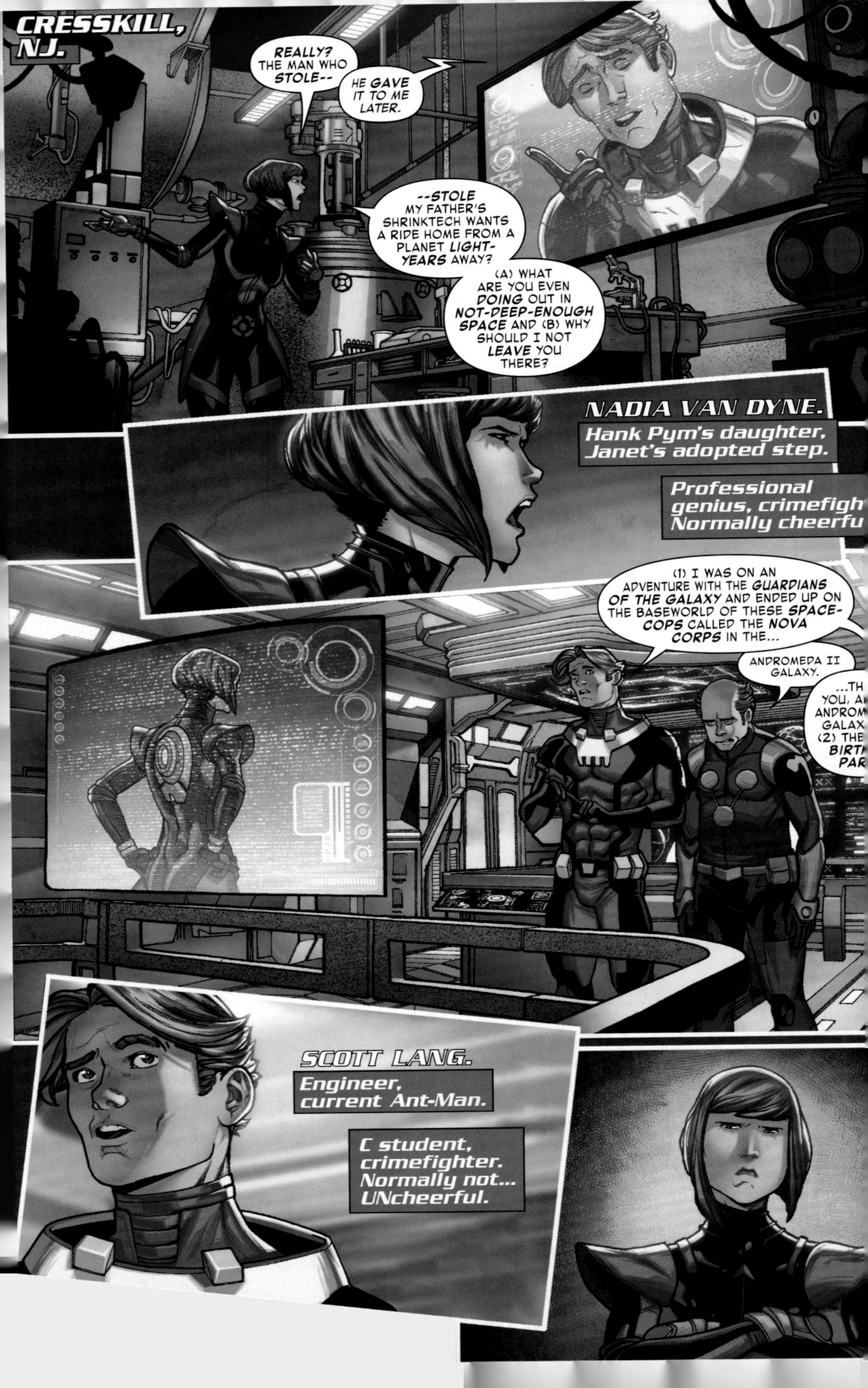
CRESSKILL, NJ.
REALLY? THE MAN WHO STOLE--
HE GAVE IT TO ME LATER.
--STOLE MY FATHER'S SHRINKTECH WANTS A RIDE HOME FROM A PLANET LIGHT-YEARS AWAY?
(A) WHAT ARE YOU EVEN DOING OUT IN NOT-DEEP-ENOUGH SPACE AND (B) WHY SHOULD I NOT LEAVE YOU THERE?
NADIA VAN DYNE.
Hank Pym's daughter, Janet's adopted step.
Professional genius, crimefigh
Normally cheerfu
(1) I WAS ON AN ADVENTURE WITH THE GUARDIANS OF THE GALAXY AND ENDED UP ON THE BASEWORLD OF THESE SPACE-COPS CALLED THE NOVA CORPS IN THE...
ANDROMEDA II GALAXY.
...TH YOU, A ANDROM GALAX (2) THE BIRT PAR
SCOTT LANG.
Engineer, current Ant-Man.
C student, crimefighter. Normally not... UNcheerful.

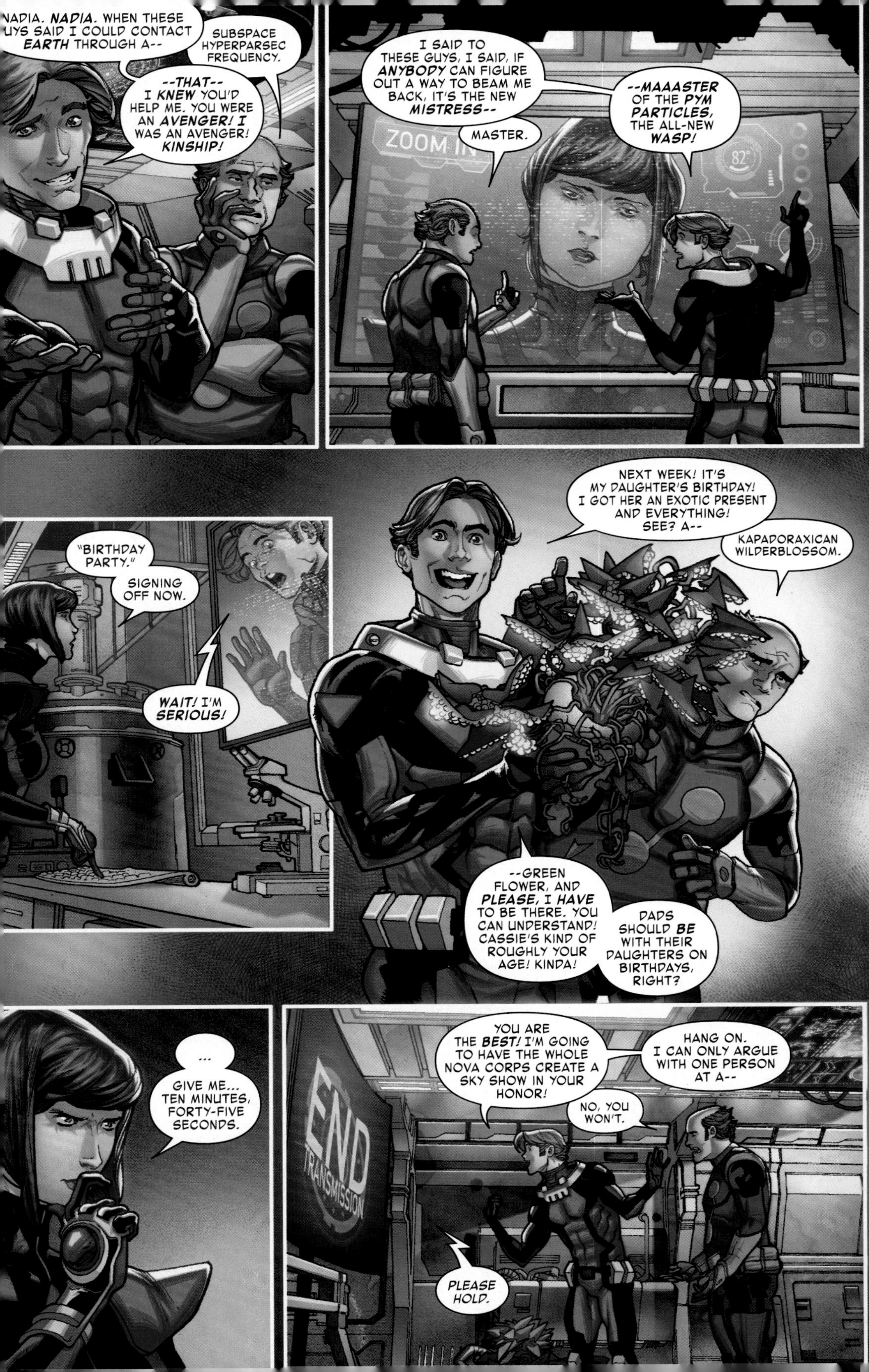
NADIA. NADIA. WHEN THESE GUYS SAID I COULD CONTACT EARTH THROUGH A--
SUBSPACE HYPERPARSEC FREQUENCY.
--THAT-- I KNEW YOU'D HELP ME. YOU WERE AN AVENGER! I WAS AN AVENGER! KINSHIP!
I SAID TO THESE GUYS, I SAID, IF ANYBODY CAN FIGURE OUT A WAY TO BEAM ME BACK, IT'S THE NEW MISTRESS--
MASTER.
--MAAASTER OF THE PYM PARTICLES, THE ALL-NEW WASP!
ZOOM IN
82°
NEXT WEEK! IT'S MY DAUGHTER'S BIRTHDAY! I GOT HER AN EXOTIC PRESENT AND EVERYTHING! SEE? A--
KAPADORAXICAN WILDERBLOSSOM.
"BIRTHDAY PARTY."
SIGNING OFF NOW.
WAIT! I'M SERIOUS!
--GREEN FLOWER, AND PLEASE, I HAVE TO BE THERE. YOU CAN UNDERSTAND! CASSIE'S KIND OF ROUGHLY YOUR AGE! KINDA!
DADS SHOULD BE WITH THEIR DAUGHTERS ON BIRTHDAYS, RIGHT?
...
GIVE ME... TEN MINUTES, FORTY-FIVE SECONDS.
END TRANSMISSION
YOU ARE THE BEST! I'M GOING TO HAVE THE WHOLE NOVA CORPS CREATE A SKY SHOW IN YOUR HONOR!
HANG ON. I CAN ONLY ARGUE WITH ONE PERSON AT A--
NO, YOU WON'T.
PLEASE HOLD.

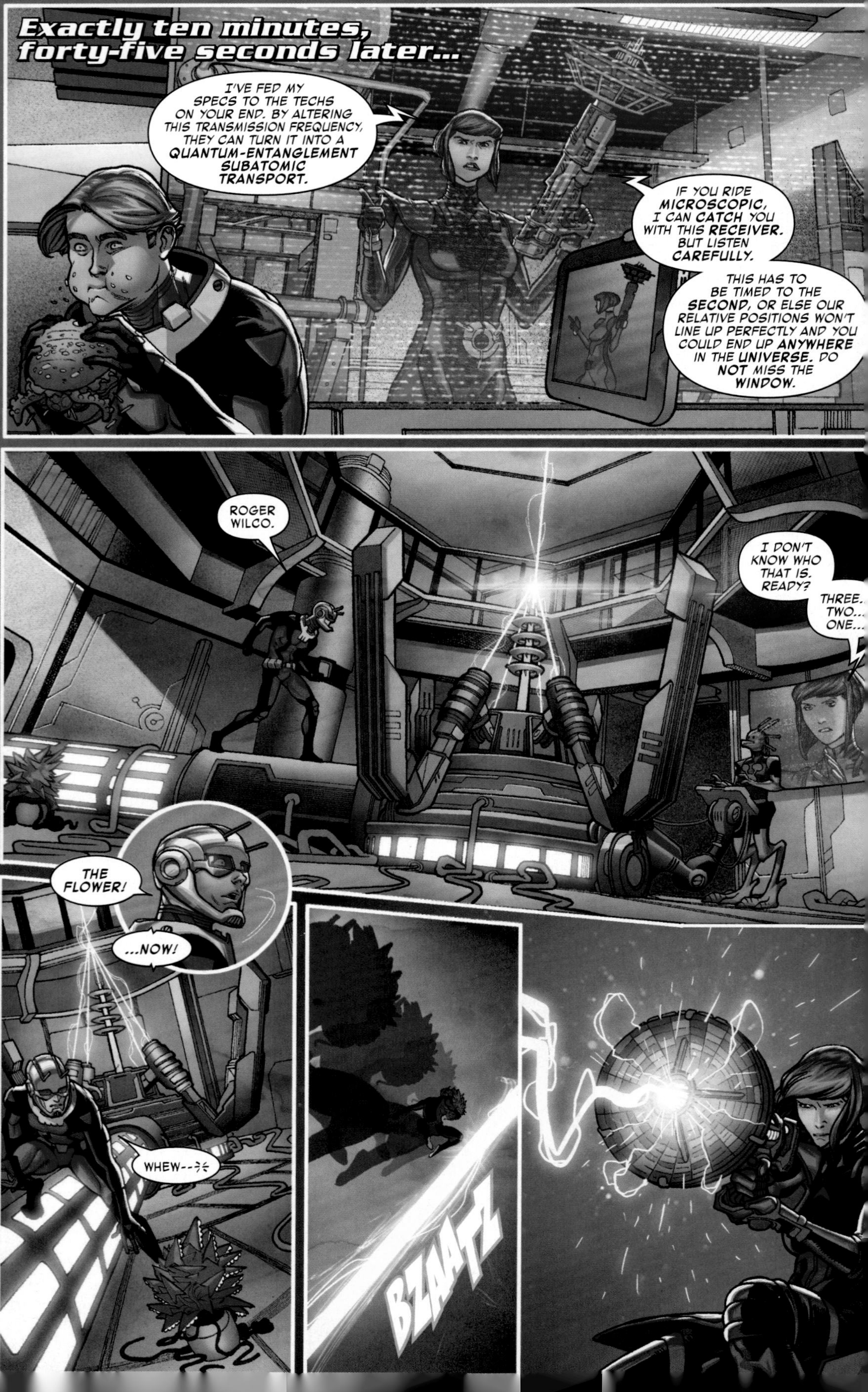
Exactly ten minutes, forty-five seconds later...
I'VE FED MY SPECS TO THE TECHS ON YOUR END. BY ALTERING THIS TRANSMISSION FREQUENCY, THEY CAN TURN IT INTO A QUANTUM-ENTANGLEMENT SUBATOMIC TRANSPORT.
IF YOU RIDE MICROSCOPIC, I CAN CATCH YOU WITH THIS RECEIVER. BUT LISTEN CAREFULLY.
THIS HAS TO BE TIMED TO THE SECOND, OR ELSE OUR RELATIVE POSITIONS WON'T LINE UP PERFECTLY AND YOU COULD END UP ANYWHERE IN THE UNIVERSE. DO NOT MISS THE WINDOW.
ROGER WILCO.
I DON'T KNOW WHO THAT IS. READY?
THREE... TWO... ONE...
THE FLOWER!
...NOW!
WHEW--
BZAATZ

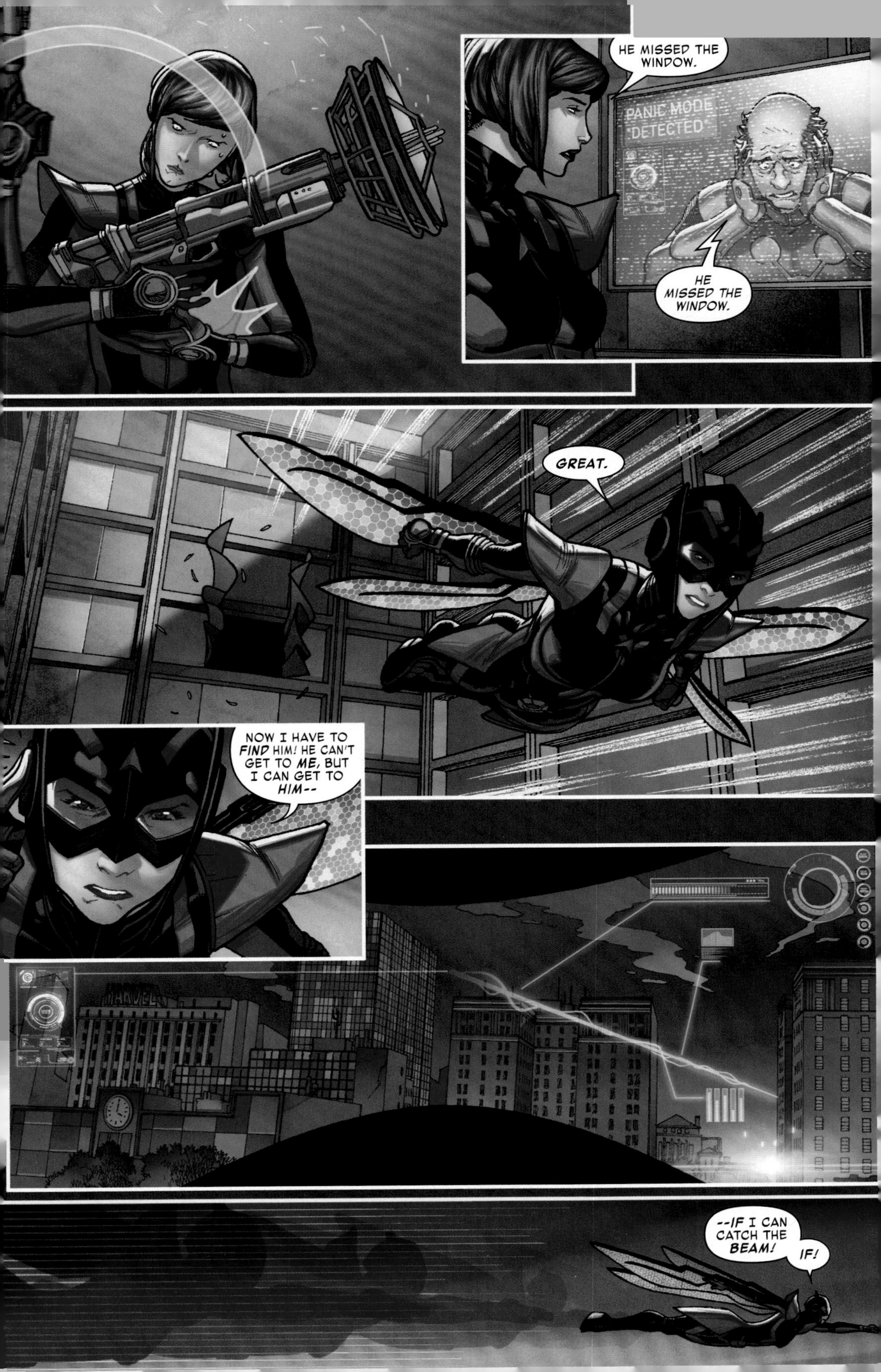
HE MISSED THE WINDOW.
PANIC MODE DETECTED
HE MISSED THE WINDOW.
GREAT.
NOW I HAVE TO FIND HIM! HE CAN'T GET TO ME, BUT I CAN GET TO HIM--
MARVEL
--IF I CAN CATCH THE BEAM!
IF!

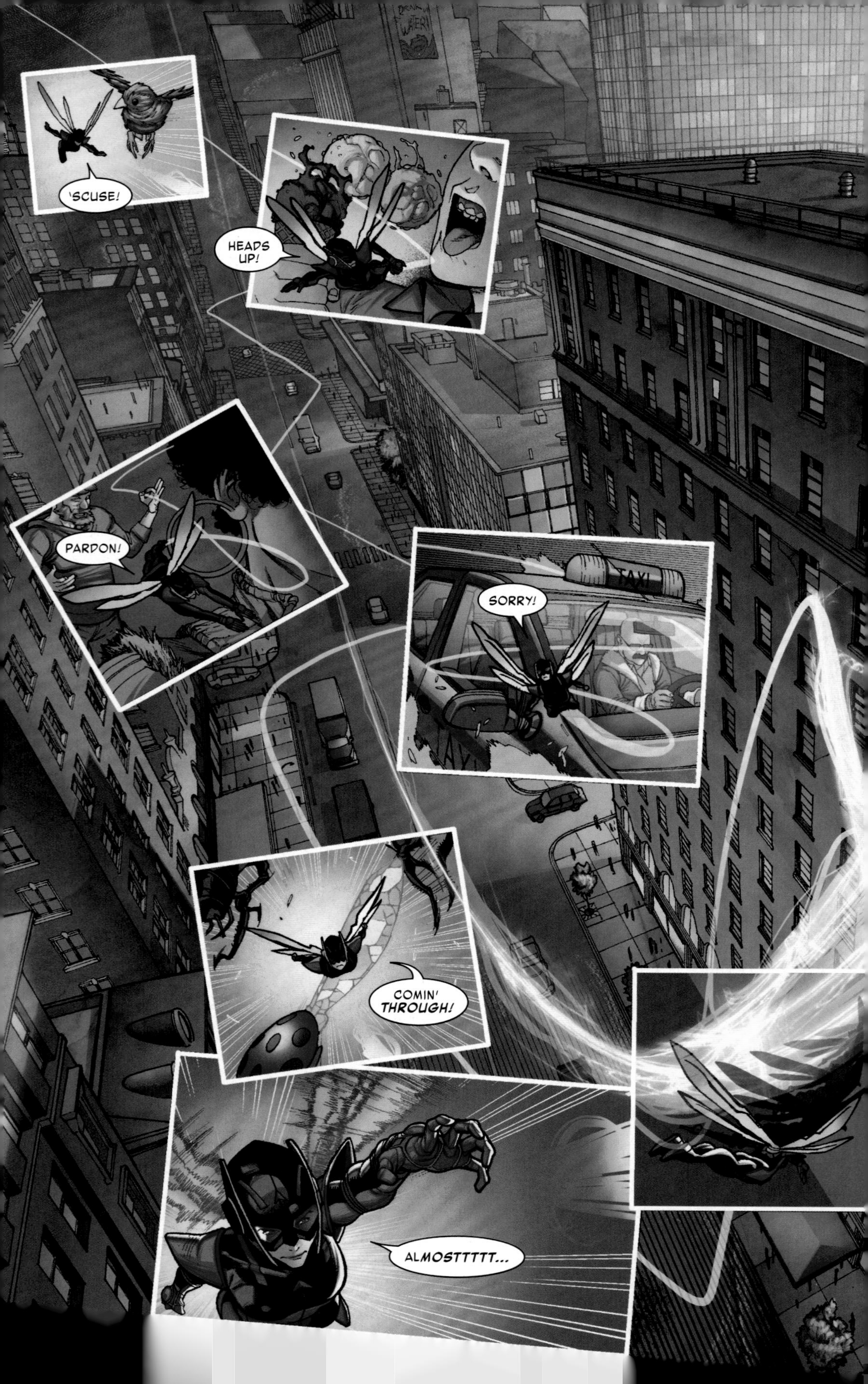
'SCUSE!
HEADS UP!
PARDON!
SORRY!
COMIN' THROUGH!
ALMOSTTTTT...

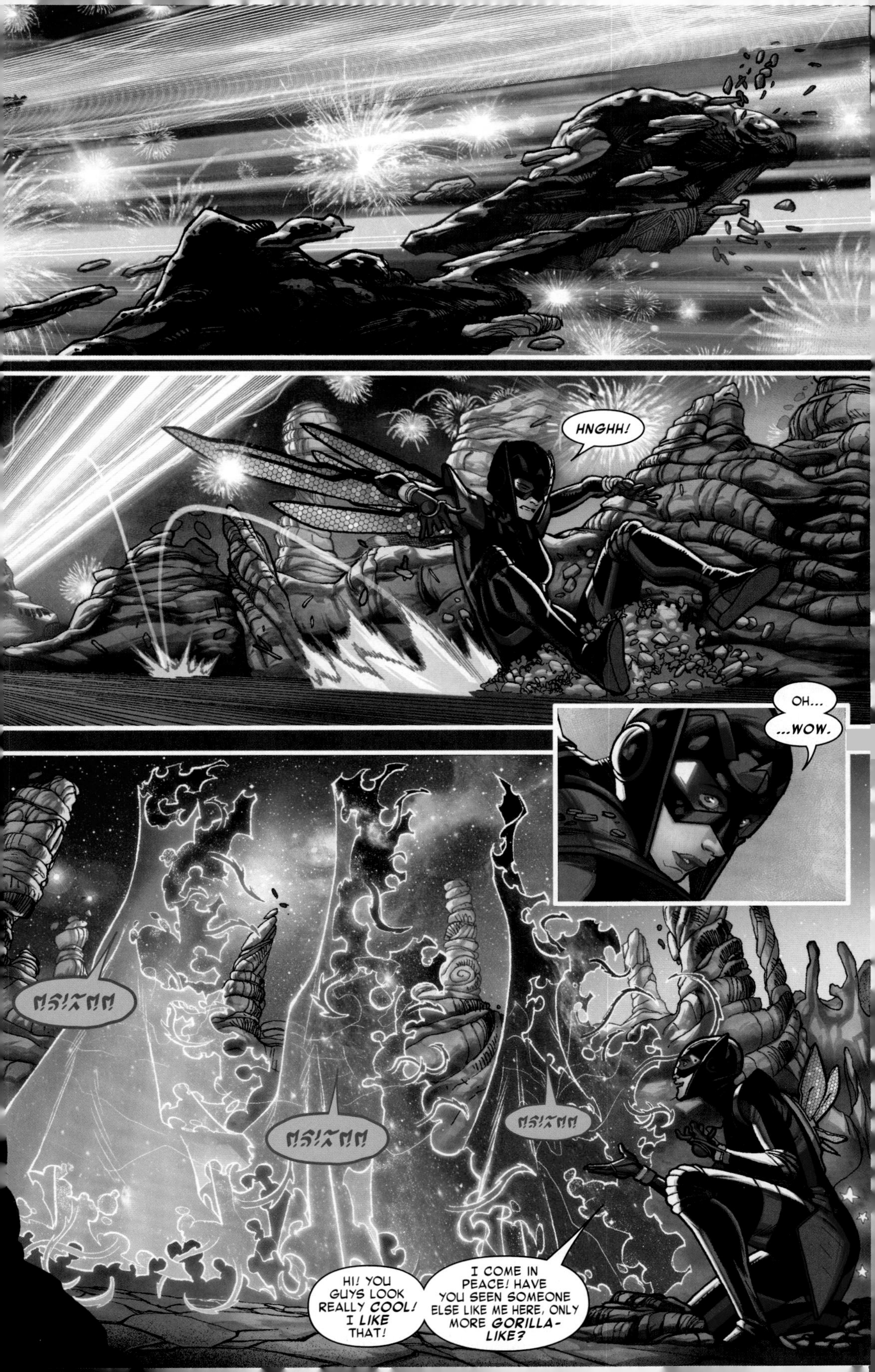
HNGHH!
OH...
...WOW.
HI! YOU GUYS LOOK REALLY COOL! I LIKE THAT!
I COME IN PEACE! HAVE YOU SEEN SOMEONE ELSE LIKE ME HERE, ONLY MORE GORILLA-LIKE?

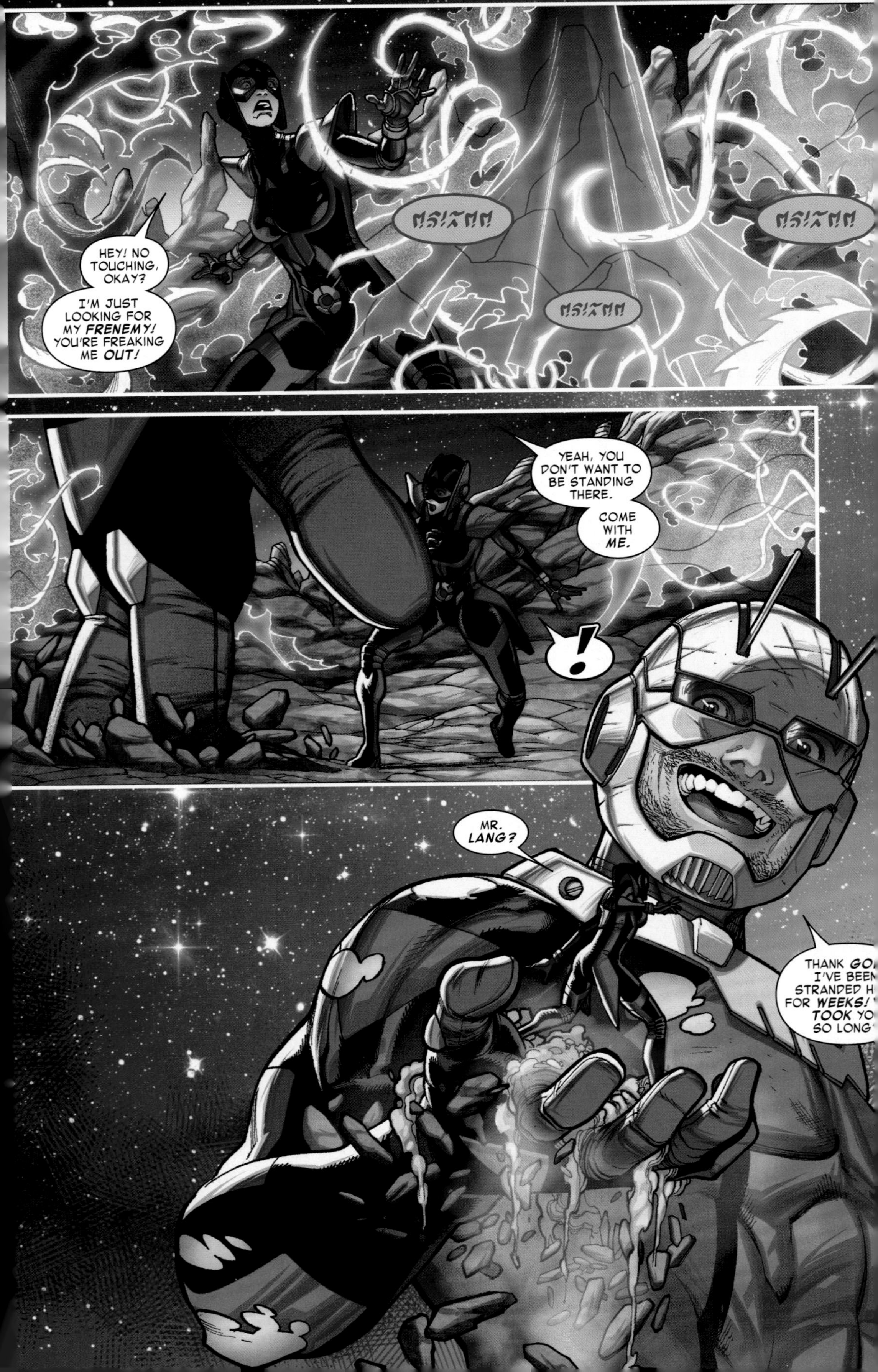
HEY! NO TOUCHING, OKAY?
I'M JUST LOOKING FOR MY FRENEMY! YOU'RE FREAKING ME OUT!
YEAH, YOU DON'T WANT TO BE STANDING THERE.
COME WITH ME.
!
MR. LANG?

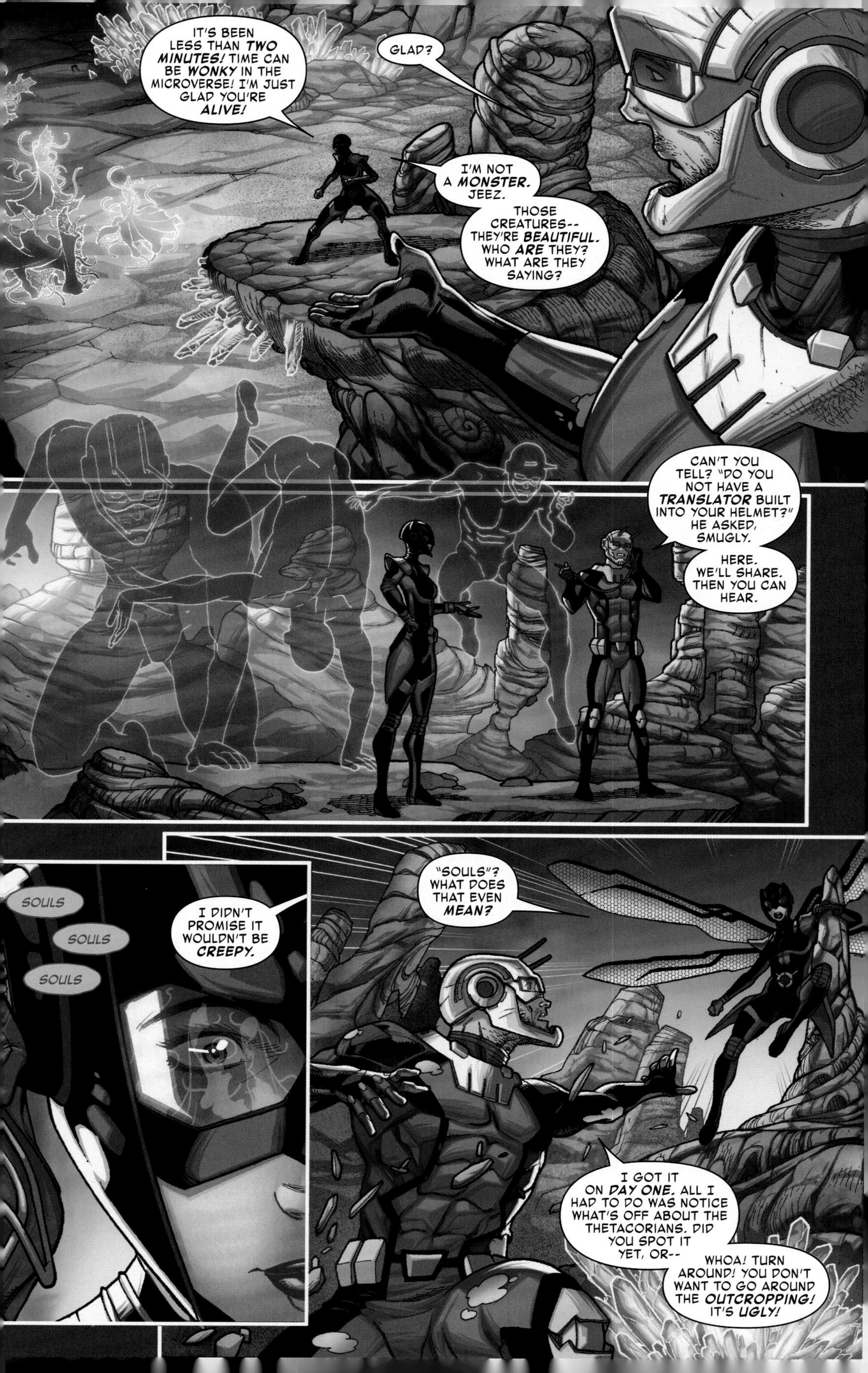

IT'S BEEN LESS THAN TWO MINUTES! TIME CAN BE WONKY IN THE MICROVERSE! I'M JUST GLAD YOU'RE ALIVE!
GLAD?
I'M NOT A MONSTER. JEEZ.
THOSE CREATURES-- THEY'RE BEAUTIFUL. WHO ARE THEY? WHAT ARE THEY SAYING?
CAN'T YOU TELL? "DO YOU NOT HAVE A TRANSLATOR BUILT INTO YOUR HELMET?" HE ASKED, SMUGLY.
HERE. WE'LL SHARE. THEN YOU CAN HEAR.
SOULS
SOULS
SOULS
I DIDN'T PROMISE IT WOULDN'T BE CREEPY.
"SOULS"? WHAT DOES THAT EVEN MEAN?
I GOT IT ON DAY ONE. ALL I HAD TO DO WAS NOTICE WHAT'S OFF ABOUT THE THETACORIANS. DID YOU SPOT IT YET, OR--
WHOA! TURN AROUND! YOU DON'T WANT TO GO AROUND THE OUTCROPPING! IT'S UGLY!

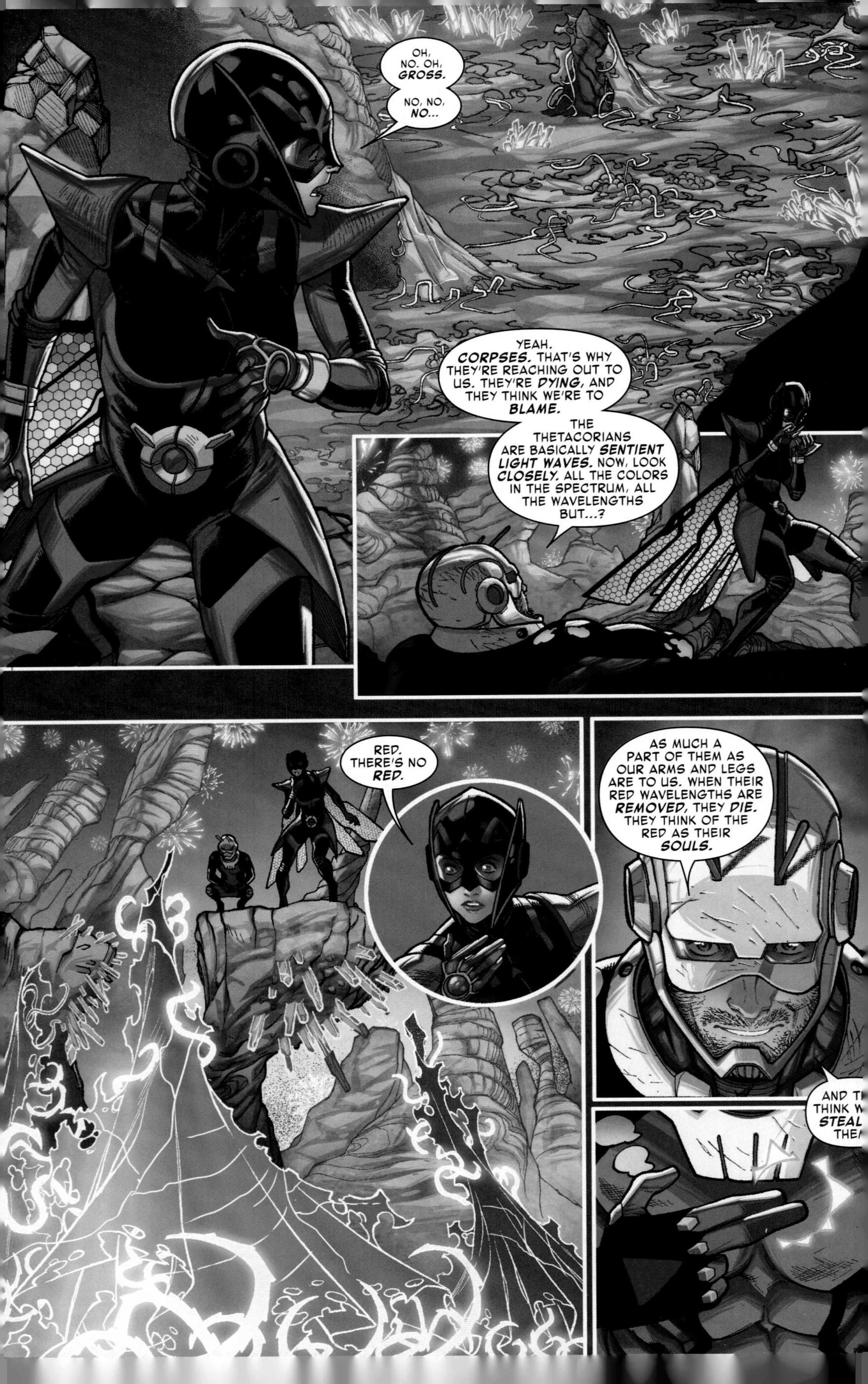
OH, NO. OH, GROSS.
NO, NO, NO...
YEAH. CORPSES. THAT'S WHY THEY'RE REACHING OUT TO US. THEY'RE DYING, AND THEY THINK WE'RE TO BLAME.
THE THETACORIANS ARE BASICALLY SENTIENT LIGHT WAVES. NOW, LOOK CLOSELY. ALL THE COLORS IN THE SPECTRUM, ALL THE WAVELENGTHS BUT...?
RED. THERE'S NO RED.
AS MUCH A PART OF THEM AS OUR ARMS AND LEGS ARE TO US. WHEN THEIR RED WAVELENGTHS ARE REMOVED, THEY DIE. THEY THINK OF THE RED AS THEIR SOULS.
AND T
THINK W
STEAL

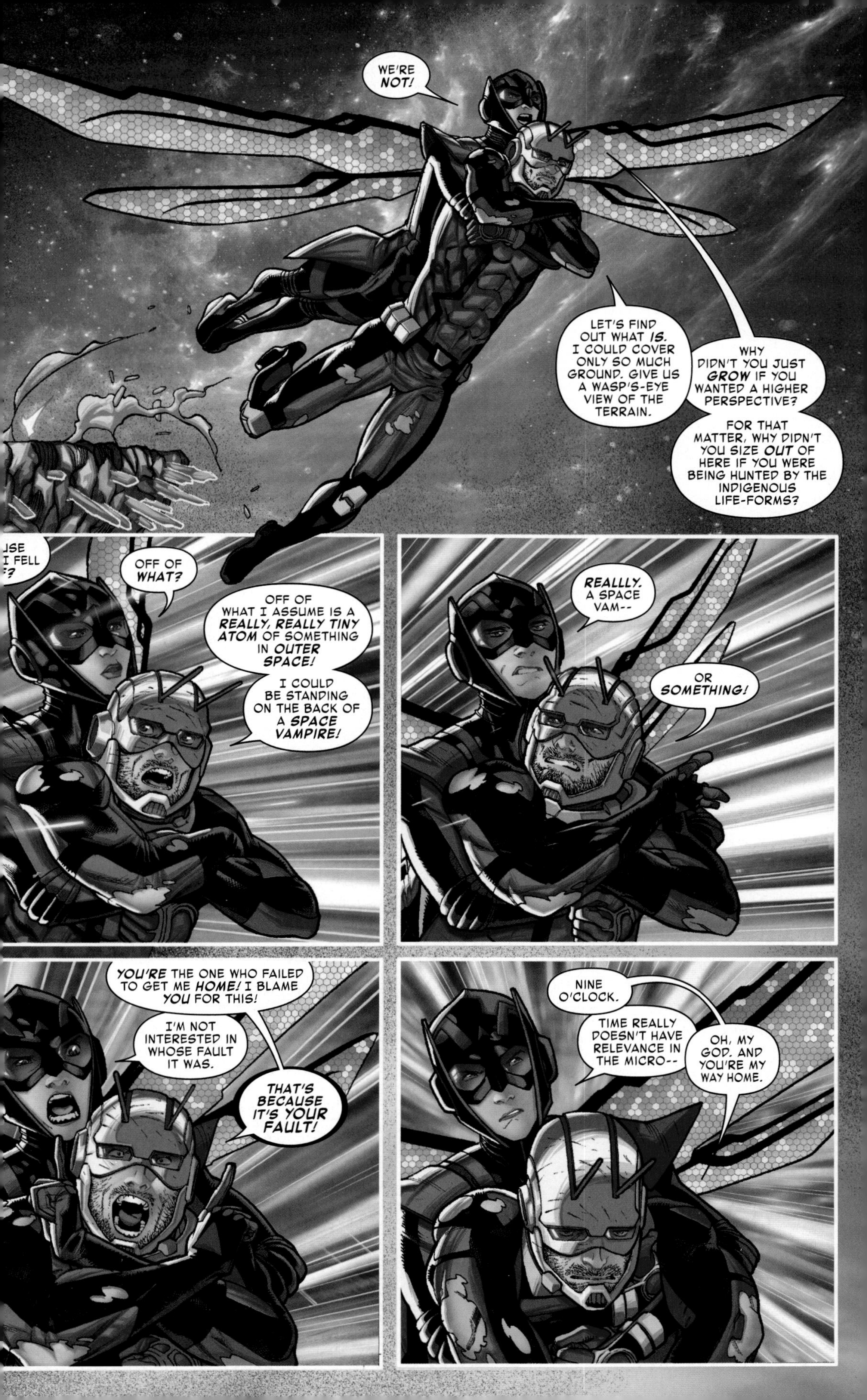

WE'RE NOT!
LET'S FIND OUT WHAT IS. I COULD COVER ONLY SO MUCH GROUND. GIVE US A WASP'S-EYE VIEW OF THE TERRAIN.
WHY DIDN'T YOU JUST GROW IF YOU WANTED A HIGHER PERSPECTIVE?
FOR THAT MATTER, WHY DIDN'T YOU SIZE OUT OF HERE IF YOU WERE BEING HUNTED BY THE INDIGENOUS LIFE-FORMS?
I FELL
OFF OF WHAT?
OFF OF WHAT I ASSUME IS A REALLY, REALLY TINY ATOM OF SOMETHING IN OUTER SPACE!
I COULD BE STANDING ON THE BACK OF A SPACE VAMPIRE!
REALLLY. A SPACE VAM--
OR SOMETHING!
YOU'RE THE ONE WHO FAILED TO GET ME HOME! I BLAME YOU FOR THIS!
I'M NOT INTERESTED IN WHOSE FAULT IT WAS.
THAT'S BECAUSE IT'S YOUR FAULT!
NINE O'CLOCK.
TIME REALLY DOESN'T HAVE RELEVANCE IN THE MICRO--
OH, MY GOD. AND YOU'RE MY WAY HOME.

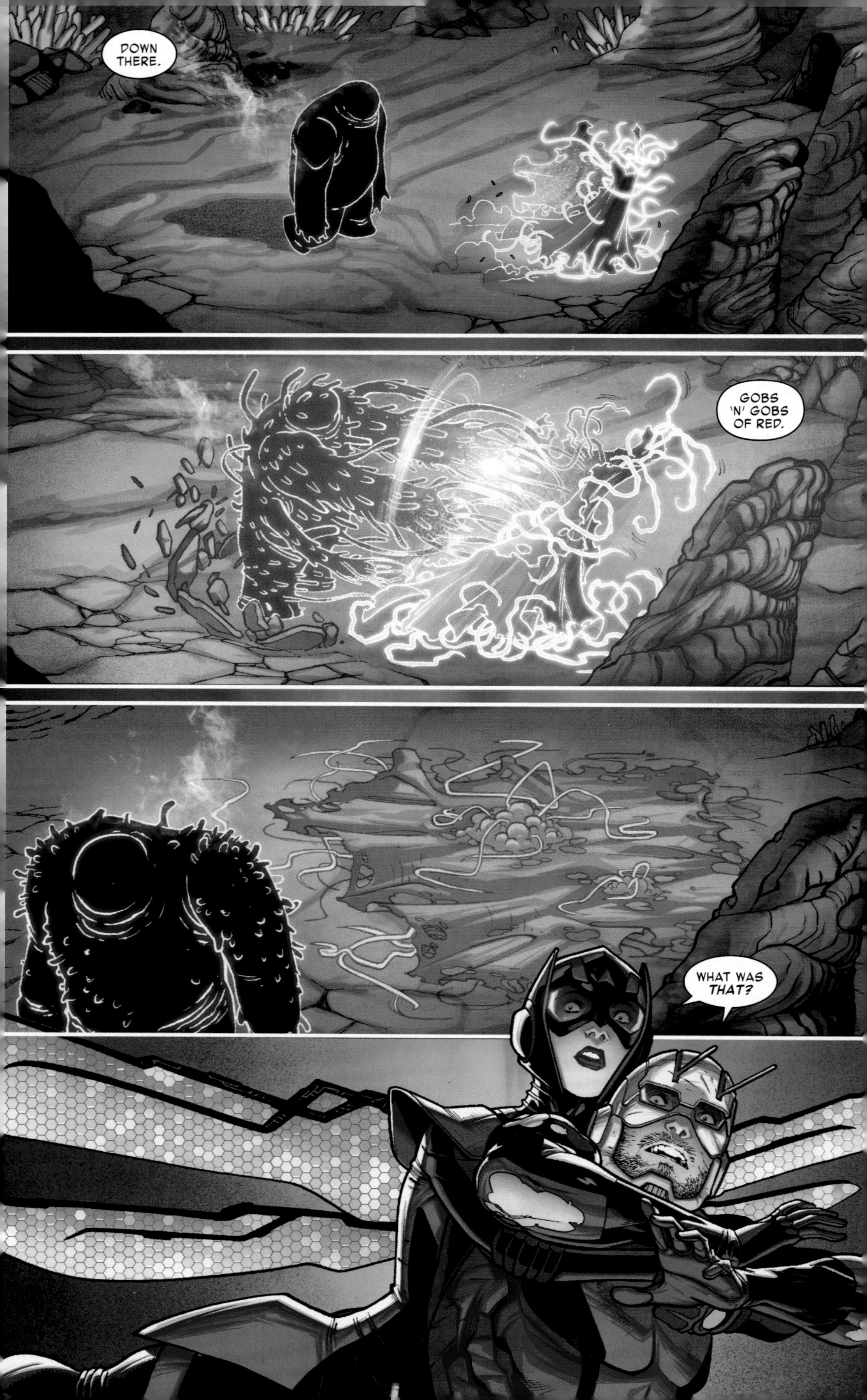
DOWN THERE.
GOBS 'N' GOBS OF RED.
WHAT WAS THAT?

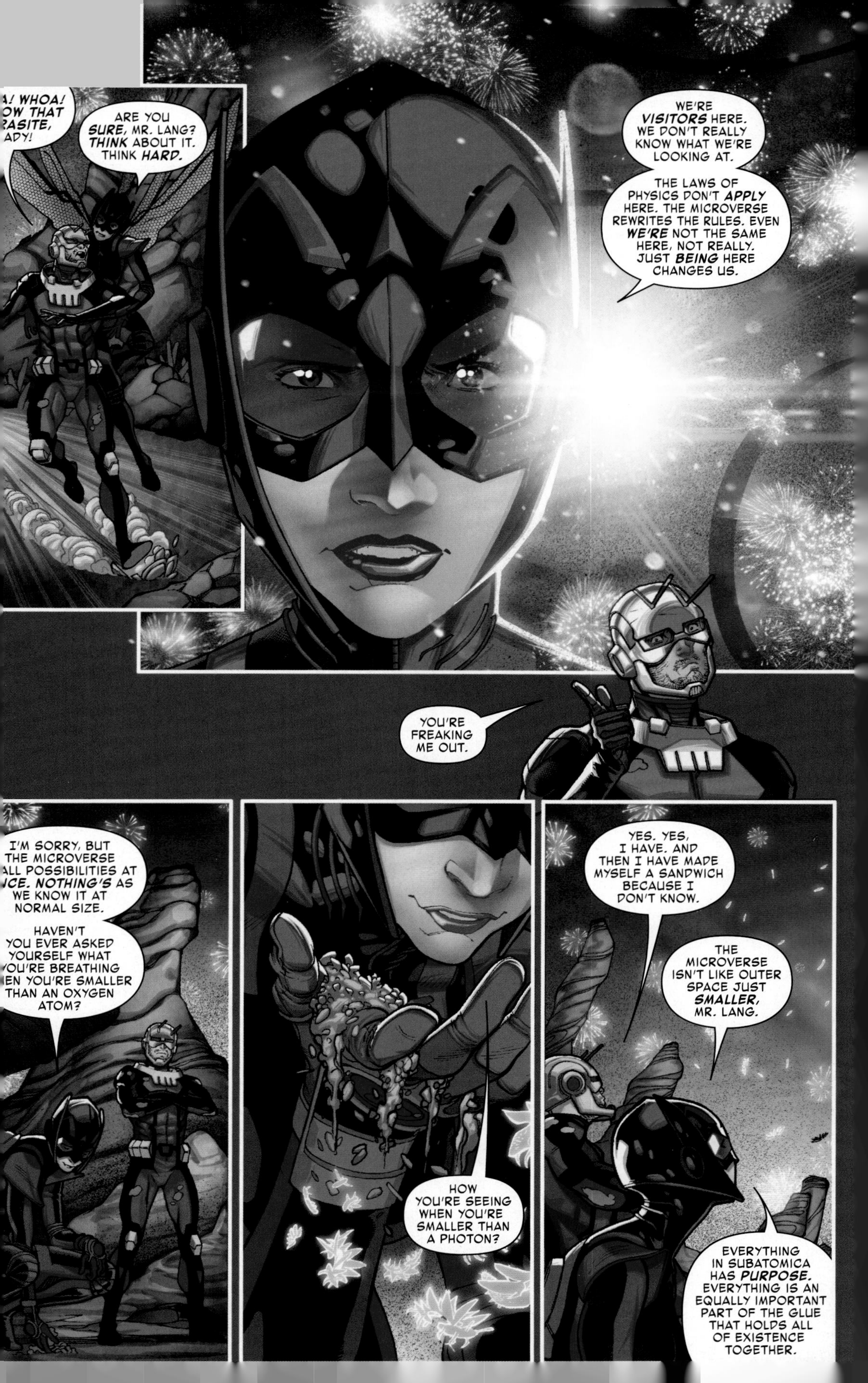

A! WHOA! OW THAT RASITE, ADY!
ARE YOU SURE, MR. LANG? THINK ABOUT IT. THINK HARD.
WE'RE VISITORS HERE. WE DON'T REALLY KNOW WHAT WE'RE LOOKING AT.
THE LAWS OF PHYSICS DON'T APPLY HERE. THE MICROVERSE REWRITES THE RULES. EVEN WE'RE NOT THE SAME HERE, NOT REALLY. JUST BEING HERE CHANGES US.
YOU'RE FREAKING ME OUT.
I'M SORRY, BUT THE MICROVERSE ALL POSSIBILITIES AT ICE. NOTHING'S AS WE KNOW IT AT NORMAL SIZE.
HAVEN'T YOU EVER ASKED YOURSELF WHAT YOU'RE BREATHING IEN YOU'RE SMALLER THAN AN OXYGEN ATOM?
HOW YOU'RE SEEING WHEN YOU'RE SMALLER THAN A PHOTON?
YES. YES, I HAVE. AND THEN I HAVE MADE MYSELF A SANDWICH BECAUSE I DON'T KNOW.
THE MICROVERSE ISN'T LIKE OUTER SPACE JUST SMALLER, MR. LANG.
EVERYTHING IN SUBATOMICA HAS PURPOSE. EVERYTHING IS AN EQUALLY IMPORTANT PART OF THE GLUE THAT HOLDS ALL OF EXISTENCE TOGETHER.

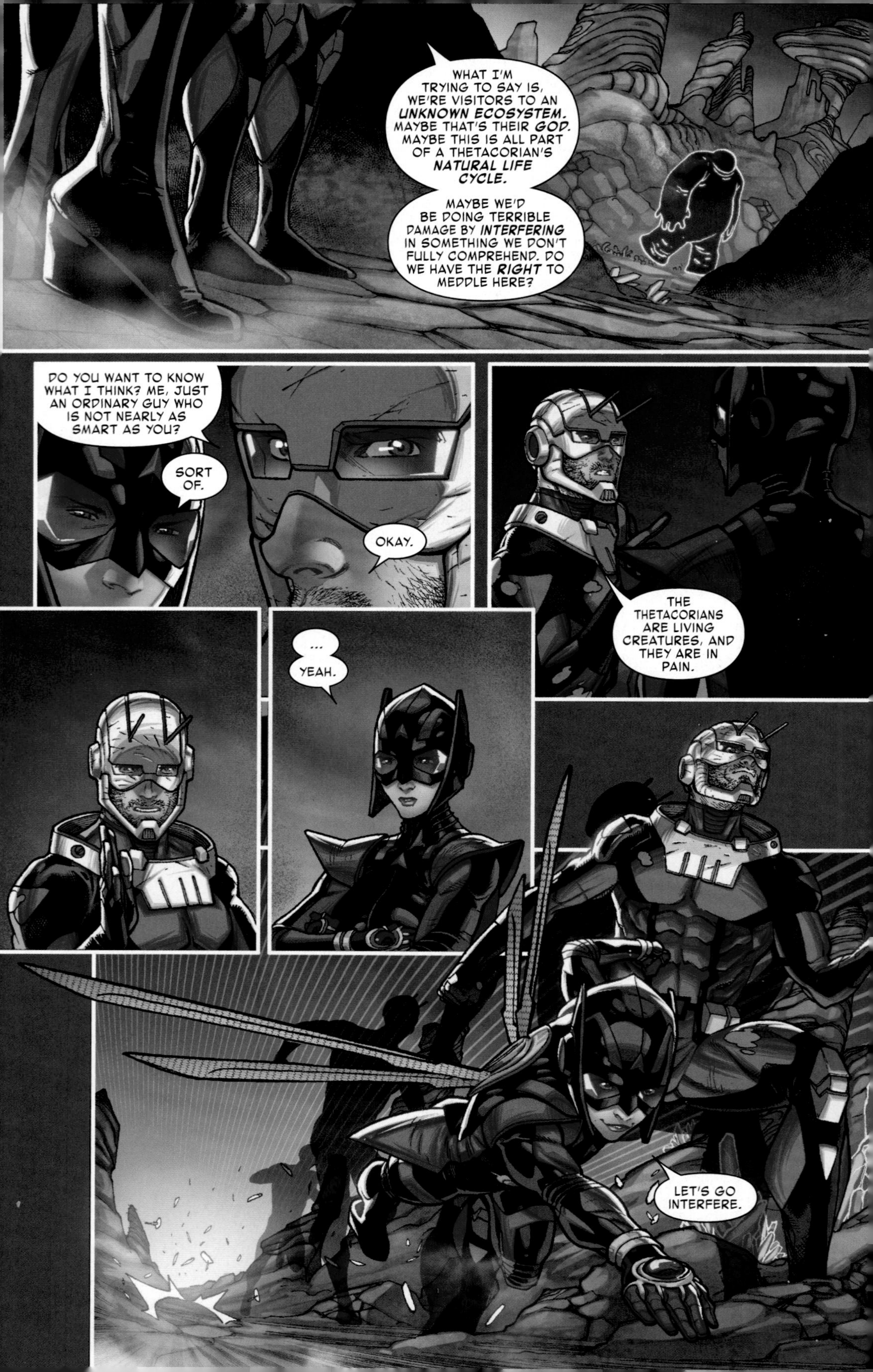
WHAT I'M TRYING TO SAY IS, WE'RE VISITORS TO AN **UNKNOWN ECOSYSTEM.** MAYBE THAT'S THEIR **GOD.** MAYBE THIS IS ALL PART OF A THETACORIAN'S **NATURAL LIFE CYCLE.**
MAYBE WE'D BE DOING TERRIBLE DAMAGE BY **INTERFERING** IN SOMETHING WE DON'T FULLY COMPREHEND. DO WE HAVE THE **RIGHT** TO MEDDLE HERE?
DO YOU WANT TO KNOW WHAT I THINK? ME, JUST AN ORDINARY GUY WHO IS NOT NEARLY AS SMART AS YOU?
SORT OF.
OKAY.
THE THETACORIANS ARE LIVING CREATURES, AND THEY ARE IN PAIN.
...
YEAH.
LET'S GO INTERFERE.

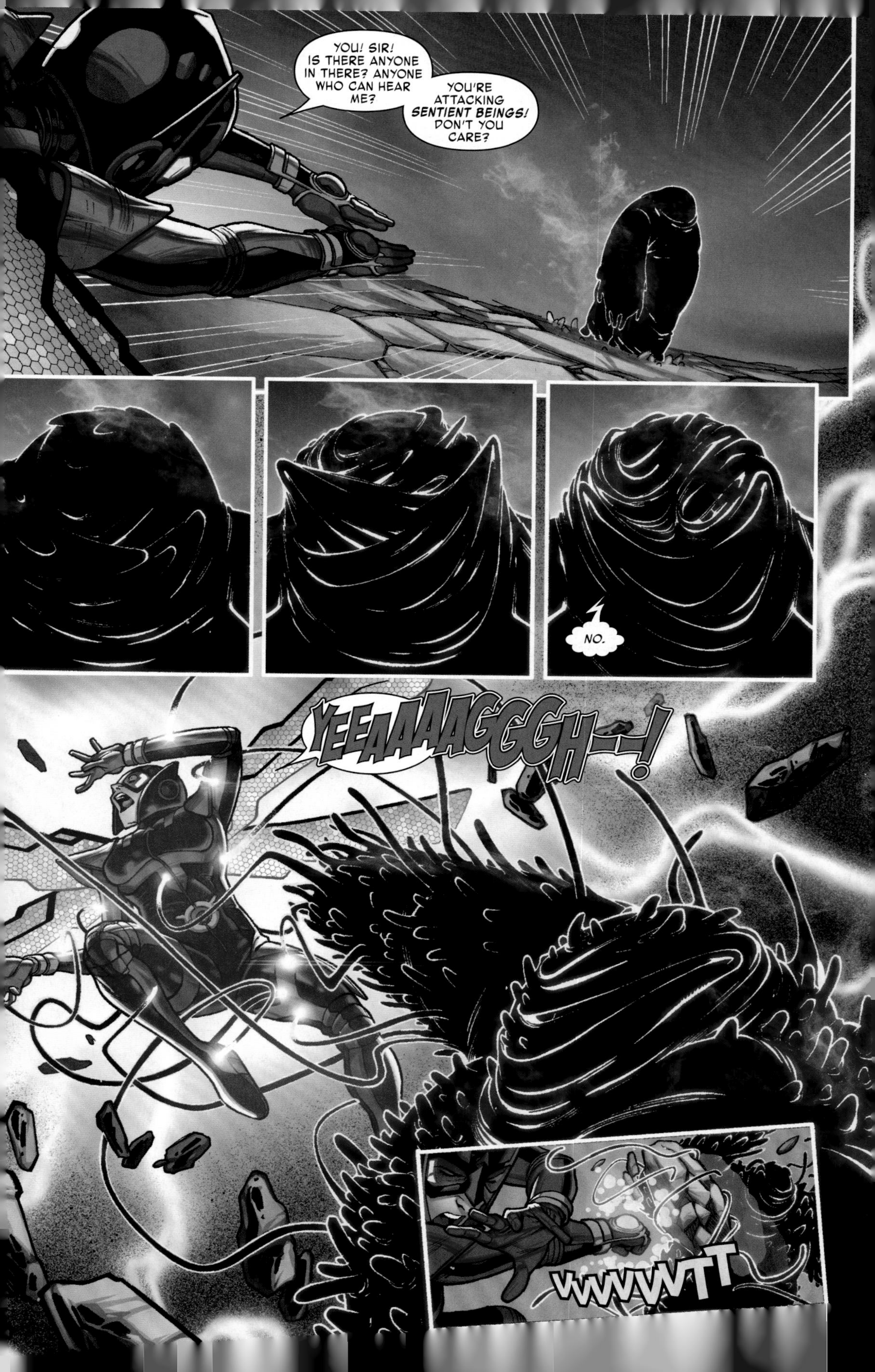
YOU! SIR! IS THERE ANYONE IN THERE? ANYONE WHO CAN HEAR ME?
YOU'RE ATTACKING SENTIENT BEINGS! DON'T YOU CARE?
NO.
YEEAAAAAGGGH--!
WWVVVTT

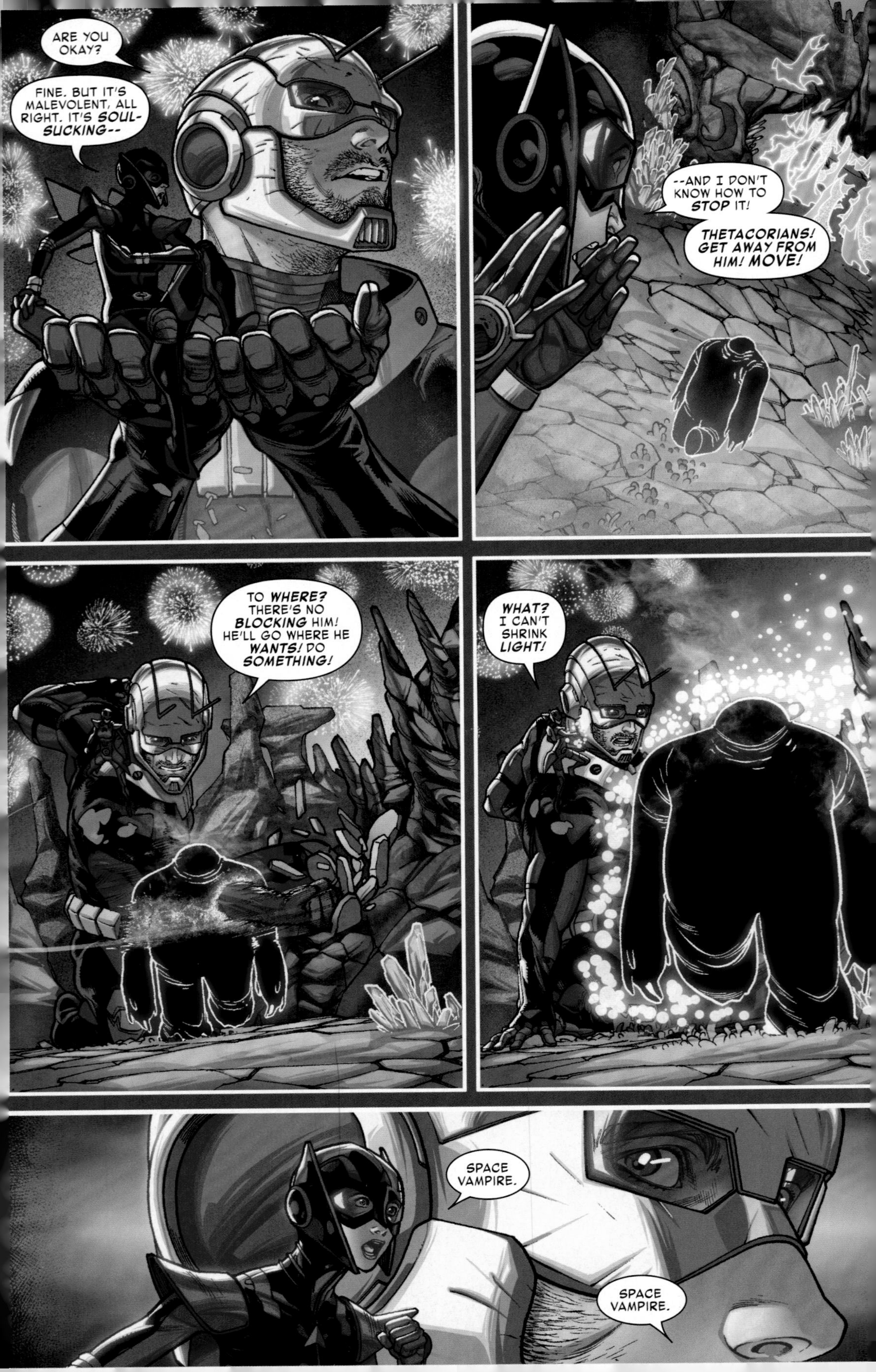
ARE YOU OKAY?
FINE. BUT IT'S MALEVOLENT, ALL RIGHT. IT'S SOUL-SUCKING--
--AND I DON'T KNOW HOW TO STOP IT!
THETACORIANS! GET AWAY FROM HIM! MOVE!
TO WHERE? THERE'S NO BLOCKING HIM! HE'LL GO WHERE HE WANTS! DO SOMETHING!
WHAT? I CAN'T SHRINK LIGHT!
SPACE VAMPIRE.
SPACE VAMPIRE.

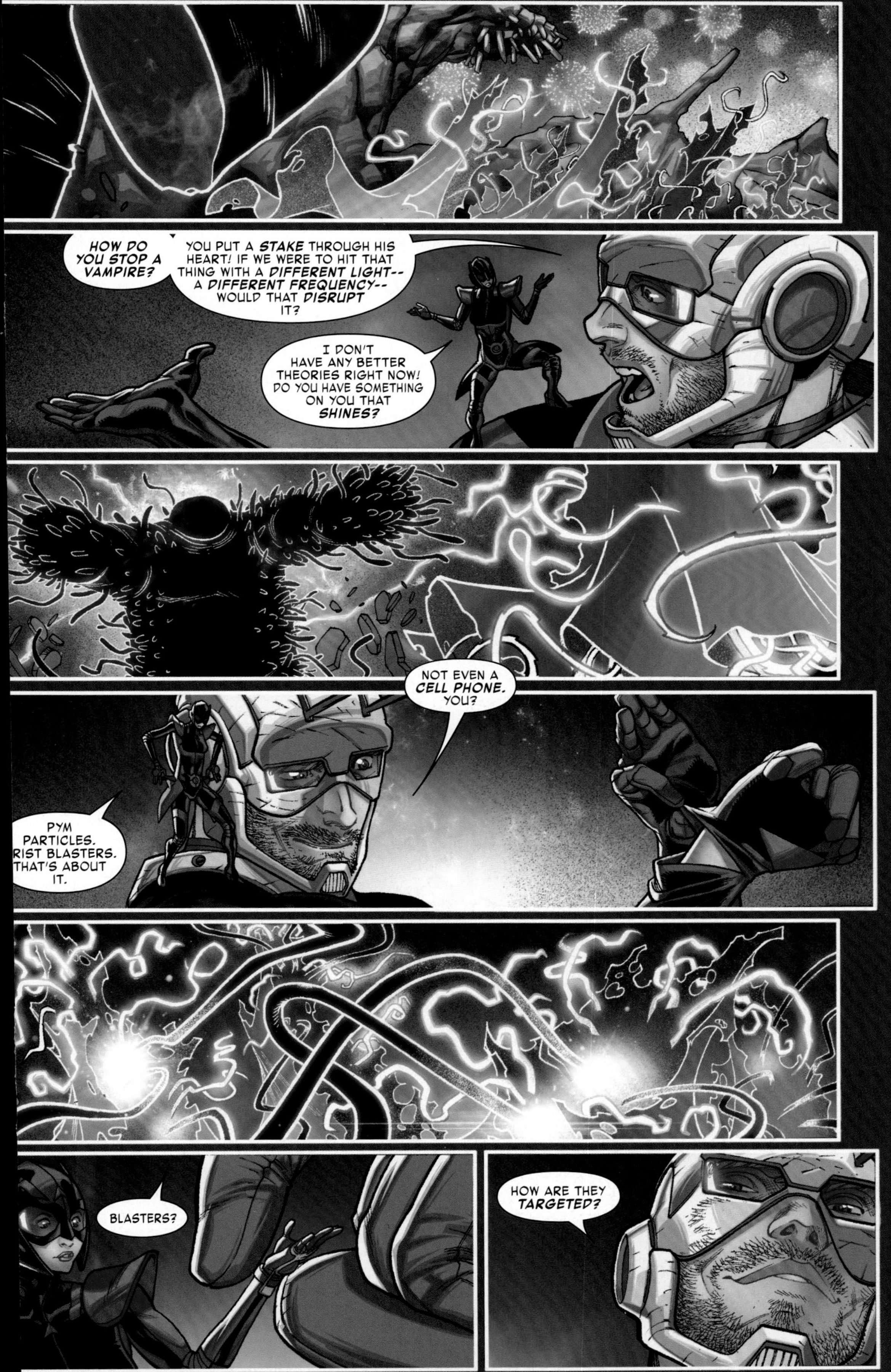
HOW DO YOU STOP A VAMPIRE?
YOU PUT A STAKE THROUGH HIS HEART! IF WE WERE TO HIT THAT THING WITH A DIFFERENT LIGHT-- A DIFFERENT FREQUENCY-- WOULD THAT DISRUPT IT?
I DON'T HAVE ANY BETTER THEORIES RIGHT NOW! DO YOU HAVE SOMETHING ON YOU THAT SHINES?
NOT EVEN A CELL PHONE. YOU?
PYM PARTICLES. RIST BLASTERS. THAT'S ABOUT IT.
BLASTERS?
HOW ARE THEY TARGETED?

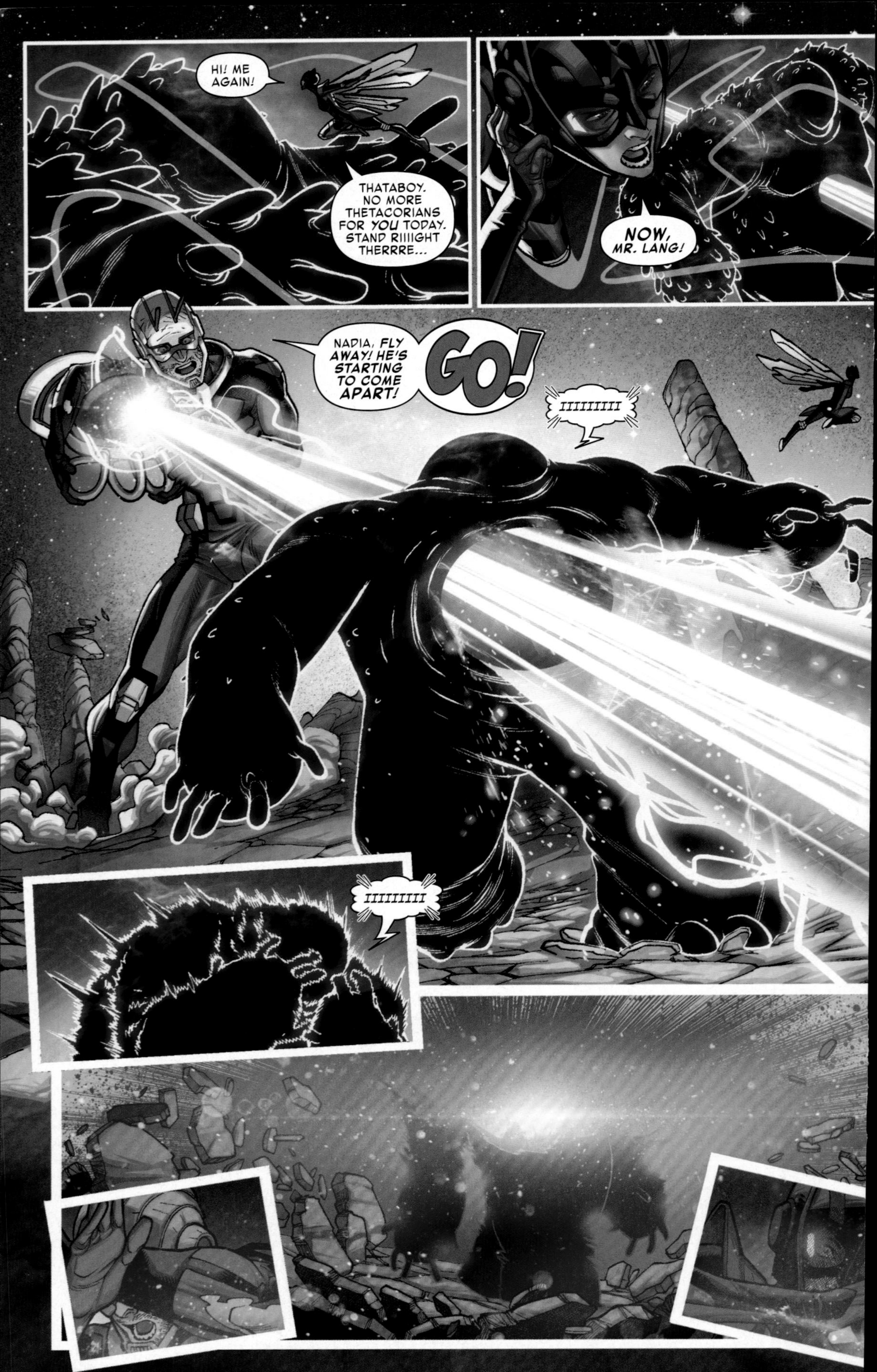
HI! ME AGAIN!
THATABOY. NO MORE THETACORIANS FOR YOU TODAY. STAND RIIIIGHT THERRRE...
NOW, MR. LANG!
NADIA, FLY AWAY! HE'S STARTING TO COME APART!
GO!
IIIIIIIII
IIIIIIIII

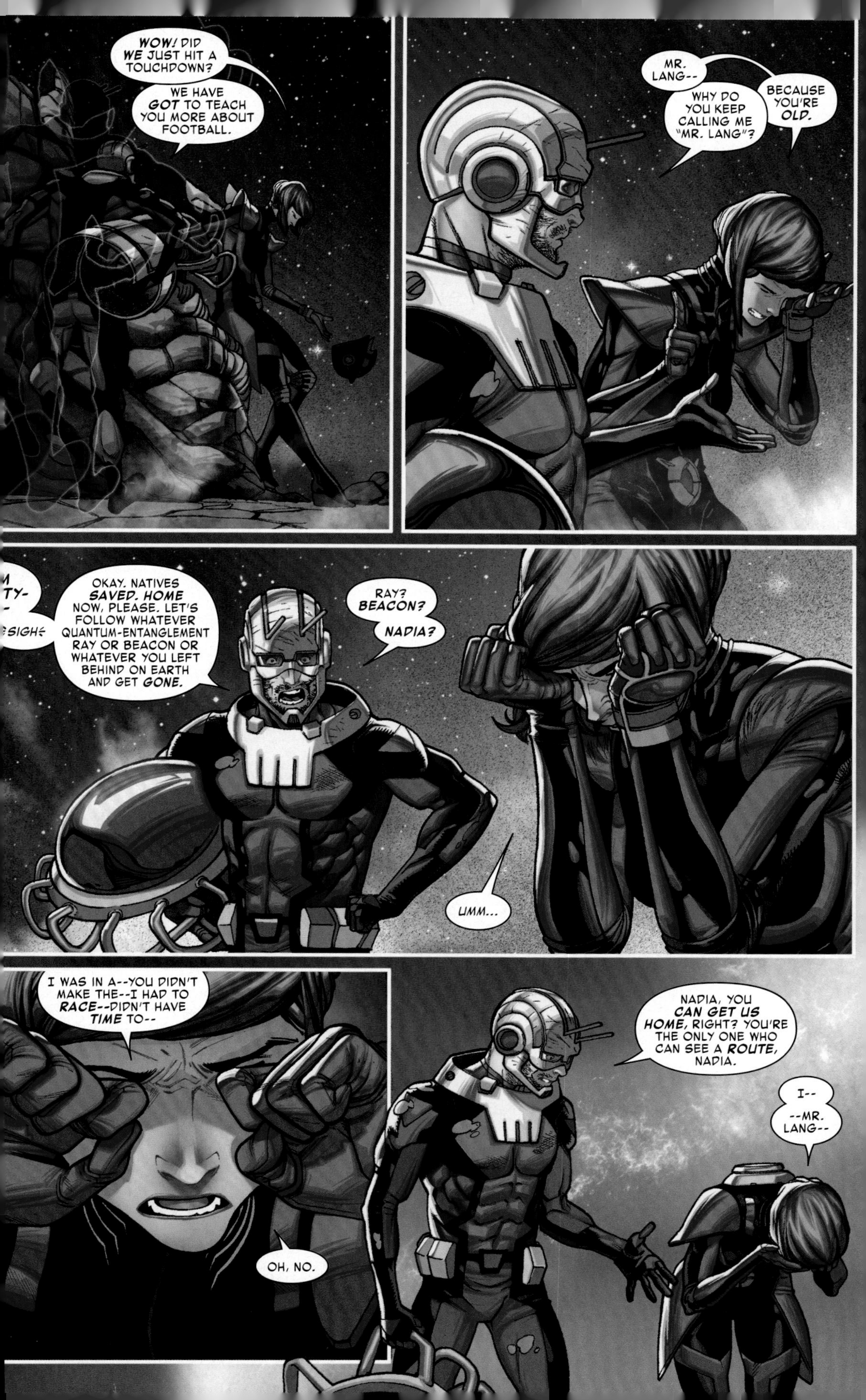
WOW! DID WE JUST HIT A TOUCHDOWN?
WE HAVE GOT TO TEACH YOU MORE ABOUT FOOTBALL.
MR. LANG--
WHY DO YOU KEEP CALLING ME "MR. LANG"?
BECAUSE YOU'RE OLD.
OKAY. NATIVES SAVED. HOME NOW, PLEASE. LET'S FOLLOW WHATEVER QUANTUM-ENTANGLEMENT RAY OR BEACON OR WHATEVER YOU LEFT BEHIND ON EARTH AND GET GONE.
RAY? BEACON?
NADIA?
UMM...
I WAS IN A--YOU DIDN'T MAKE THE--I HAD TO RACE--DIDN'T HAVE TIME TO--
OH, NO.
NADIA, YOU CAN GET US HOME, RIGHT? YOU'RE THE ONLY ONE WHO CAN SEE A ROUTE, NADIA.
I--
--MR. LANG--

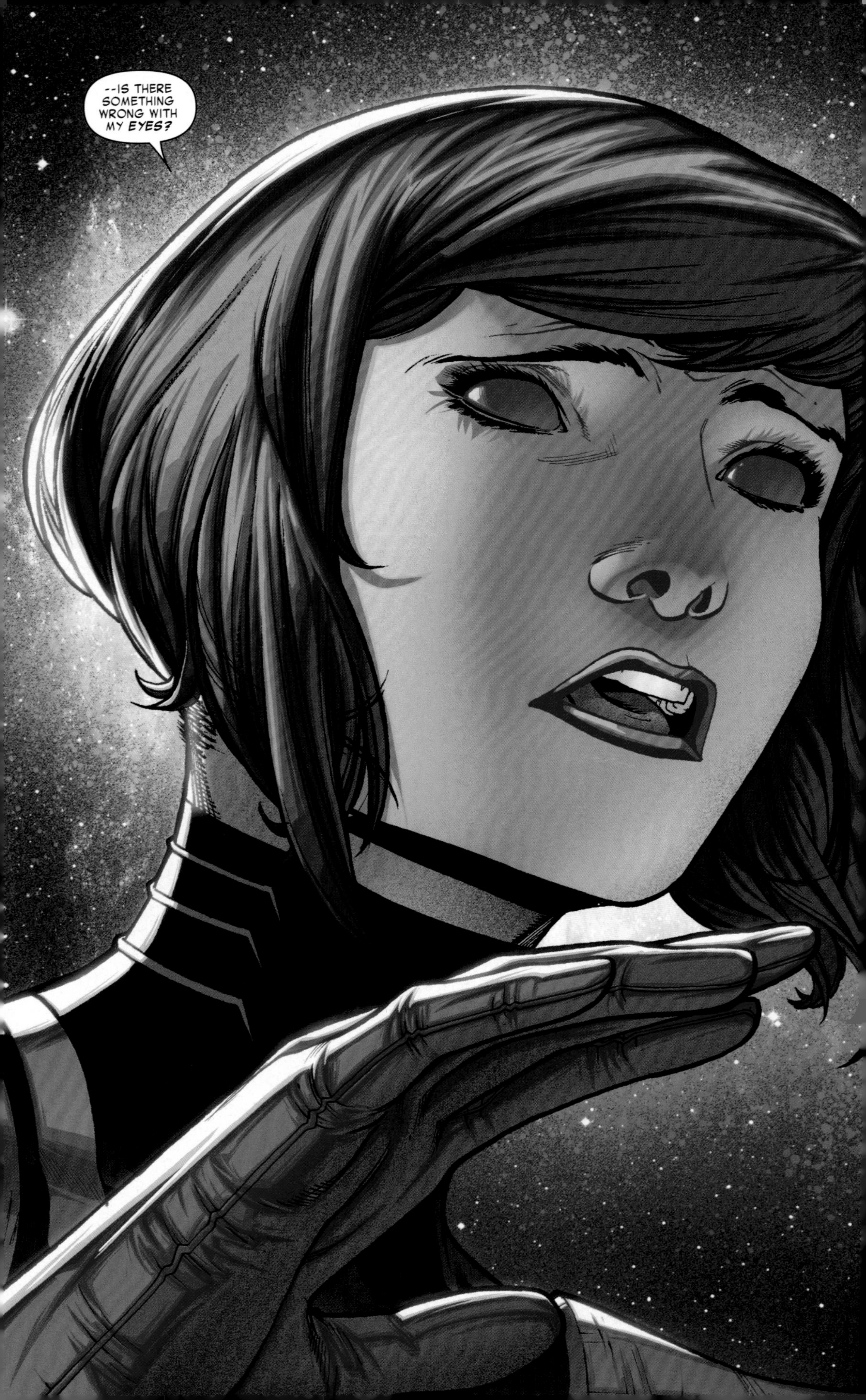
--IS THERE SOMETHING WRONG WITH MY EYES?

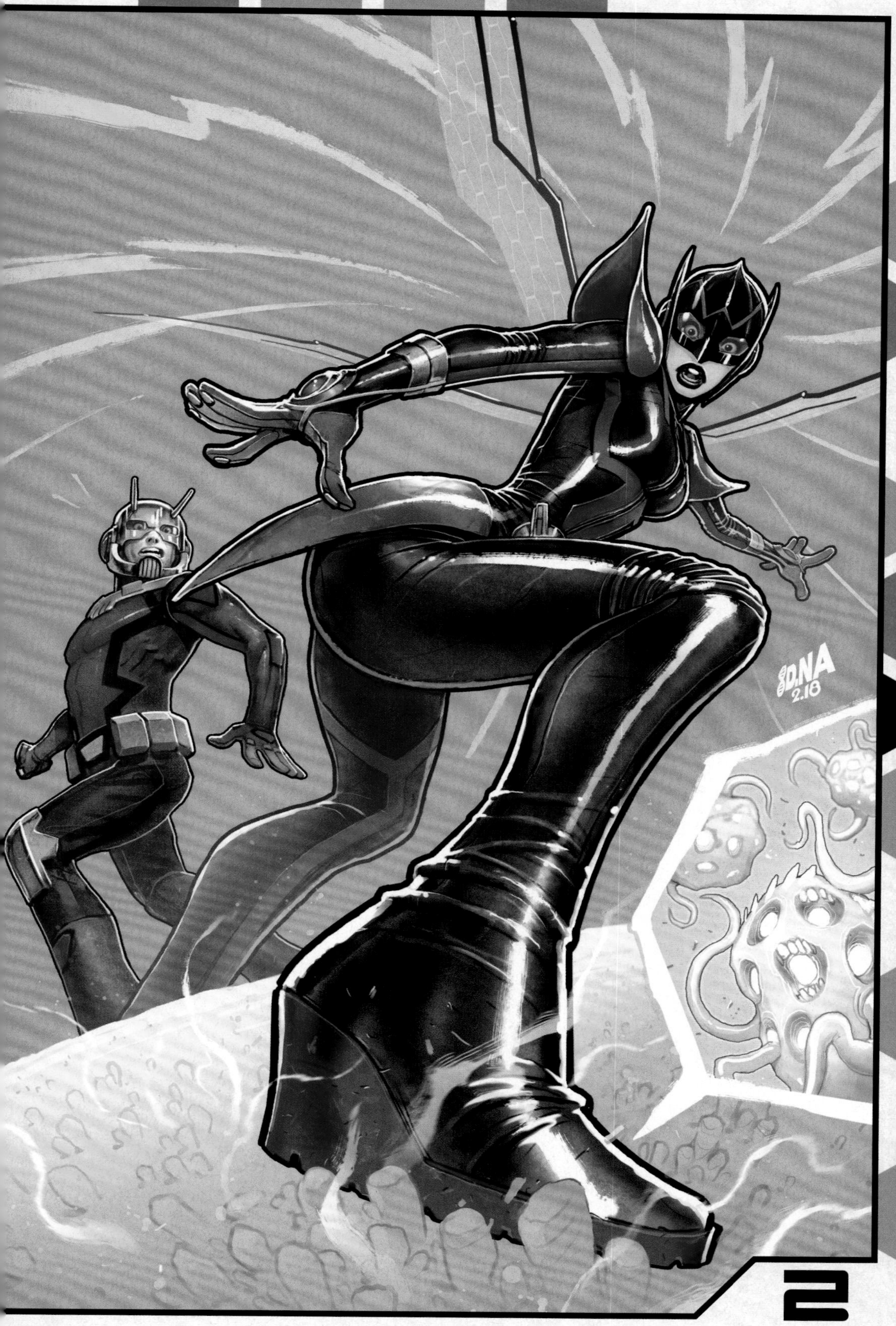
D.NA
2.18
2

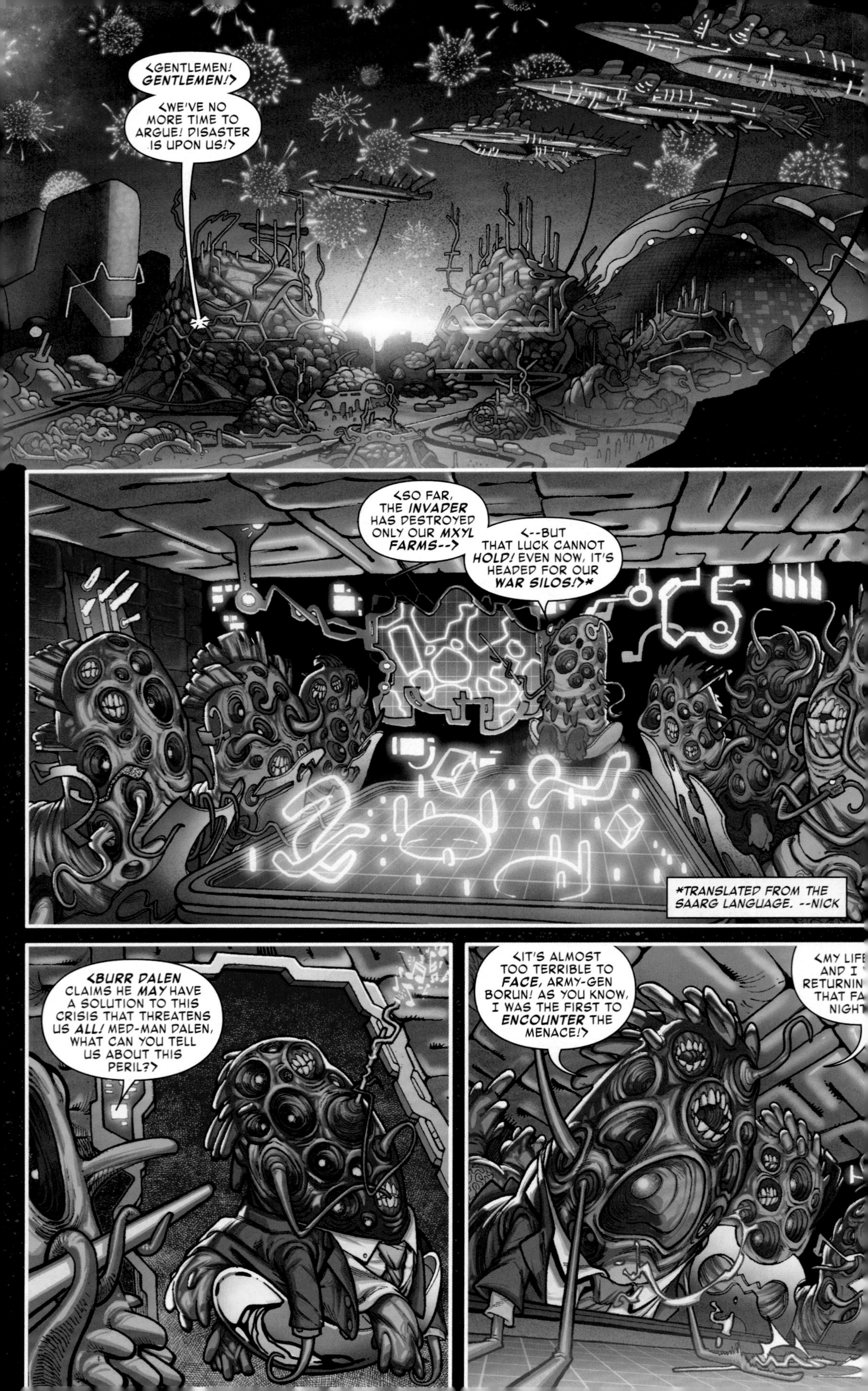
<GENTLEMEN! GENTLEMEN!>
<WE'VE NO MORE TIME TO ARGUE! DISASTER IS UPON US!>
<SO FAR, THE INVADER HAS DESTROYED ONLY OUR MXYL FARMS-->
<--BUT THAT LUCK CANNOT HOLD! EVEN NOW, IT'S HEADED FOR OUR WAR SILOS!>*
*TRANSLATED FROM THE SAARG LANGUAGE. --NICK
<BURR DALEN CLAIMS HE MAY HAVE A SOLUTION TO THIS CRISIS THAT THREATENS US ALL! MED-MAN DALEN, WHAT CAN YOU TELL US ABOUT THIS PERIL?>
<IT'S ALMOST TOO TERRIBLE TO FACE, ARMY-GEN BORUN! AS YOU KNOW, I WAS THE FIRST TO ENCOUNTER THE MENACE!>

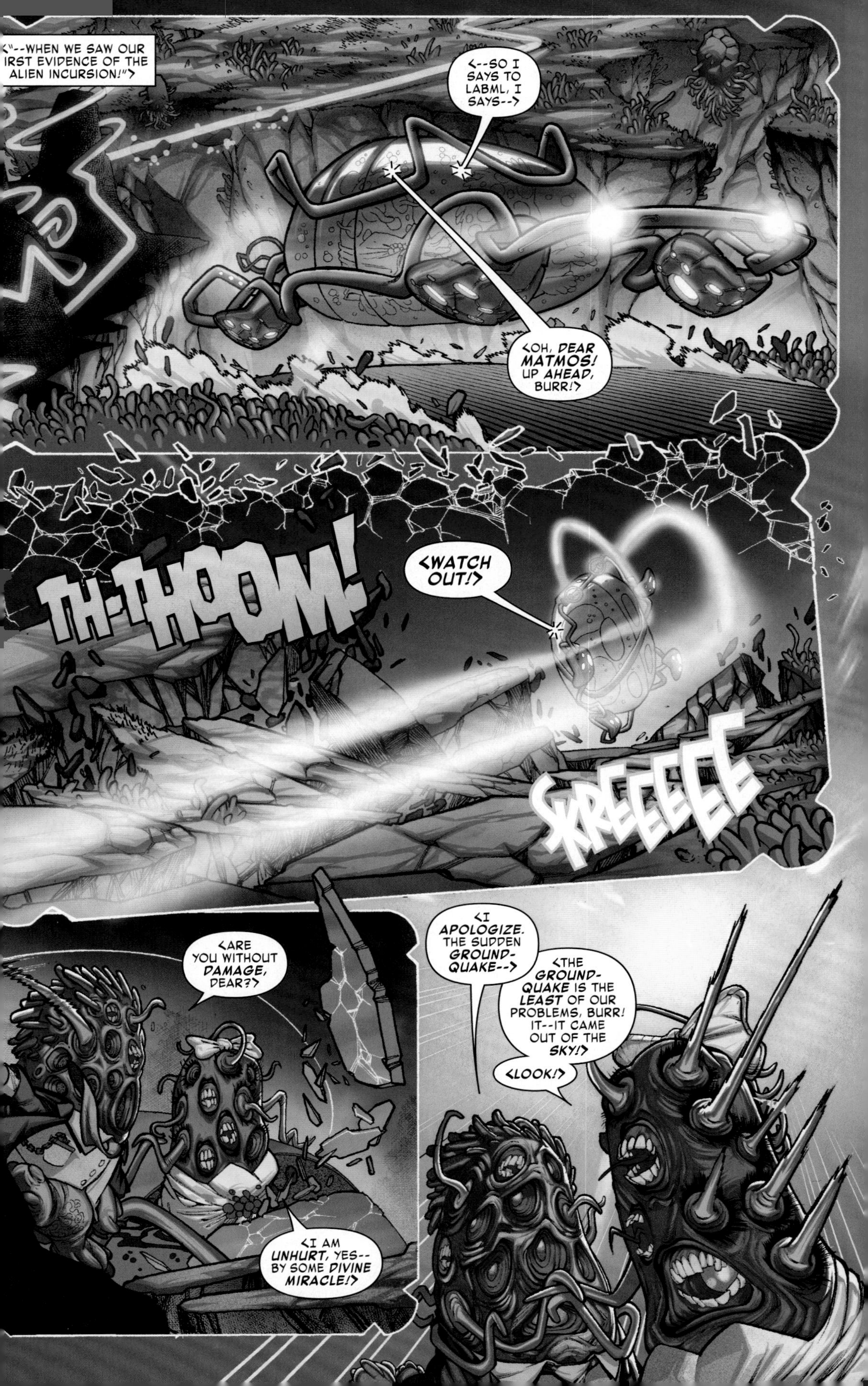
<"--WHEN WE SAW OUR IRST EVIDENCE OF THE ALIEN INCURSION!">
<--SO I SAYS TO LABML, I SAYS-->
<OH, DEAR MATMOS! UP AHEAD, BURR!>
TH-THOOM!
<WATCH OUT!>
SKREEEEE
<ARE YOU WITHOUT DAMAGE, DEAR?>
<I AM UNHURT, YES-- BY SOME DIVINE MIRACLE!>
<I APOLOGIZE. THE SUDDEN GROUND-QUAKE-->
<THE GROUND-QUAKE IS THE LEAST OF OUR PROBLEMS, BURR! IT--IT CAME OUT OF THE SKY!>
<LOOK!>

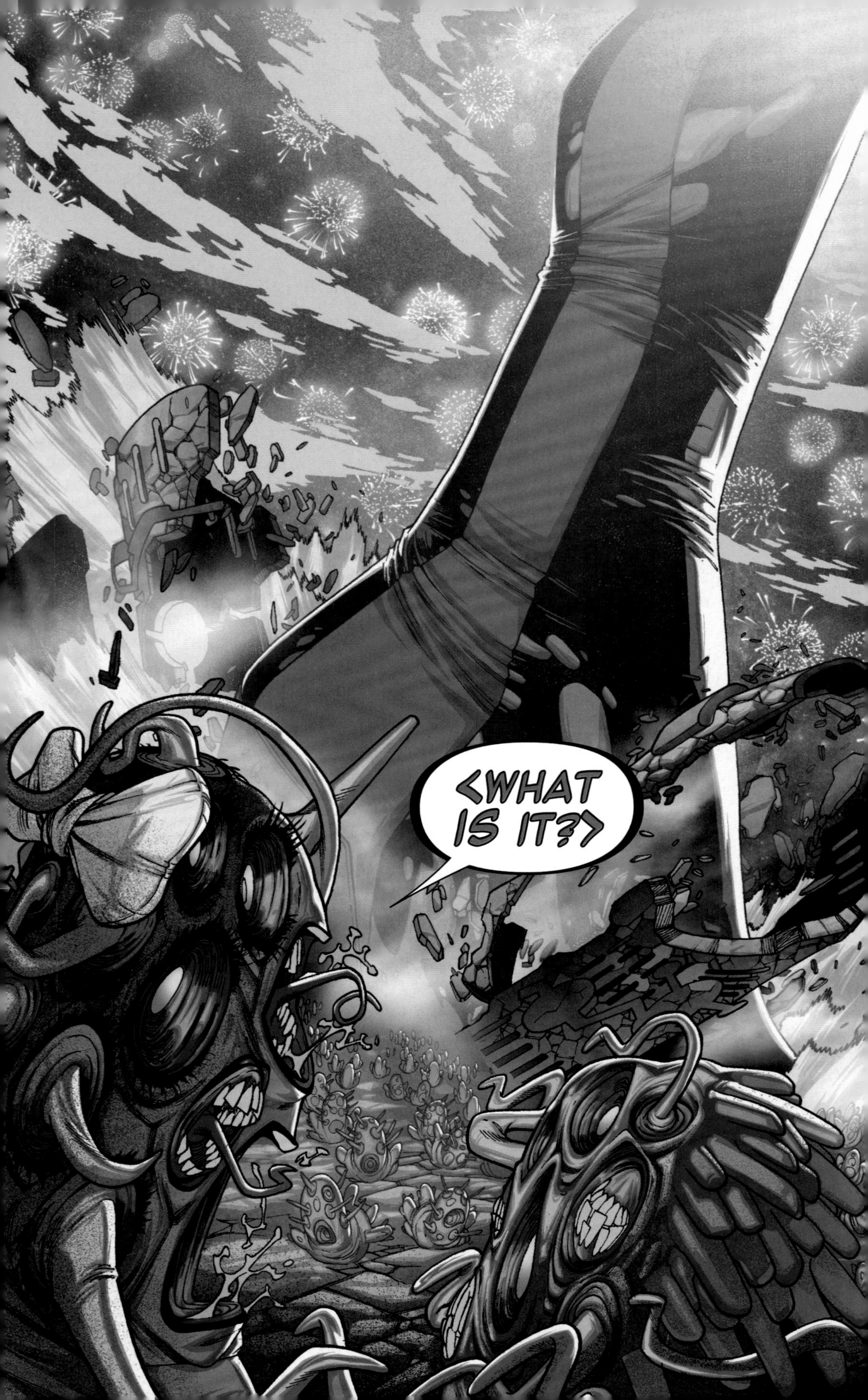
<WHAT IS IT?>

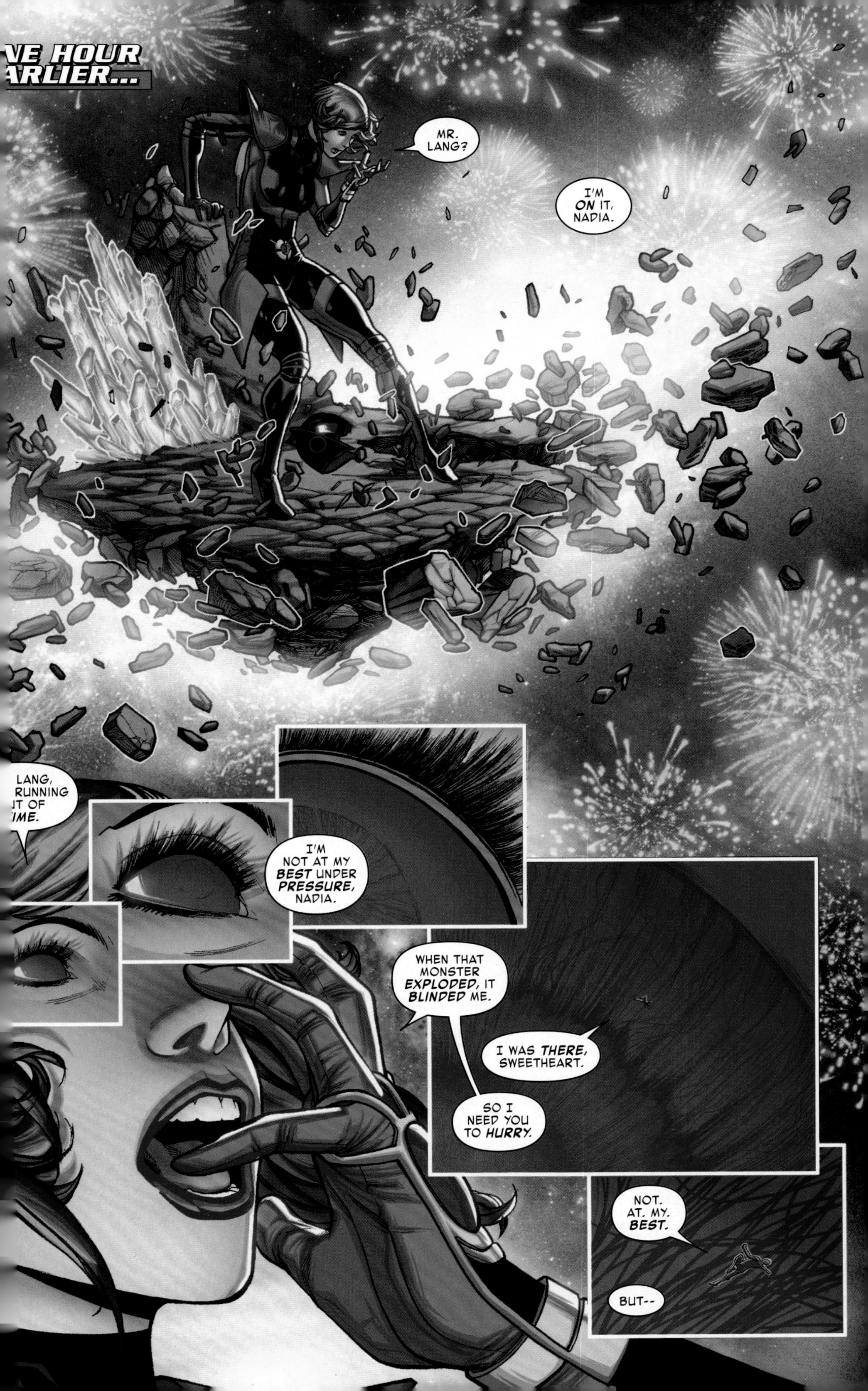
NE HOUR ARLIER...
MR. LANG?
I'M ON IT, NADIA.
LANG, RUNNING IT OF IME.
I'M NOT AT MY BEST UNDER PRESSURE, NADIA.
WHEN THAT MONSTER EXPLODED, IT BLINDED ME.
I WAS THERE, SWEETHEART.
SO I NEED YOU TO HURRY.
NOT. AT. MY. BEST.
BUT--

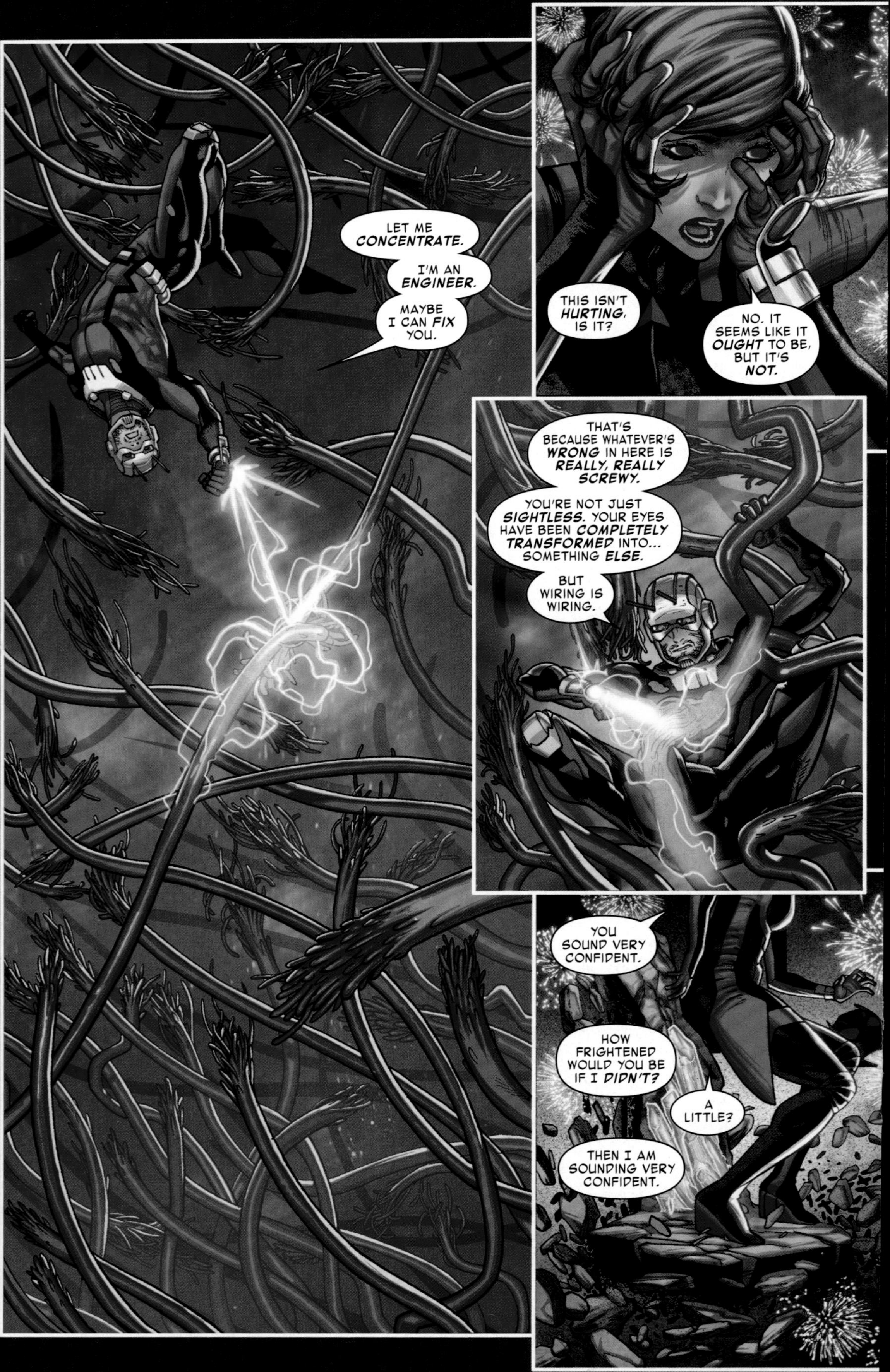
LET ME CONCENTRATE.
I'M AN ENGINEER.
MAYBE I CAN FIX YOU.
THIS ISN'T HURTING, IS IT?
NO. IT SEEMS LIKE IT OUGHT TO BE, BUT IT'S NOT.
THAT'S BECAUSE WHATEVER'S WRONG IN HERE IS REALLY, REALLY SCREWY.
YOU'RE NOT JUST SIGHTLESS. YOUR EYES HAVE BEEN COMPLETELY TRANSFORMED INTO... SOMETHING ELSE.
BUT WIRING IS WIRING.
YOU SOUND VERY CONFIDENT.
HOW FRIGHTENED WOULD YOU BE IF I DIDN'T?
A LITTLE?
THEN I AM SOUNDING VERY CONFIDENT.

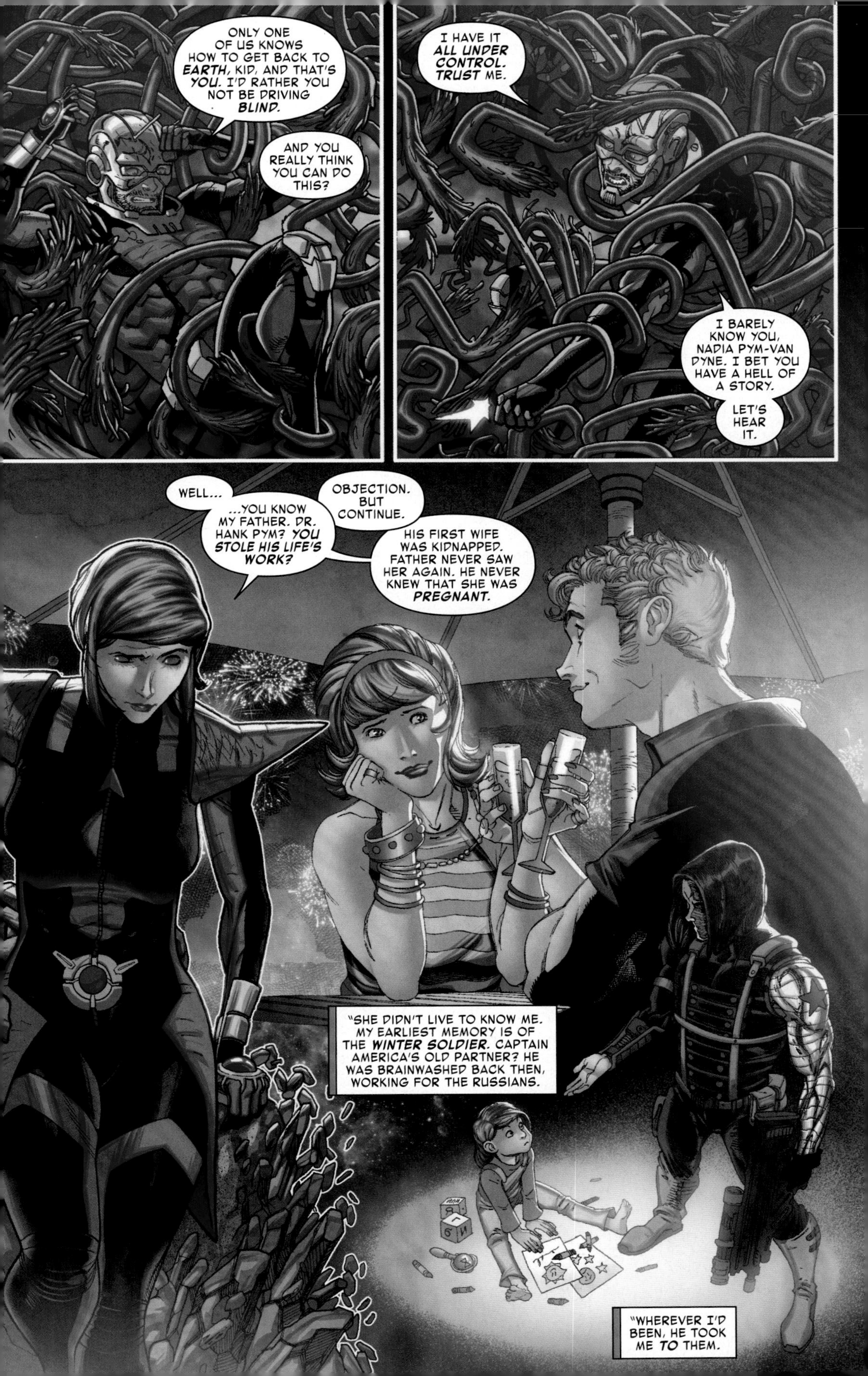
ONLY ONE OF US KNOWS HOW TO GET BACK TO EARTH, KID, AND THAT'S YOU. I'D RATHER YOU NOT BE DRIVING BLIND.
AND YOU REALLY THINK YOU CAN DO THIS?
I HAVE IT ALL UNDER CONTROL. TRUST ME.
I BARELY KNOW YOU, NADIA PYM-VAN DYNE. I BET YOU HAVE A HELL OF A STORY.
LET'S HEAR IT.
WELL...
...YOU KNOW MY FATHER. DR. HANK PYM? YOU STOLE HIS LIFE'S WORK?
OBJECTION. BUT CONTINUE.
HIS FIRST WIFE WAS KIDNAPPED. FATHER NEVER SAW HER AGAIN. HE NEVER KNEW THAT SHE WAS PREGNANT.
"SHE DIDN'T LIVE TO KNOW ME. MY EARLIEST MEMORY IS OF THE WINTER SOLDIER. CAPTAIN AMERICA'S OLD PARTNER? HE WAS BRAINWASHED BACK THEN, WORKING FOR THE RUSSIANS.
"WHEREVER I'D BEEN, HE TOOK ME TO THEM.

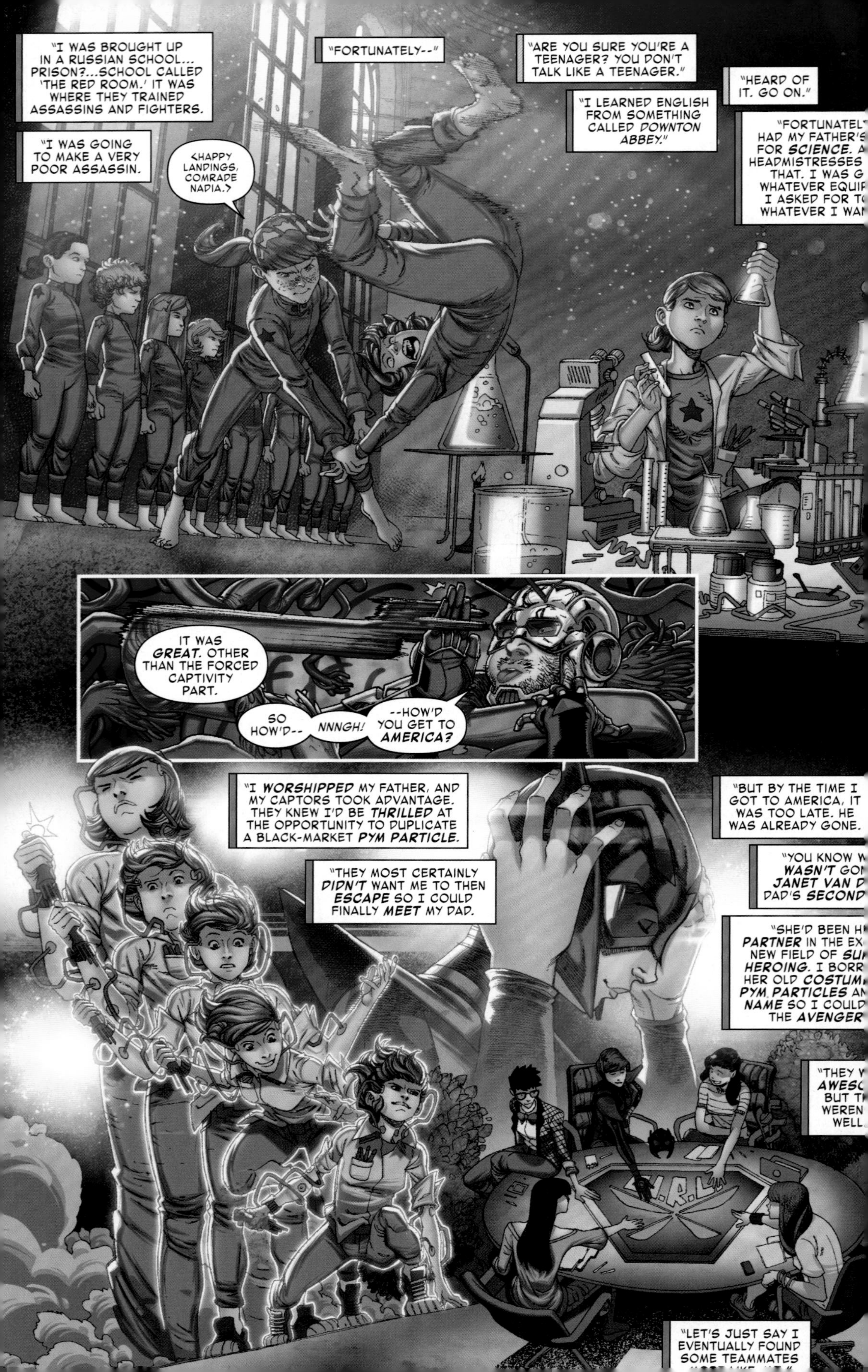
"I WAS BROUGHT UP IN A RUSSIAN SCHOOL... PRISON?...SCHOOL CALLED 'THE RED ROOM.' IT WAS WHERE THEY TRAINED ASSASSINS AND FIGHTERS.
"I WAS GOING TO MAKE A VERY POOR ASSASSIN.
<HAPPY LANDINGS, COMRADE NADIA.>
"FORTUNATELY--"
"ARE YOU SURE YOU'RE A TEENAGER? YOU DON'T TALK LIKE A TEENAGER."
"I LEARNED ENGLISH FROM SOMETHING CALLED *DOWNTON ABBEY*."
"HEARD OF IT. GO ON."
"FORTUNATEL HAD MY FATHER'S FOR *SCIENCE*. A HEADMISTRESSES THAT. I WAS G WHATEVER EQUIP I ASKED FOR TO WHATEVER I WAN
IT WAS *GREAT*. OTHER THAN THE FORCED CAPTIVITY PART.
SO HOW'D--
NNNGH!
--HOW'D YOU GET TO *AMERICA?*
"I *WORSHIPPED* MY FATHER, AND MY CAPTORS TOOK ADVANTAGE. THEY KNEW I'D BE *THRILLED* AT THE OPPORTUNITY TO DUPLICATE A BLACK-MARKET *PYM PARTICLE*.
"THEY MOST CERTAINLY *DIDN'T* WANT ME TO THEN *ESCAPE* SO I COULD FINALLY *MEET* MY DAD.
"BUT BY THE TIME I GOT TO AMERICA, IT WAS TOO LATE. HE WAS ALREADY GONE.
"YOU KNOW W *WASN'T* GO *JANET VAN D* DAD'S *SECOND*
"SHE'D BEEN H *PARTNER* IN THE EX NEW FIELD OF *SU HEROING*. I BORR HER OLD *COSTUM PYM PARTICLES* AN *NAME* SO I COULD THE *AVENGER*
"THEY *AWESO* BUT T WEREN WELL
"LET'S JUST SAY I EVENTUALLY FOUND SOME TEAMMATES

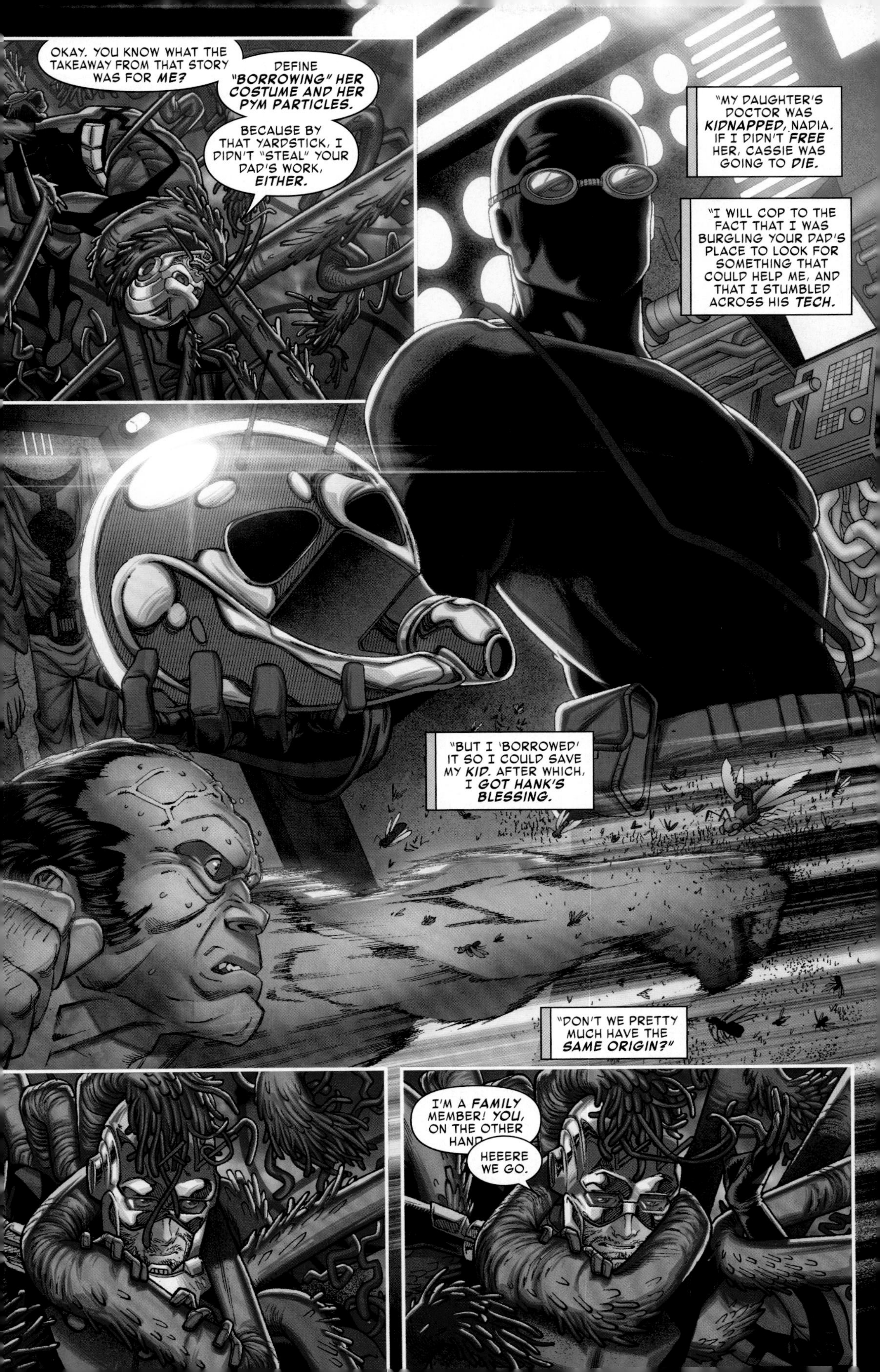
OKAY. YOU KNOW WHAT THE TAKEAWAY FROM THAT STORY WAS FOR *ME?*
DEFINE *"BORROWING" HER COSTUME AND HER PYM PARTICLES.*
BECAUSE BY THAT YARDSTICK, I DIDN'T "STEAL" YOUR DAD'S WORK, *EITHER.*
"MY DAUGHTER'S DOCTOR WAS *KIDNAPPED,* NADIA. IF I DIDN'T *FREE* HER, CASSIE WAS GOING TO *DIE.*
"I WILL COP TO THE FACT THAT I WAS BURGLING YOUR DAD'S PLACE TO LOOK FOR SOMETHING THAT COULD HELP ME, AND THAT I STUMBLED ACROSS HIS *TECH.*
"BUT I 'BORROWED' IT SO I COULD SAVE MY *KID.* AFTER WHICH, I *GOT HANK'S BLESSING.*
"DON'T WE PRETTY MUCH HAVE THE *SAME ORIGIN?"*
I'M A *FAMILY* MEMBER! *YOU,* ON THE OTHER HAND
HEEERE WE GO.

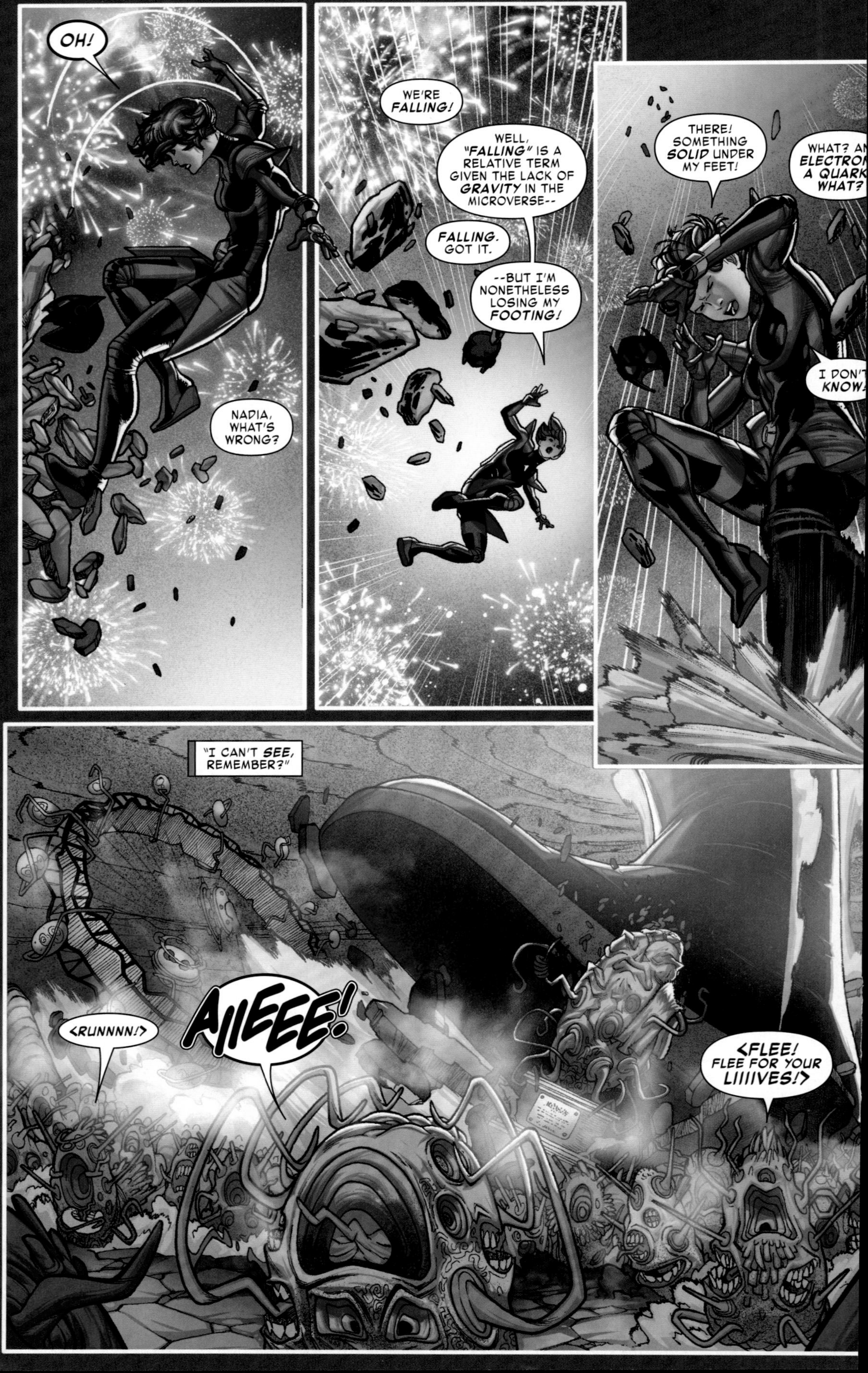
OH!
NADIA, WHAT'S WRONG?
WE'RE FALLING!
WELL, "FALLING" IS A RELATIVE TERM GIVEN THE LACK OF GRAVITY IN THE MICROVERSE--
FALLING. GOT IT.
--BUT I'M NONETHELESS LOSING MY FOOTING!
THERE! SOMETHING SOLID UNDER MY FEET!
"I CAN'T SEE, REMEMBER?"
<RUNNNN!>
AIIEEE!
<FLEE! FLEE FOR YOUR LIIIIVES!>

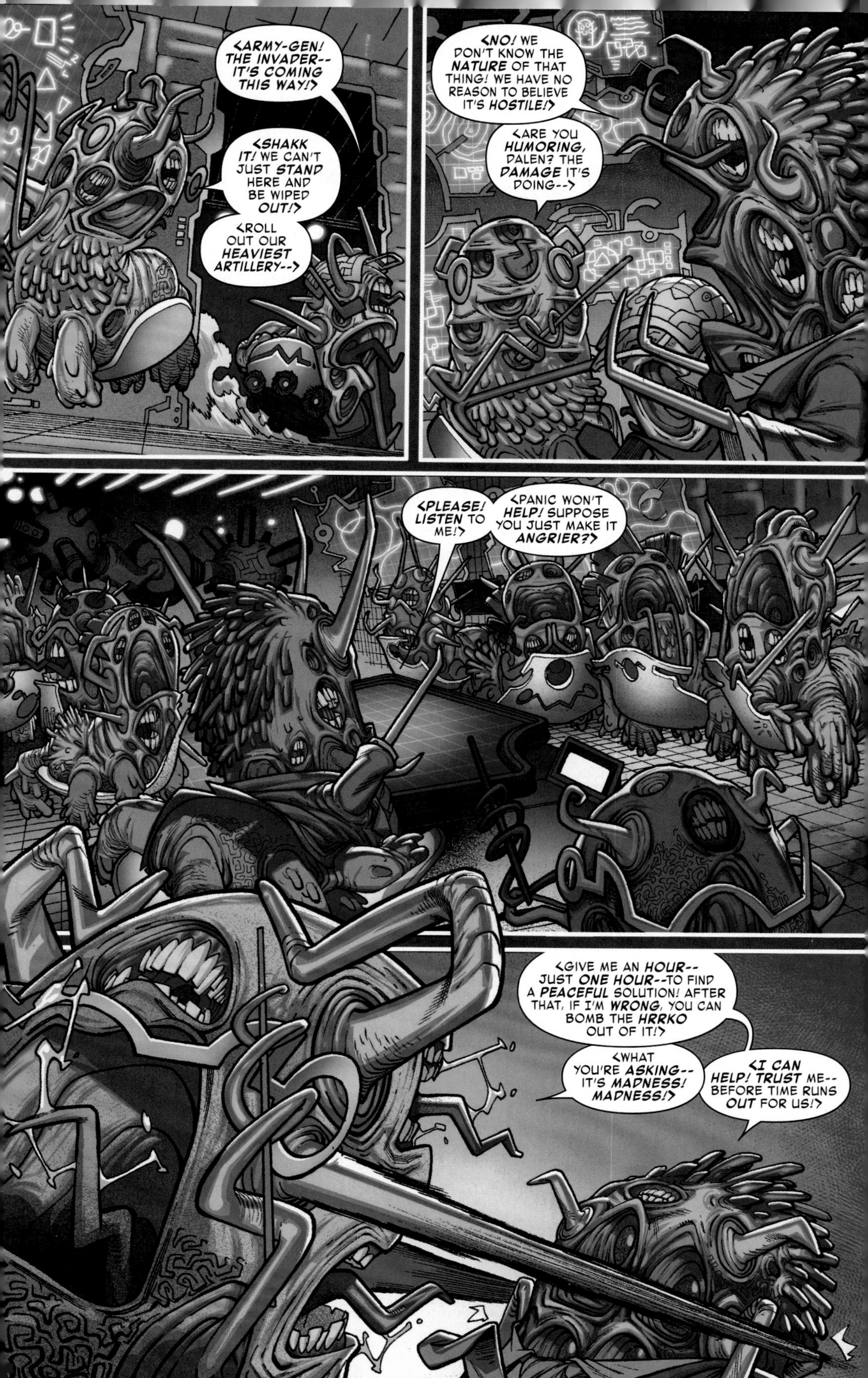

<ARMY-GEN! THE INVADER-- IT'S COMING THIS WAY!>
<SHAKK IT! WE CAN'T JUST STAND HERE AND BE WIPED OUT!>
<ROLL OUT OUR HEAVIEST ARTILLERY-->
<NO! WE DON'T KNOW THE NATURE OF THAT THING! WE HAVE NO REASON TO BELIEVE IT'S HOSTILE!>
<ARE YOU HUMORING, DALEN? THE DAMAGE IT'S DOING-->
<PLEASE! LISTEN TO ME!>
<PANIC WON'T HELP! SUPPOSE YOU JUST MAKE IT ANGRIER?>
<GIVE ME AN HOUR-- JUST ONE HOUR--TO FIND A PEACEFUL SOLUTION! AFTER THAT, IF I'M WRONG, YOU CAN BOMB THE HRRKO OUT OF IT!>
<WHAT YOU'RE ASKING-- IT'S MADNESS! MADNESS!>
<I CAN HELP! TRUST ME-- BEFORE TIME RUNS OUT FOR US!>

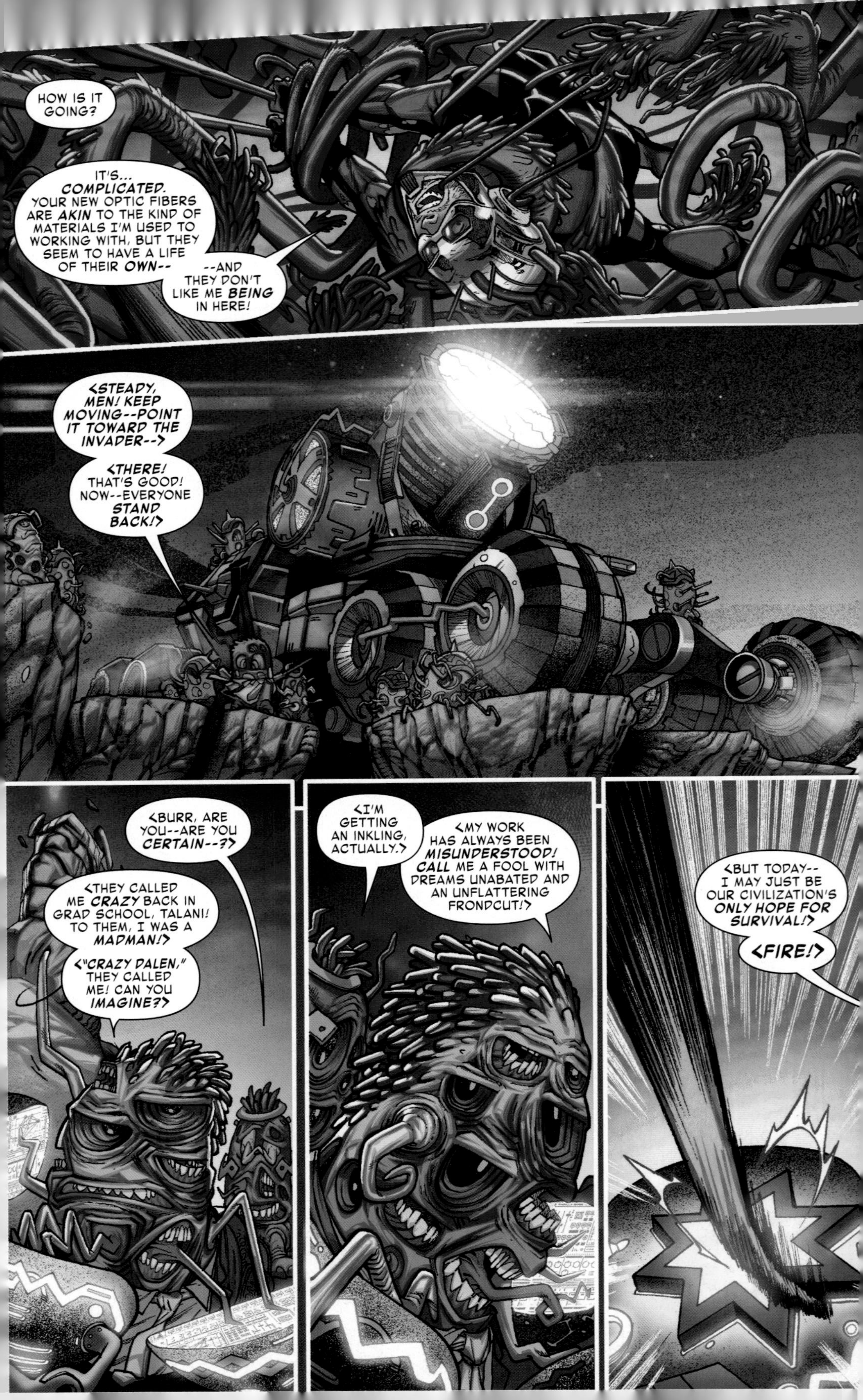
HOW IS IT GOING?
IT'S... COMPLICATED. YOUR NEW OPTIC FIBERS ARE AKIN TO THE KIND OF MATERIALS I'M USED TO WORKING WITH, BUT THEY SEEM TO HAVE A LIFE OF THEIR OWN--
--AND THEY DON'T LIKE ME BEING IN HERE!
<STEADY, MEN! KEEP MOVING--POINT IT TOWARD THE INVADER-->
<THERE! THAT'S GOOD! NOW--EVERYONE STAND BACK!>
<BURR, ARE YOU--ARE YOU CERTAIN--?>
<THEY CALLED ME CRAZY BACK IN GRAD SCHOOL, TALANI! TO THEM, I WAS A MADMAN!>
<"CRAZY DALEN," THEY CALLED ME! CAN YOU IMAGINE?>
<I'M GETTING AN INKLING, ACTUALLY.>
<MY WORK HAS ALWAYS BEEN MISUNDERSTOOD! CALL ME A FOOL WITH DREAMS UNABATED AND AN UNFLATTERING FRONDCUT!>
<BUT TODAY-- I MAY JUST BE OUR CIVILIZATION'S ONLY HOPE FOR SURVIVAL!>
<FIRE!>

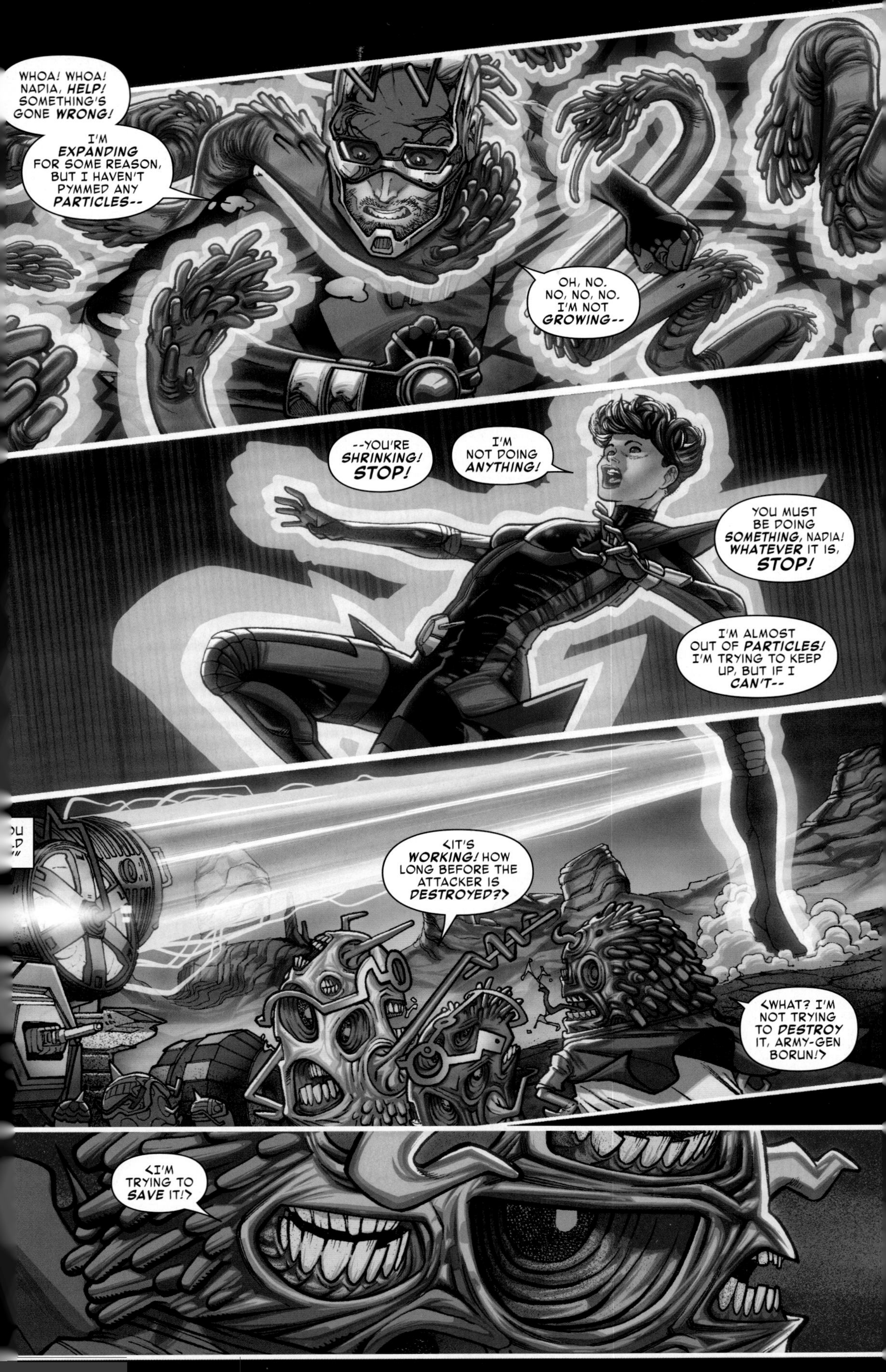
WHOA! WHOA! NADIA, HELP! SOMETHING'S GONE WRONG!
I'M EXPANDING FOR SOME REASON, BUT I HAVEN'T PYMMED ANY PARTICLES--
OH, NO. NO, NO, NO. I'M NOT GROWING--
--YOU'RE SHRINKING! STOP!
I'M NOT DOING ANYTHING!
YOU MUST BE DOING SOMETHING, NADIA! WHATEVER IT IS, STOP!
I'M ALMOST OUT OF PARTICLES! I'M TRYING TO KEEP UP, BUT IF I CAN'T--
<IT'S WORKING! HOW LONG BEFORE THE ATTACKER IS DESTROYED?>
<WHAT? I'M NOT TRYING TO DESTROY IT, ARMY-GEN BORUN!>
<I'M TRYING TO SAVE IT!>

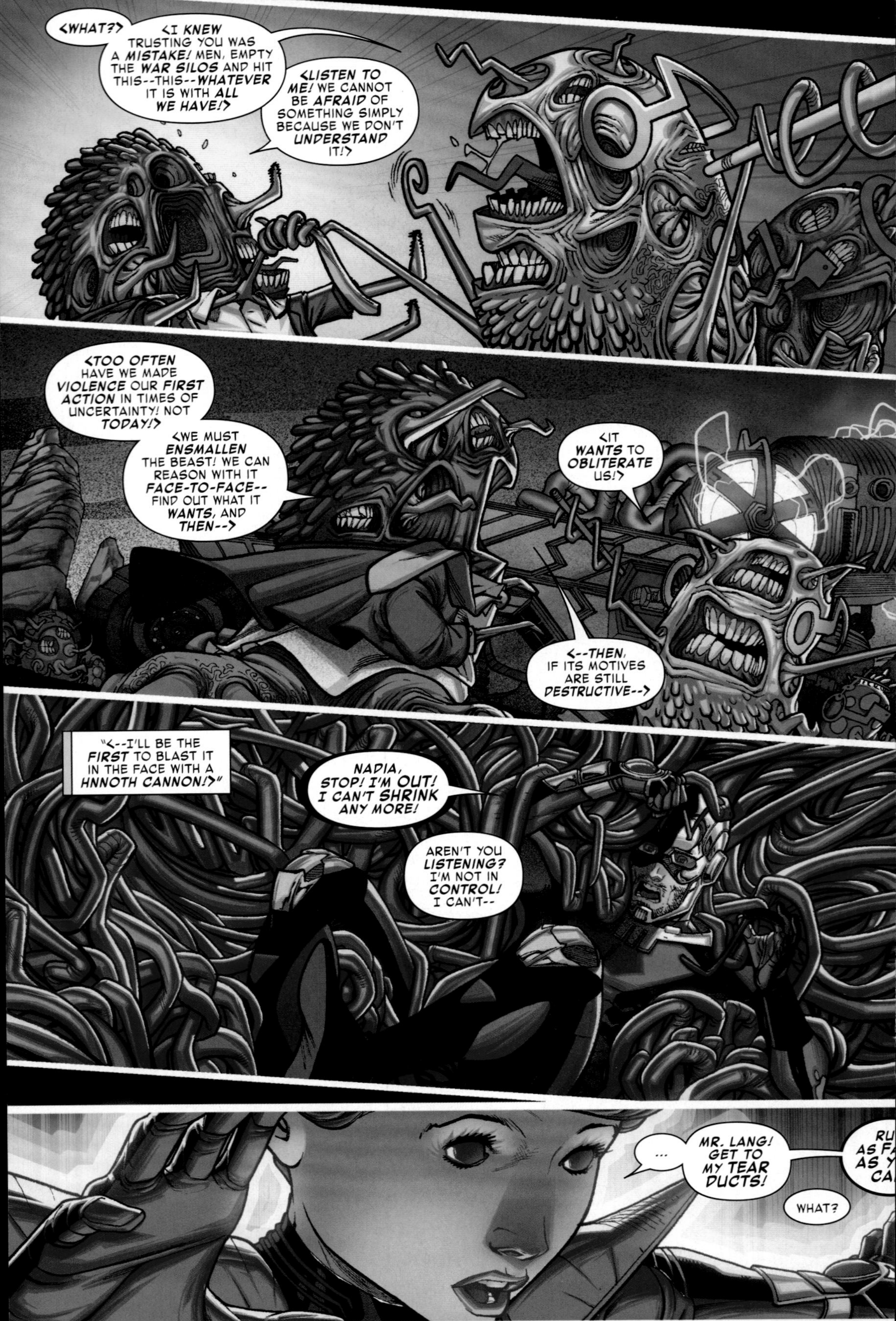
<WHAT?>
<I KNEW TRUSTING YOU WAS A MISTAKE! MEN, EMPTY THE WAR SILOS AND HIT THIS--THIS--WHATEVER IT IS WITH ALL WE HAVE!>
<LISTEN TO ME! WE CANNOT BE AFRAID OF SOMETHING SIMPLY BECAUSE WE DON'T UNDERSTAND IT!>
<TOO OFTEN HAVE WE MADE VIOLENCE OUR FIRST ACTION IN TIMES OF UNCERTAINTY! NOT TODAY!>
<WE MUST ENSMALLEN THE BEAST! WE CAN REASON WITH IT FACE-TO-FACE--FIND OUT WHAT IT WANTS, AND THEN-->
<IT WANTS TO OBLITERATE US!>
<--THEN, IF ITS MOTIVES ARE STILL DESTRUCTIVE-->
"<--I'LL BE THE FIRST TO BLAST IT IN THE FACE WITH A HNNOTH CANNON!>"
NADIA, STOP! I'M OUT! I CAN'T SHRINK ANY MORE!
AREN'T YOU LISTENING? I'M NOT IN CONTROL! I CAN'T--
...
MR. LANG! GET TO MY TEAR DUCTS!
WHAT?

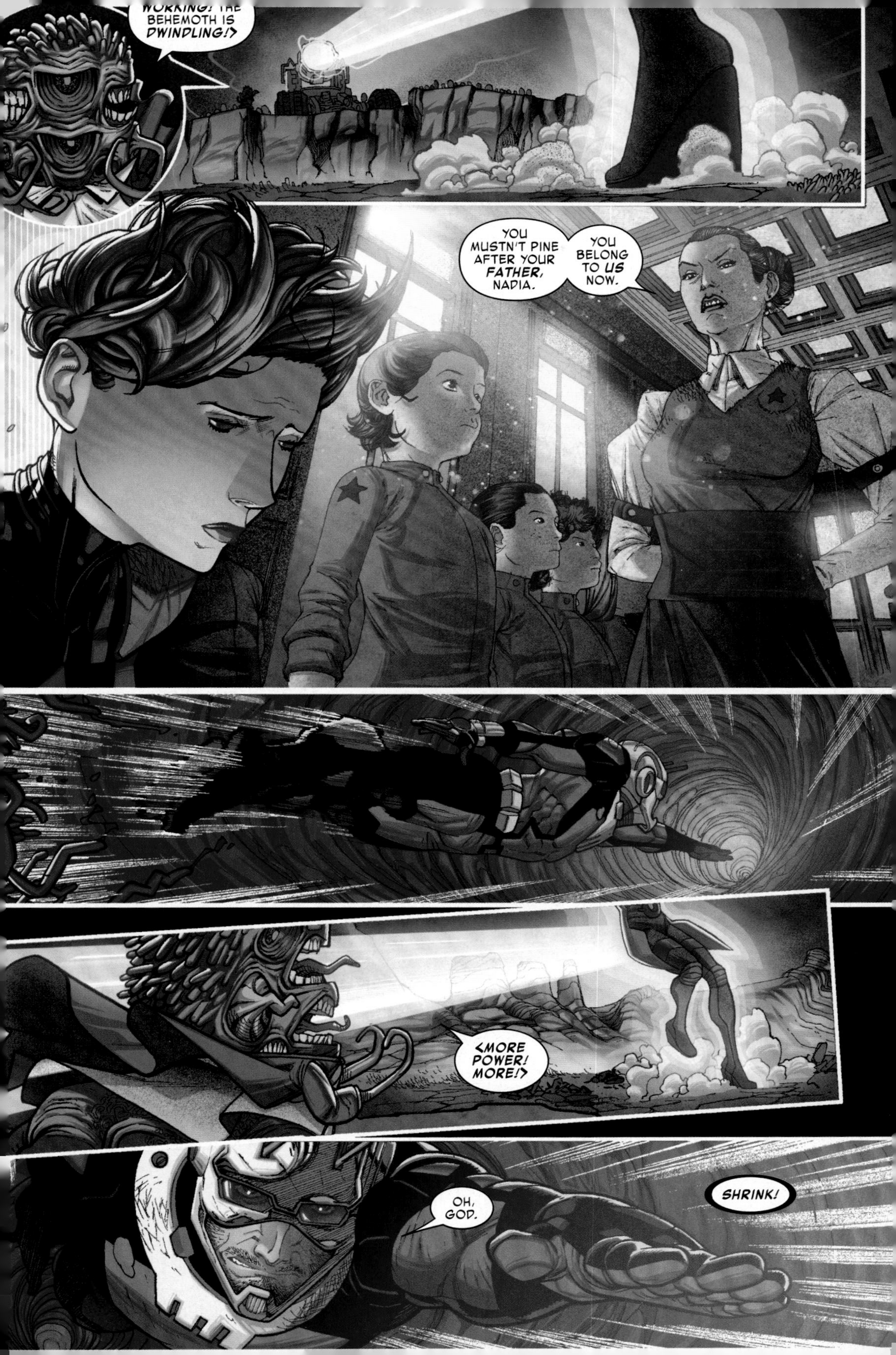
WORKING! THE BEHEMOTH IS DWINDLING!>
YOU MUSTN'T PINE AFTER YOUR FATHER, NADIA.
YOU BELONG TO US NOW.
<MORE POWER! MORE!>
OH, GOD.
SHRINK!

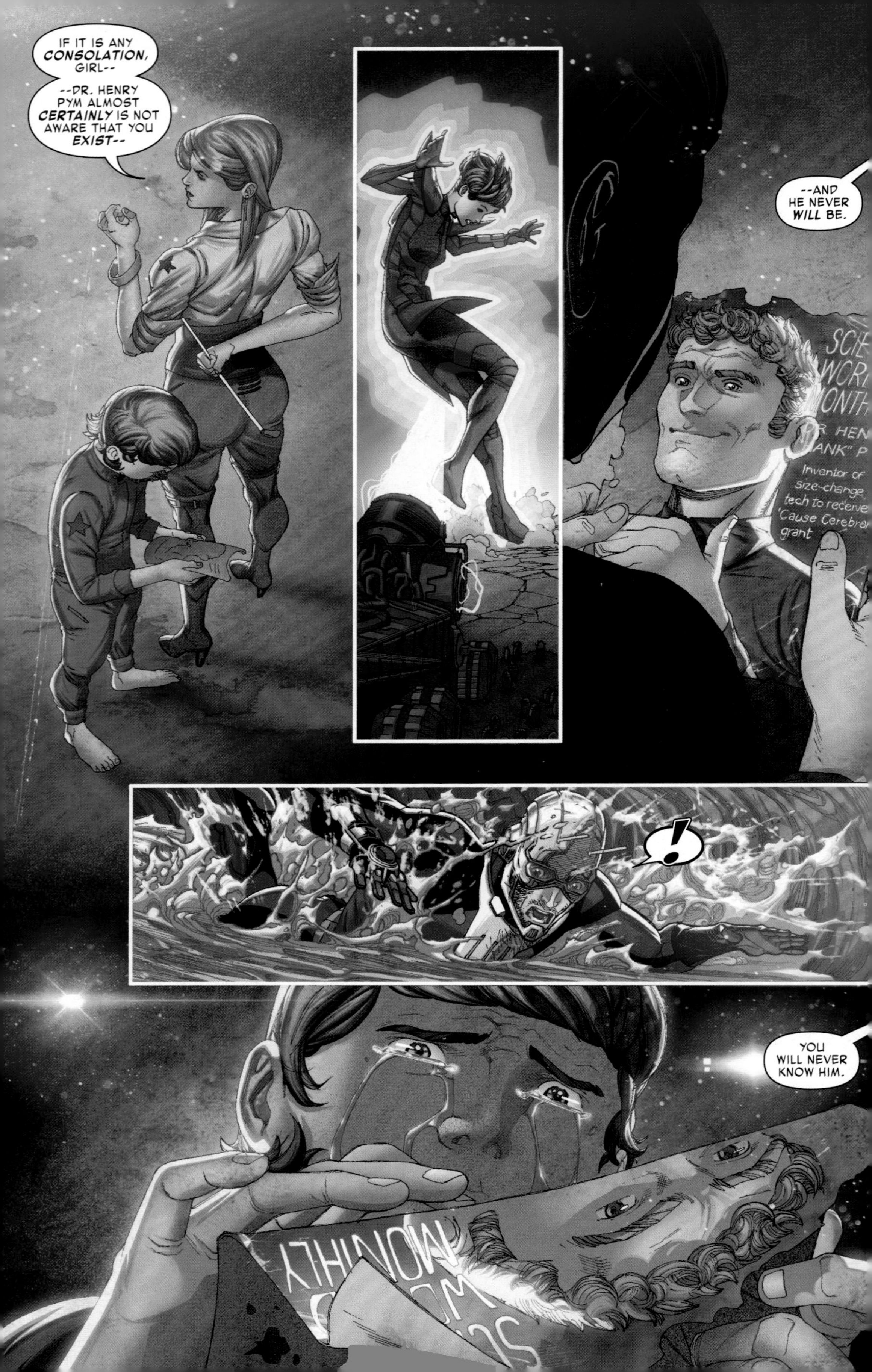

IF IT IS ANY CONSOLATION, GIRL--
--DR. HENRY PYM ALMOST CERTAINLY IS NOT AWARE THAT YOU EXIST--
--AND HE NEVER WILL BE.
!
YOU WILL NEVER KNOW HIM.

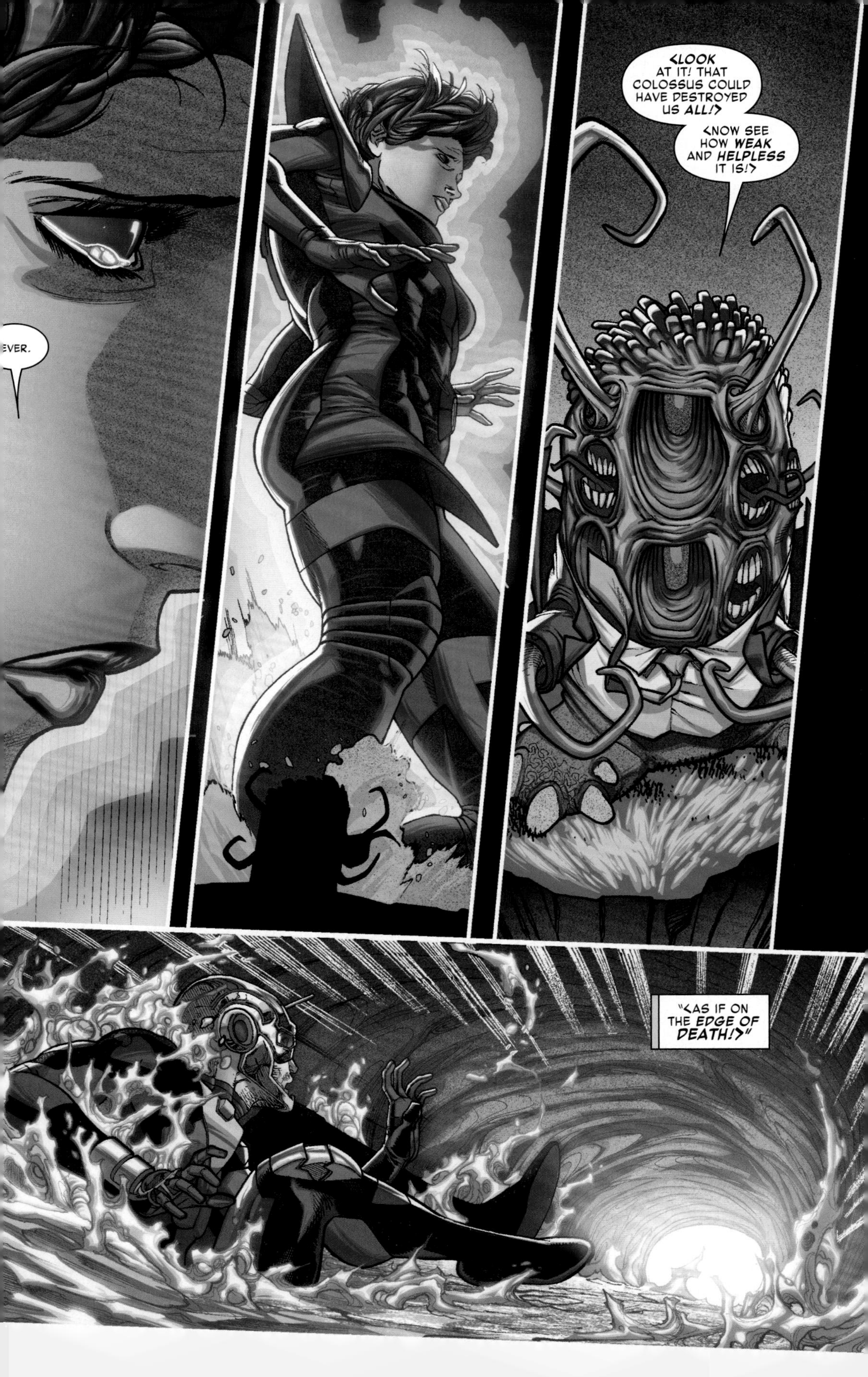

EVER.
<LOOK AT IT! THAT COLOSSUS COULD HAVE DESTROYED US ALL!>
<NOW SEE HOW WEAK AND HELPLESS IT IS!>
"<AS IF ON THE EDGE OF DEATH!>"

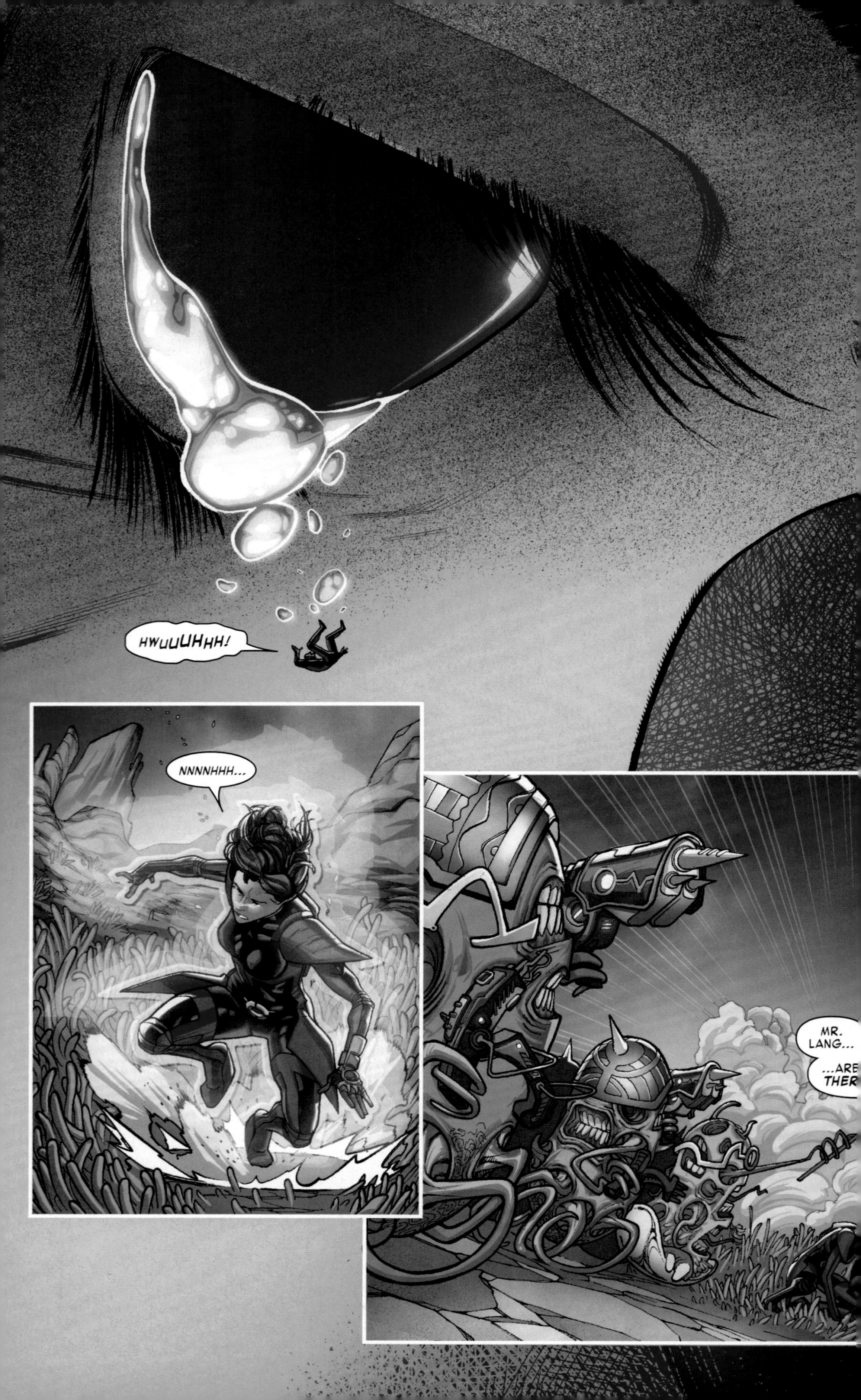
HWUUUHHH!
NNNNHHH...
MR. LANG...

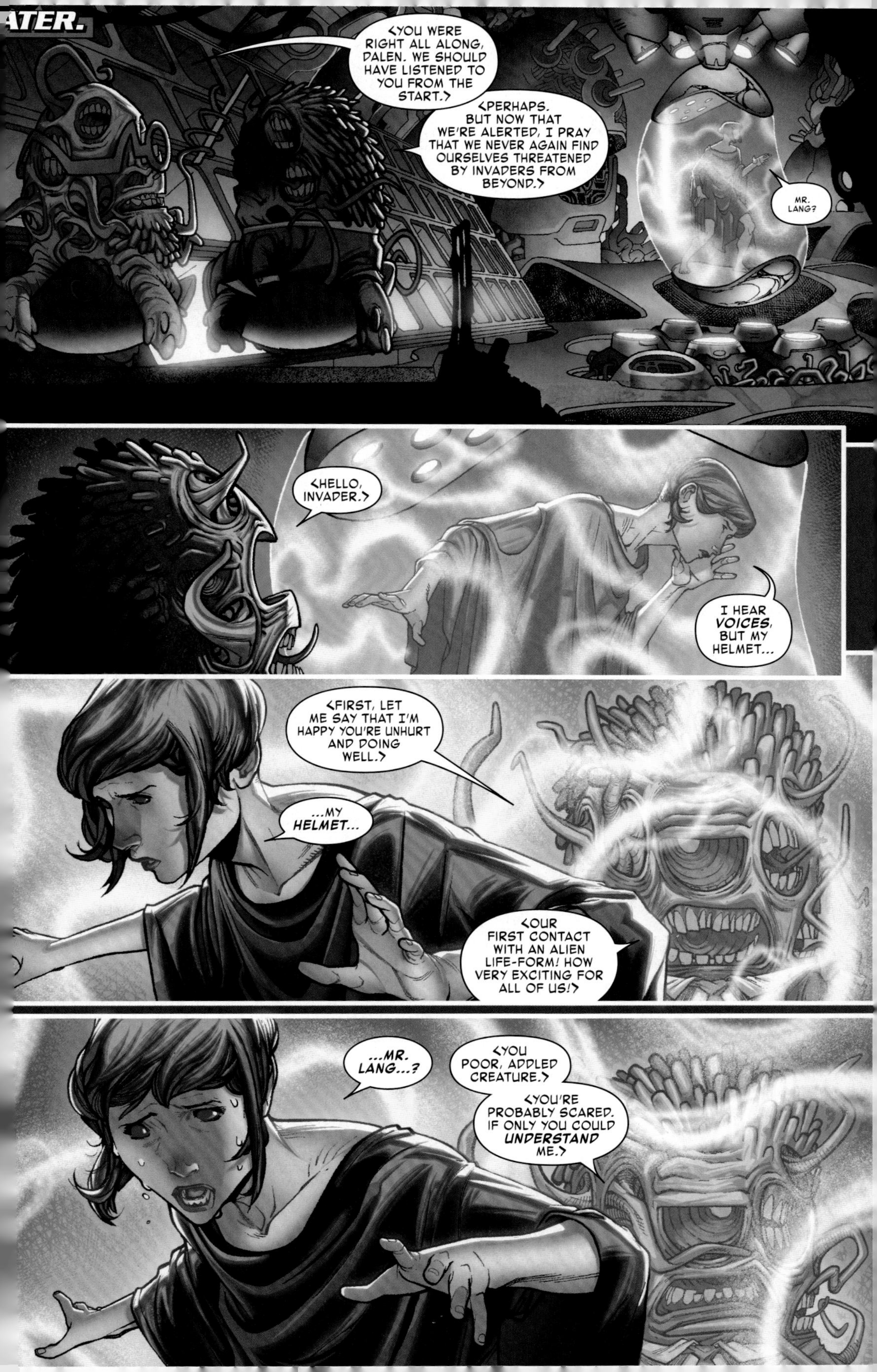
ATER.
<YOU WERE RIGHT ALL ALONG, DALEN. WE SHOULD HAVE LISTENED TO YOU FROM THE START.>
<PERHAPS. BUT NOW THAT WE'RE ALERTED, I PRAY THAT WE NEVER AGAIN FIND OURSELVES THREATENED BY INVADERS FROM BEYOND.>
MR. LANG?
<HELLO, INVADER.>
I HEAR VOICES, BUT MY HELMET...
<FIRST, LET ME SAY THAT I'M HAPPY YOU'RE UNHURT AND DOING WELL.>
...MY HELMET...
<OUR FIRST CONTACT WITH AN ALIEN LIFE-FORM! HOW VERY EXCITING FOR ALL OF US!>
...MR. LANG...?
<YOU POOR, ADDLED CREATURE.>
<YOU'RE PROBABLY SCARED. IF ONLY YOU COULD UNDERSTAND ME.>

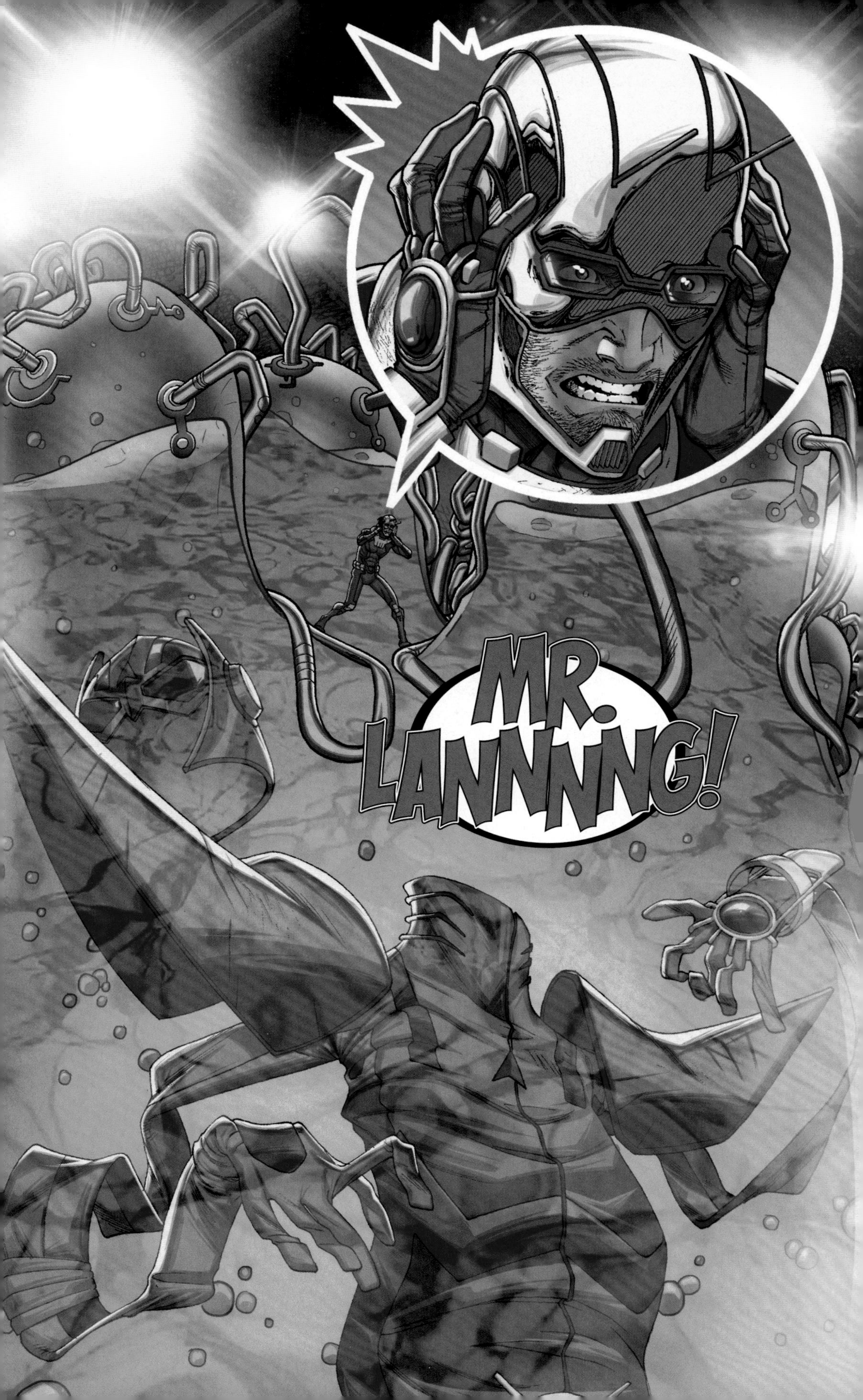
MR. LANNNNG!

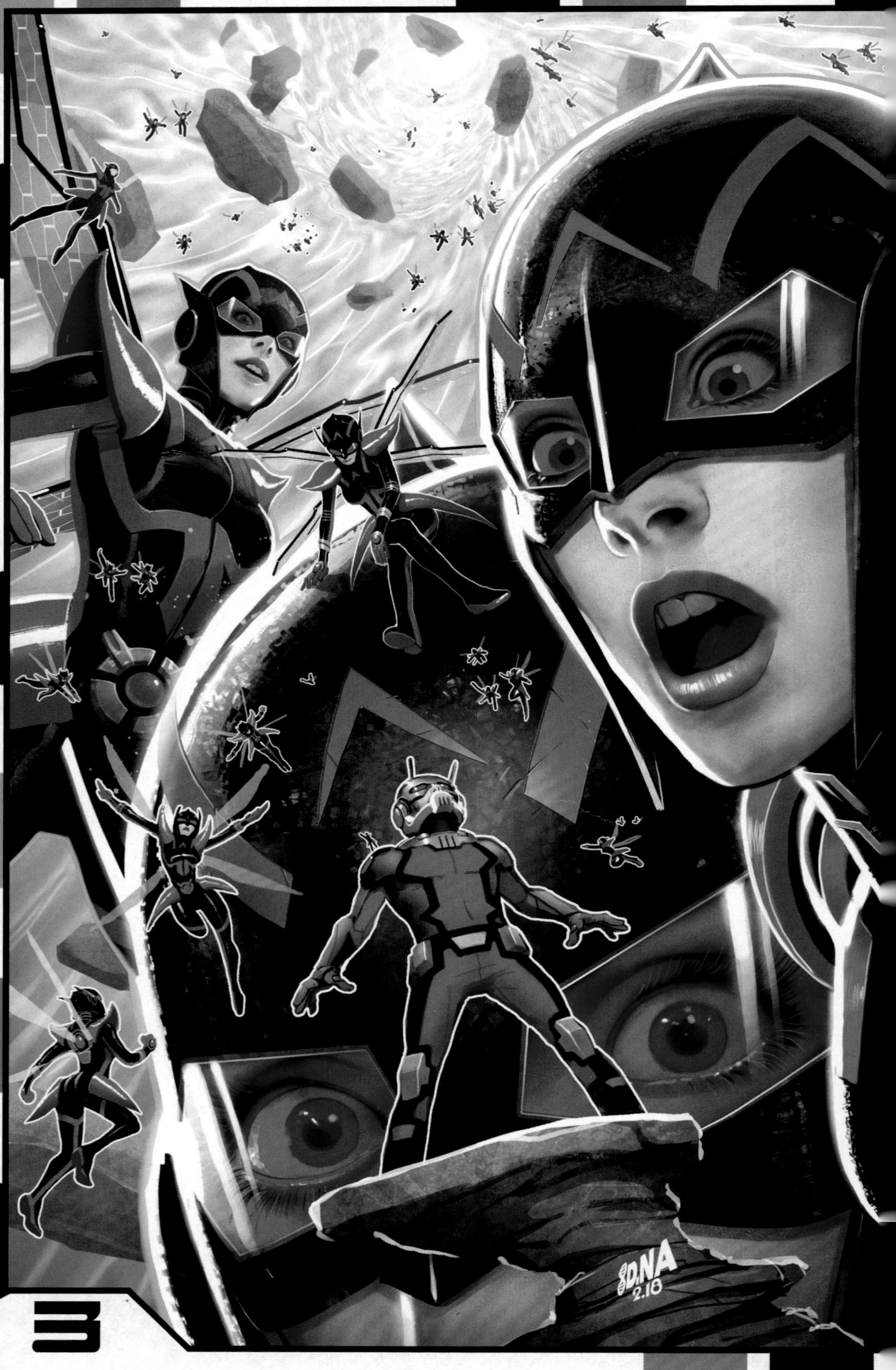
D.NA
2.18
3

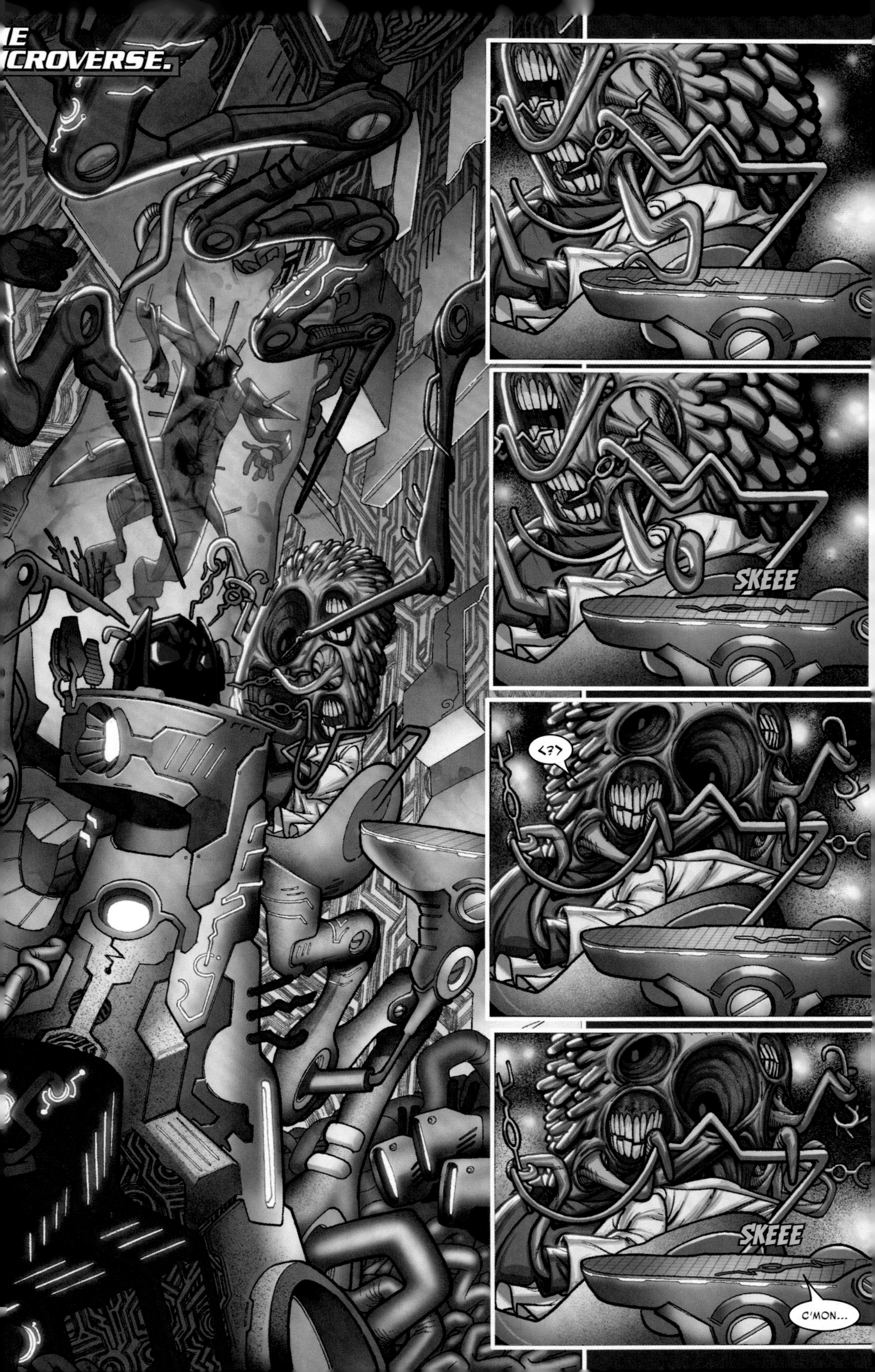

…E
…CROVERSE.
SKEEE
<?>
SKEEE
C'MON...

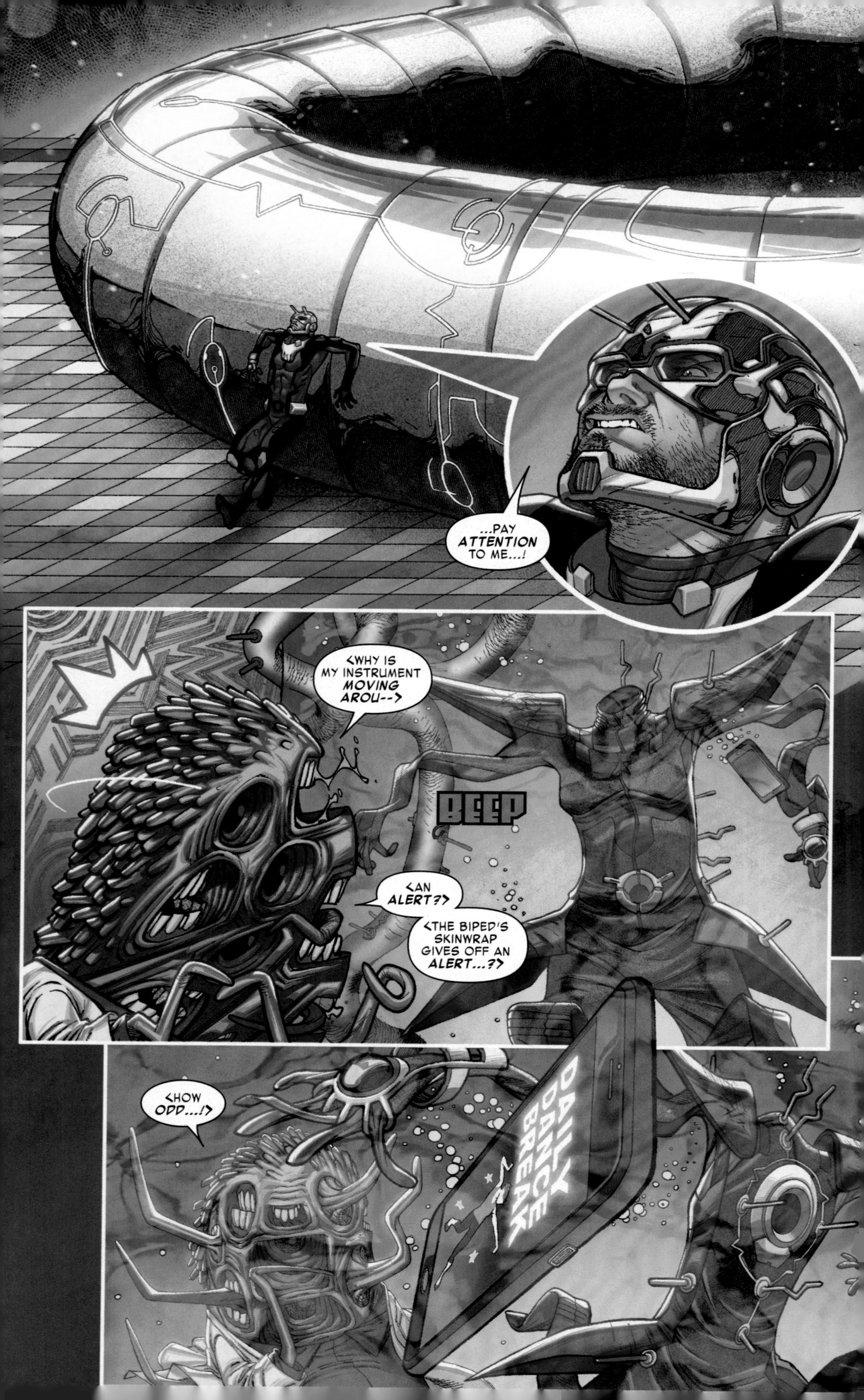
...PAY ATTENTION TO ME...!
<WHY IS MY INSTRUMENT MOVING AROU-->
BEEP
<AN ALERT?>
<THE BIPED'S SKINWRAP GIVES OFF AN ALERT...?>
<HOW ODD...!>
DAILY DANCE BREAK

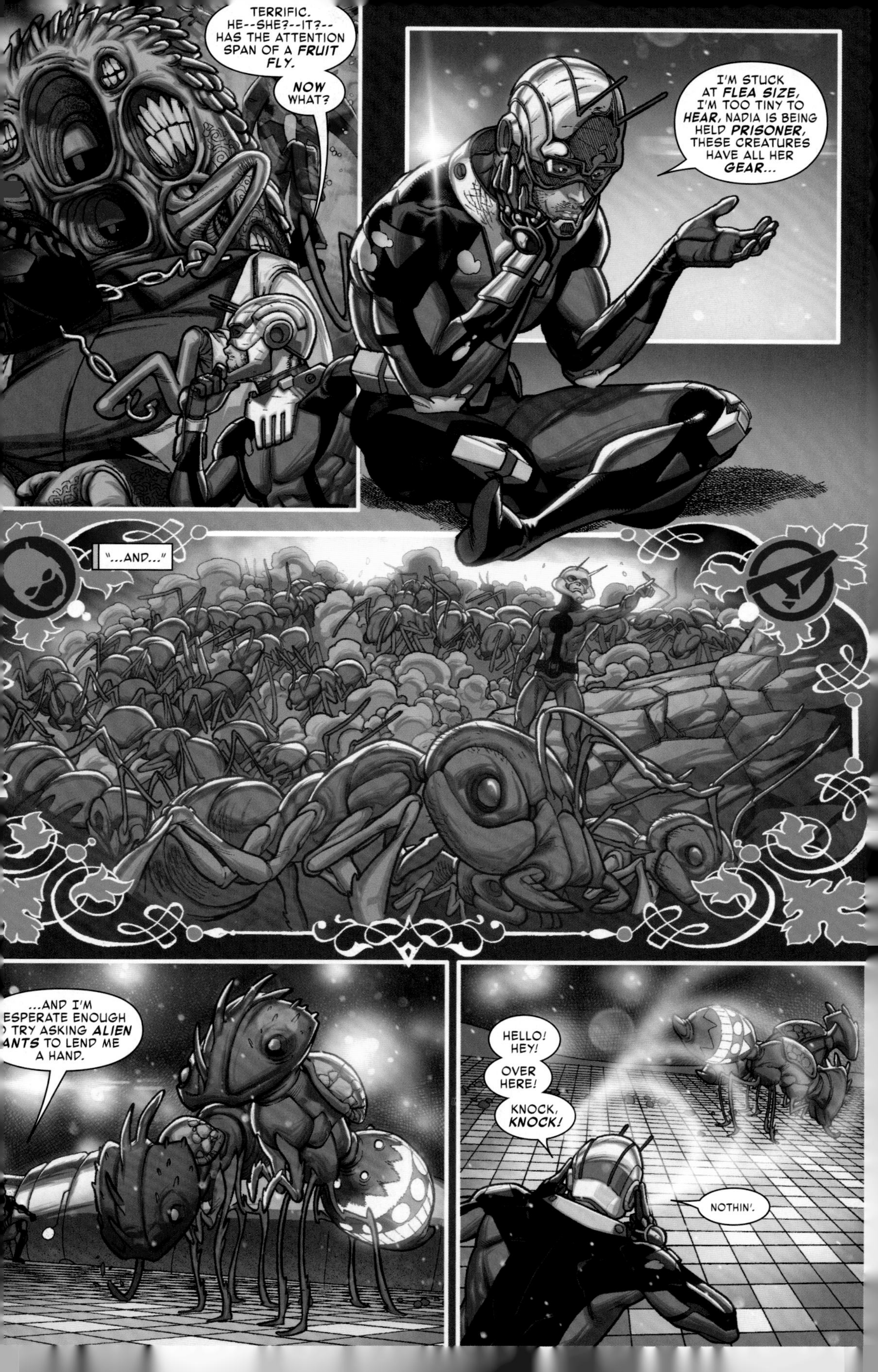
TERRIFIC. HE--SHE?--IT?-- HAS THE ATTENTION SPAN OF A FRUIT FLY.
NOW WHAT?
I'M STUCK AT FLEA SIZE, I'M TOO TINY TO HEAR, NADIA IS BEING HELD PRISONER, THESE CREATURES HAVE ALL HER GEAR...
"...AND..."
...AND I'M ESPERATE ENOUGH O TRY ASKING ALIEN ANTS TO LEND ME A HAND.
HELLO! HEY!
OVER HERE!
KNOCK, KNOCK!
NOTHIN'.

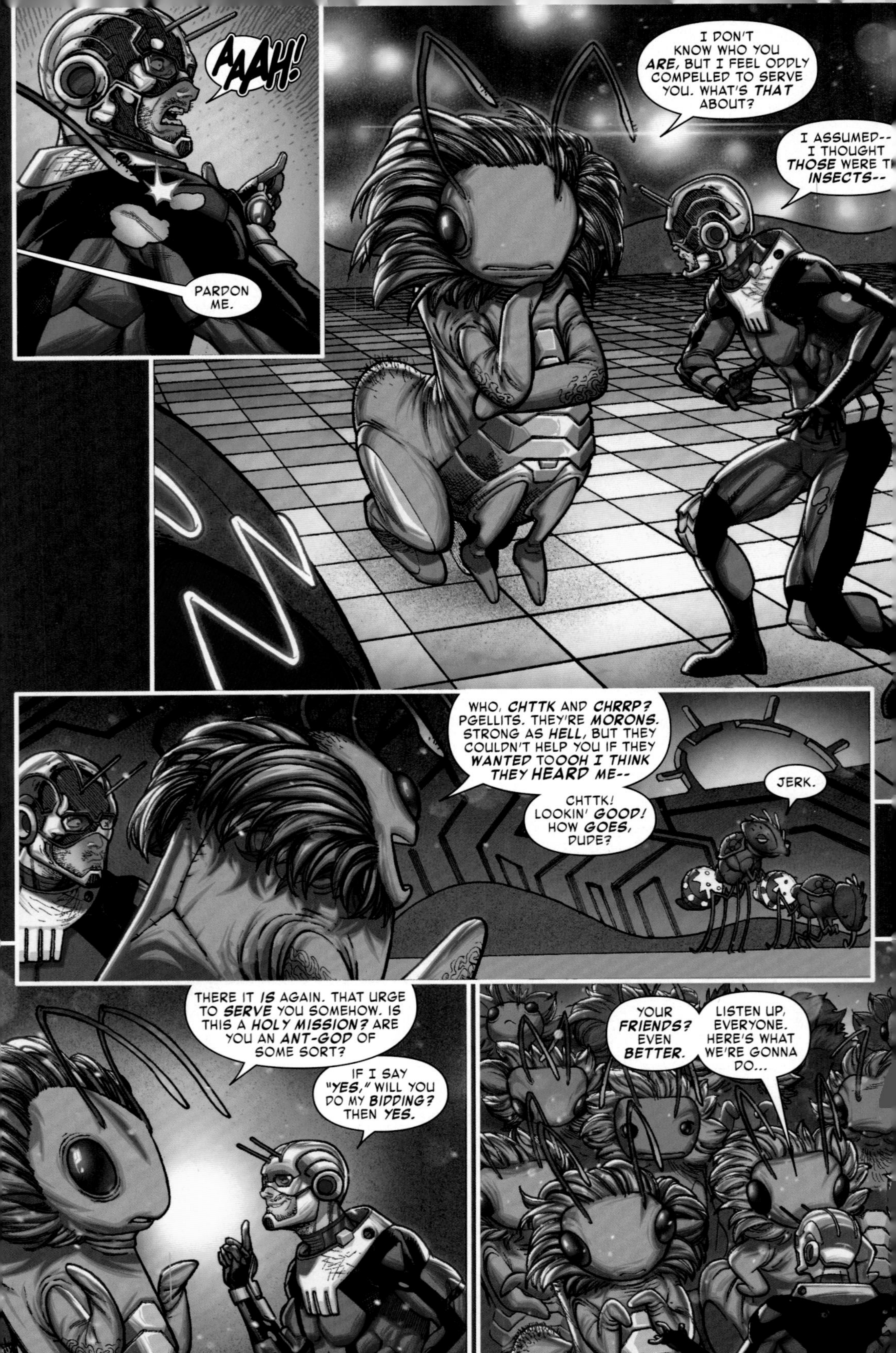
AAAH!
PARDON ME.
I DON'T KNOW WHO YOU ARE, BUT I FEEL ODDLY COMPELLED TO SERVE YOU. WHAT'S THAT ABOUT?
I ASSUMED-- I THOUGHT THOSE WERE T
INSECTS--
WHO, CHTTK AND CHRRP? PGELLITS. THEY'RE MORONS. STRONG AS HELL, BUT THEY COULDN'T HELP YOU IF THEY WANTED TOOOH I THINK THEY HEARD ME--
JERK.
CHTTK! LOOKIN' GOOD! HOW GOES, DUDE?
THERE IT IS AGAIN. THAT URGE TO SERVE YOU SOMEHOW. IS THIS A HOLY MISSION? ARE YOU AN ANT-GOD OF SOME SORT?
IF I SAY "YES," WILL YOU DO MY BIDDING? THEN YES.
YOUR FRIENDS? EVEN BETTER.
LISTEN UP, EVERYONE. HERE'S WHAT WE'RE GONNA DO...

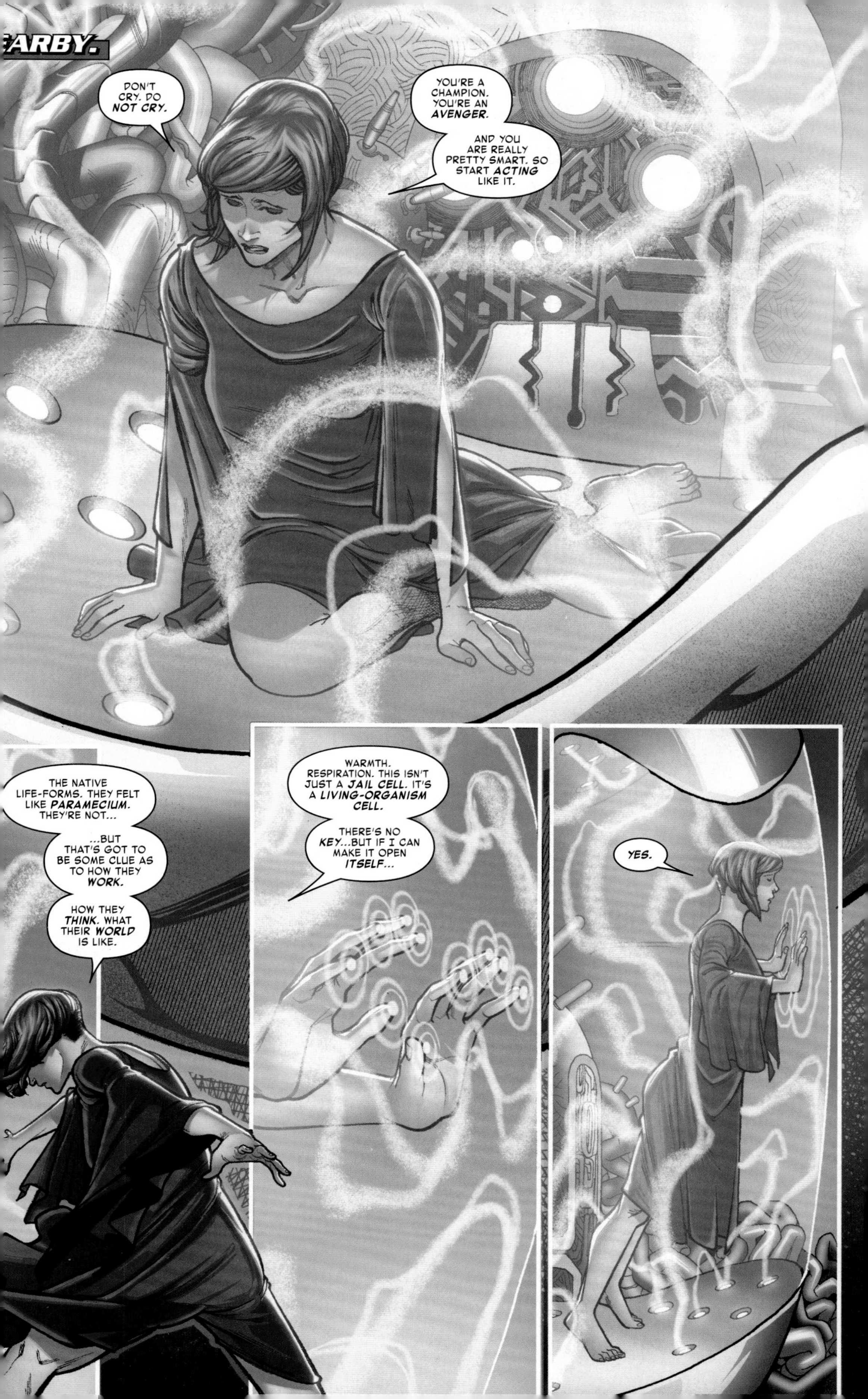
ARBY.
DON'T CRY. DO NOT CRY.
YOU'RE A CHAMPION. YOU'RE AN AVENGER.
AND YOU ARE REALLY PRETTY SMART. SO START ACTING LIKE IT.
THE NATIVE LIFE-FORMS. THEY FELT LIKE PARAMECIUM. THEY'RE NOT...
...BUT THAT'S GOT TO BE SOME CLUE AS TO HOW THEY WORK.
HOW THEY THINK. WHAT THEIR WORLD IS LIKE.
WARMTH. RESPIRATION. THIS ISN'T JUST A JAIL CELL. IT'S A LIVING-ORGANISM CELL.
THERE'S NO KEY...BUT IF I CAN MAKE IT OPEN ITSELF...
YES.

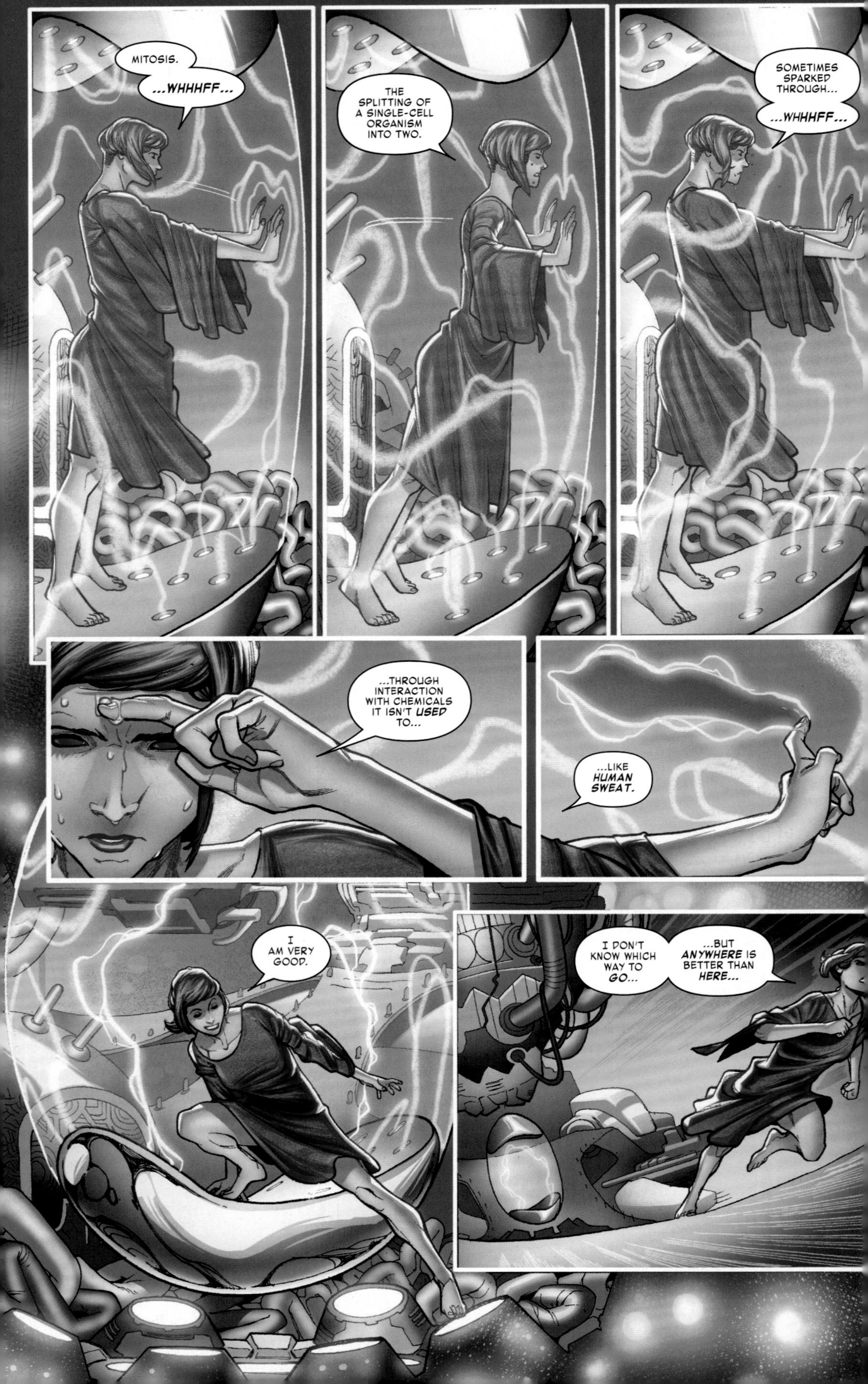
MITOSIS.
...WHHHFF...
THE SPLITTING OF A SINGLE-CELL ORGANISM INTO TWO.
SOMETIMES SPARKED THROUGH...
...WHHHFF...
...THROUGH INTERACTION WITH CHEMICALS IT ISN'T USED TO...
...LIKE HUMAN SWEAT.
I AM VERY GOOD.
I DON'T KNOW WHICH WAY TO GO...
...BUT ANYWHERE IS BETTER THAN HERE...

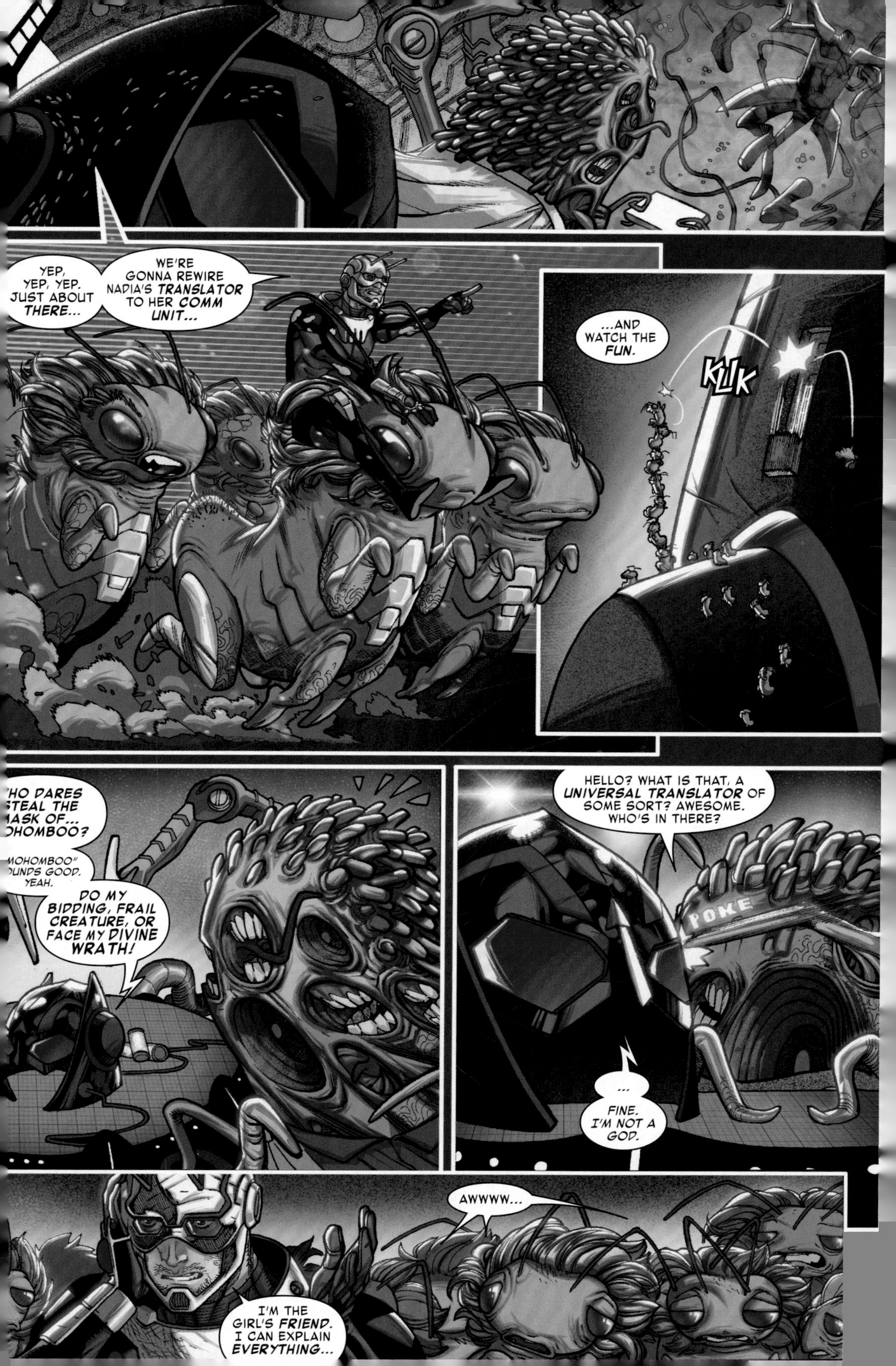

YEP, YEP, YEP. JUST ABOUT THERE...
WE'RE GONNA REWIRE NADIA'S TRANSLATOR TO HER COMM UNIT...
...AND WATCH THE FUN.
KLIK
HO DARES STEAL THE ASK OF... OHOMBOO?
MOHOMBOO" OUNDS GOOD. YEAH.
DO MY BIDDING, FRAIL CREATURE, OR FACE MY DIVINE WRATH!
HELLO? WHAT IS THAT, A UNIVERSAL TRANSLATOR OF SOME SORT? AWESOME. WHO'S IN THERE?
POKE
... FINE. I'M NOT A GOD.
AWWWW...
I'M THE GIRL'S FRIEND. I CAN EXPLAIN EVERYTHING...

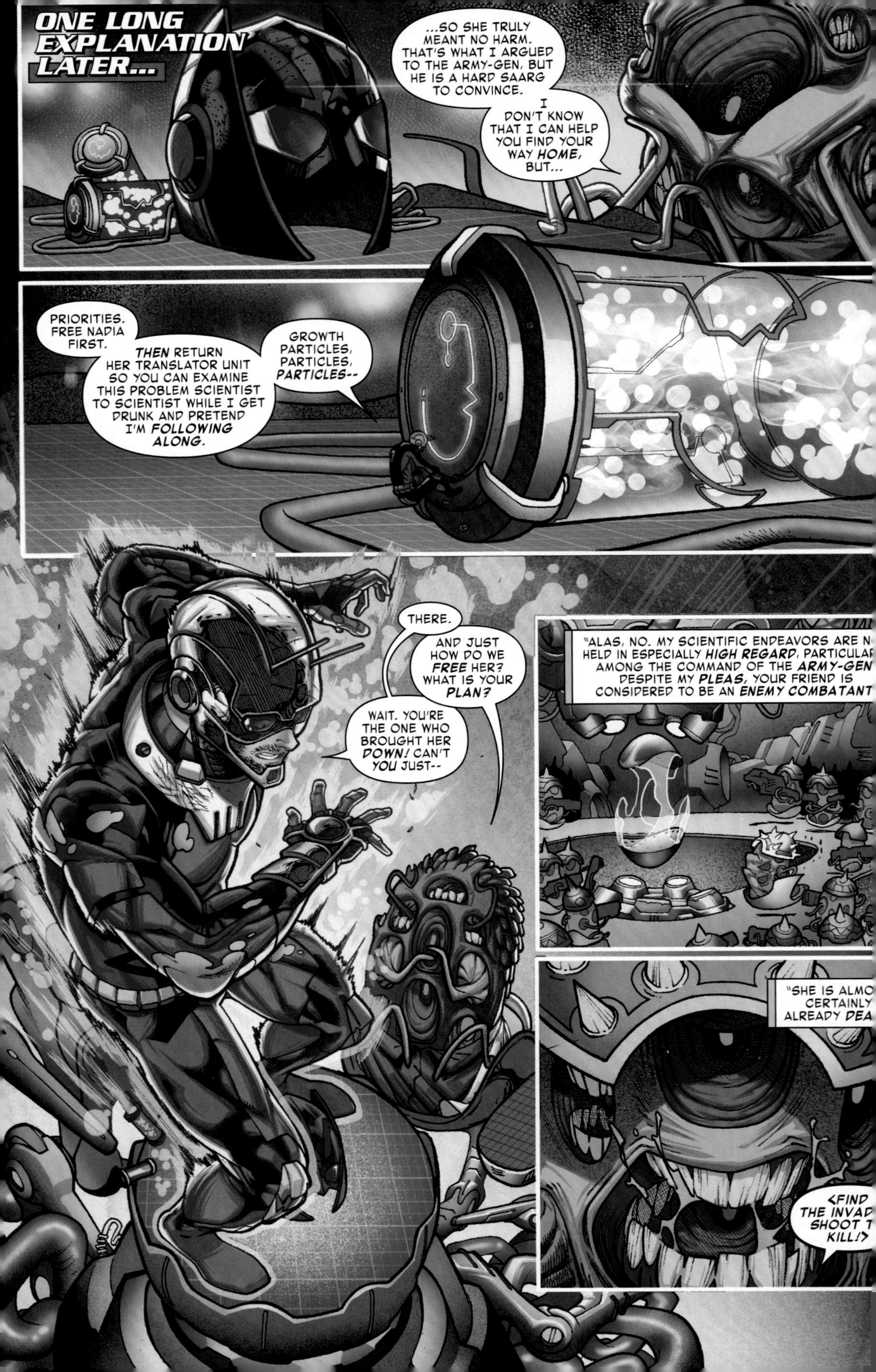

ONE LONG EXPLANATION LATER...
...SO SHE TRULY MEANT NO HARM. THAT'S WHAT I ARGUED TO THE ARMY-GEN, BUT HE IS A HARD SAARG TO CONVINCE.
I DON'T KNOW THAT I CAN HELP YOU FIND YOUR WAY HOME, BUT...
PRIORITIES. FREE NADIA FIRST.
THEN RETURN HER TRANSLATOR UNIT SO YOU CAN EXAMINE THIS PROBLEM SCIENTIST TO SCIENTIST WHILE I GET DRUNK AND PRETEND I'M FOLLOWING ALONG.
GROWTH PARTICLES, PARTICLES, PARTICLES--
THERE.
AND JUST HOW DO WE FREE HER? WHAT IS YOUR PLAN?
WAIT. YOU'RE THE ONE WHO BROUGHT HER DOWN! CAN'T YOU JUST--
"ALAS, NO. MY SCIENTIFIC ENDEAVORS ARE N HELD IN ESPECIALLY HIGH REGARD, PARTICULAR AMONG THE COMMAND OF THE ARMY-GEN DESPITE MY PLEAS, YOUR FRIEND IS CONSIDERED TO BE AN ENEMY COMBATANT
"SHE IS ALMO CERTAINLY ALREADY DEA
<FIND THE INVAD SHOOT T KILL!>

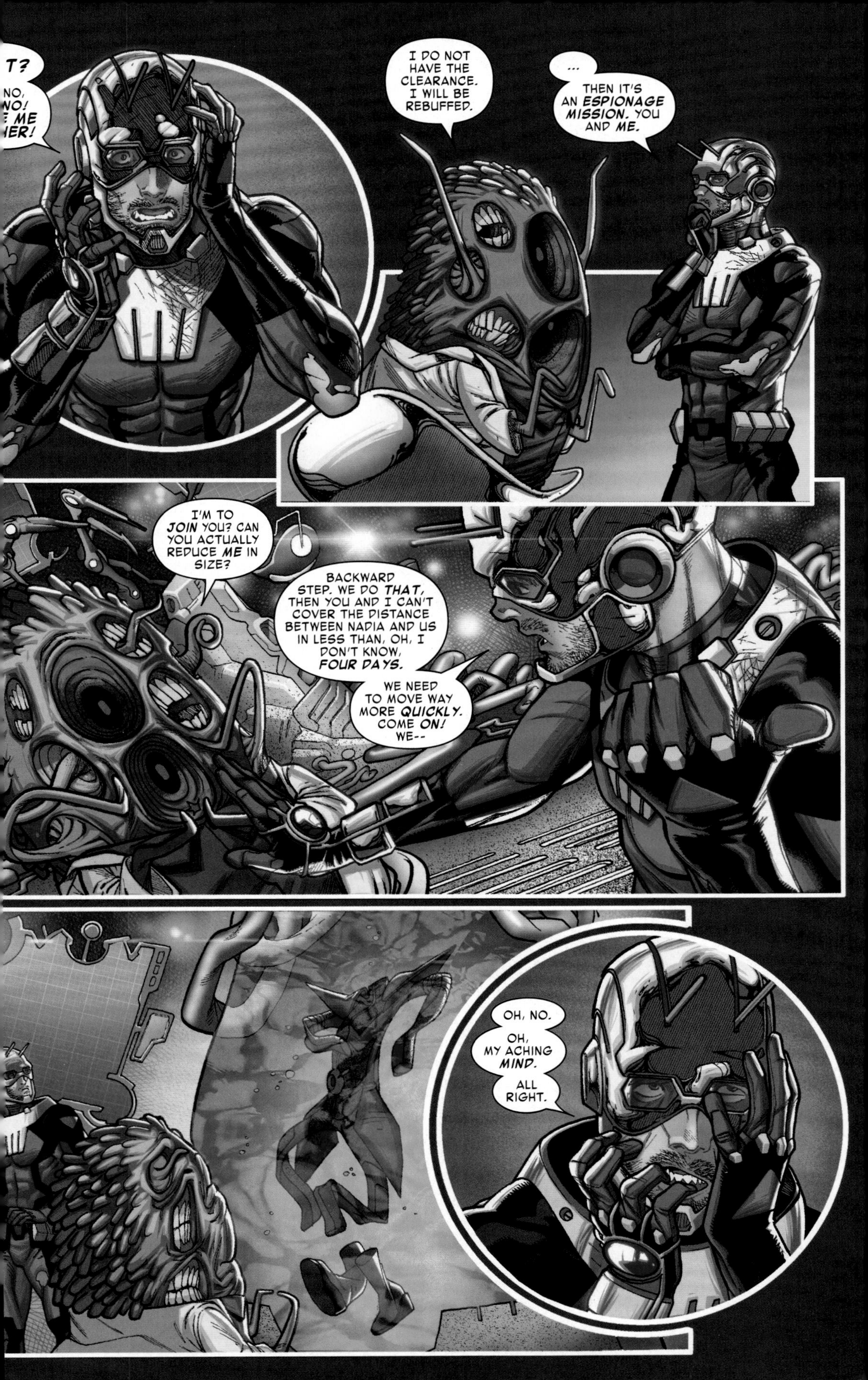
NO, NO!
I DO NOT HAVE THE CLEARANCE. I WILL BE REBUFFED.
...
THEN IT'S AN ESPIONAGE MISSION. YOU AND ME.
I'M TO JOIN YOU? CAN YOU ACTUALLY REDUCE ME IN SIZE?
BACKWARD STEP. WE DO THAT, THEN YOU AND I CAN'T COVER THE DISTANCE BETWEEN NADIA AND US IN LESS THAN, OH, I DON'T KNOW, FOUR DAYS.
WE NEED TO MOVE WAY MORE QUICKLY. COME ON! WE--
OH, NO.
OH, MY ACHING MIND.
ALL RIGHT.

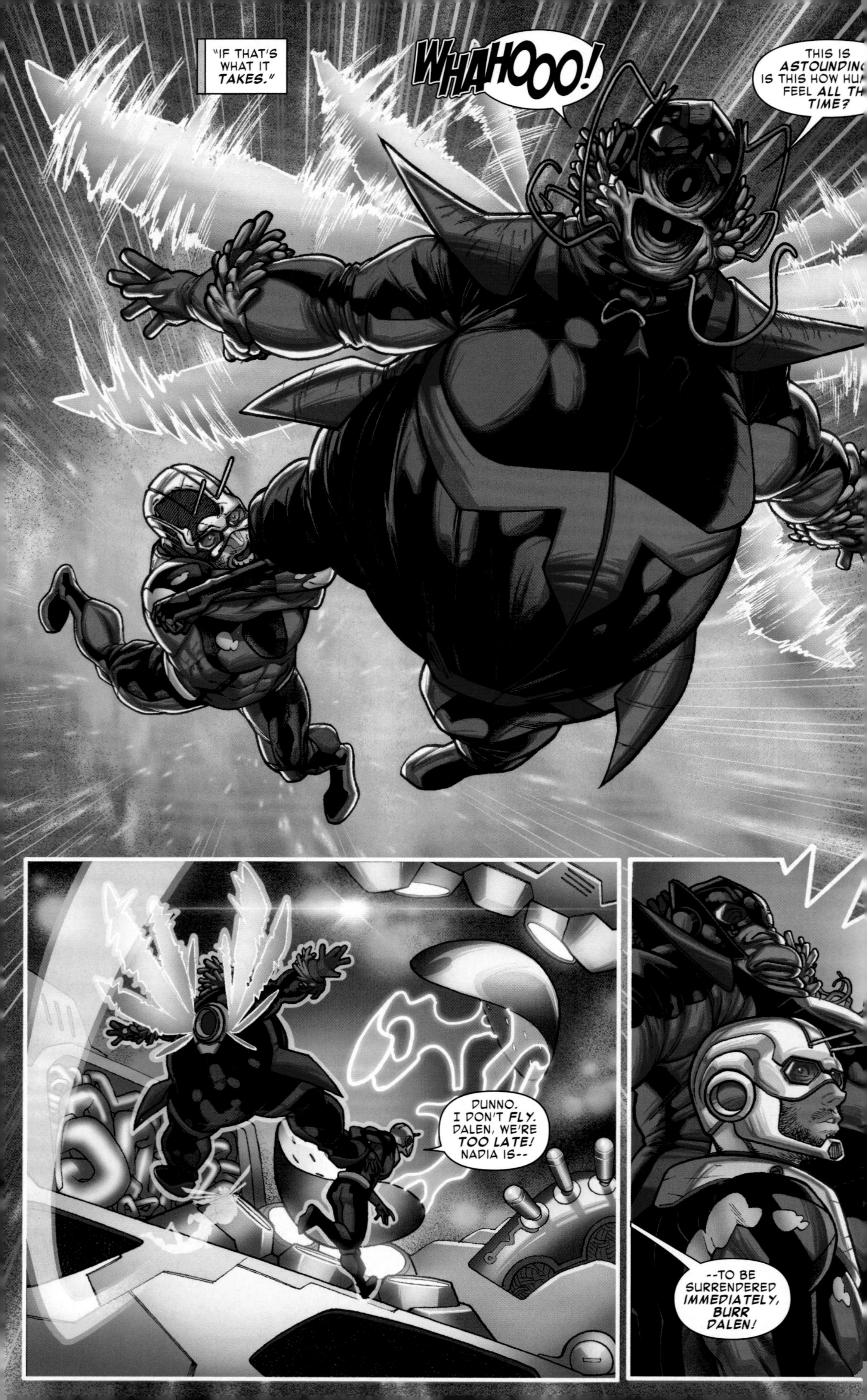
"IF THAT'S WHAT IT TAKES."
WHAHOOO!
THIS IS ASTOUNDIN IS THIS HOW HU FEEL ALL TH TIME?
DUNNO. I DON'T FLY. DALEN, WE'RE TOO LATE! NADIA IS--
--TO BE SURRENDERED IMMEDIATELY, BURR DALEN!

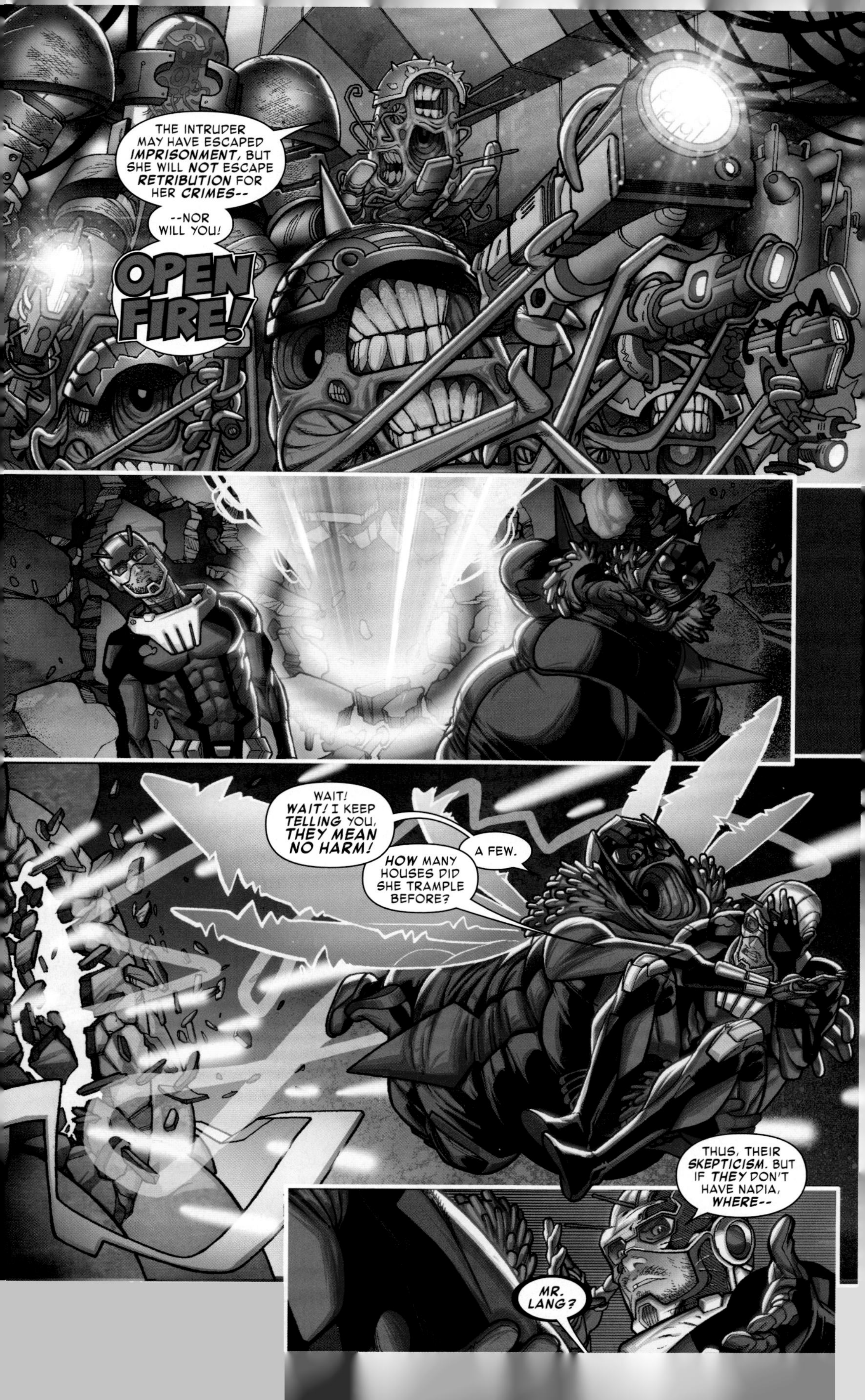

THE INTRUDER MAY HAVE ESCAPED IMPRISONMENT, BUT SHE WILL NOT ESCAPE RETRIBUTION FOR HER CRIMES--
--NOR WILL YOU!
OPEN FIRE!
WAIT! WAIT! I KEEP TELLING YOU, THEY MEAN NO HARM!
HOW MANY HOUSES DID SHE TRAMPLE BEFORE?
A FEW.
THUS, THEIR SKEPTICISM. BUT IF THEY DON'T HAVE NADIA, WHERE--
MR. LANG?

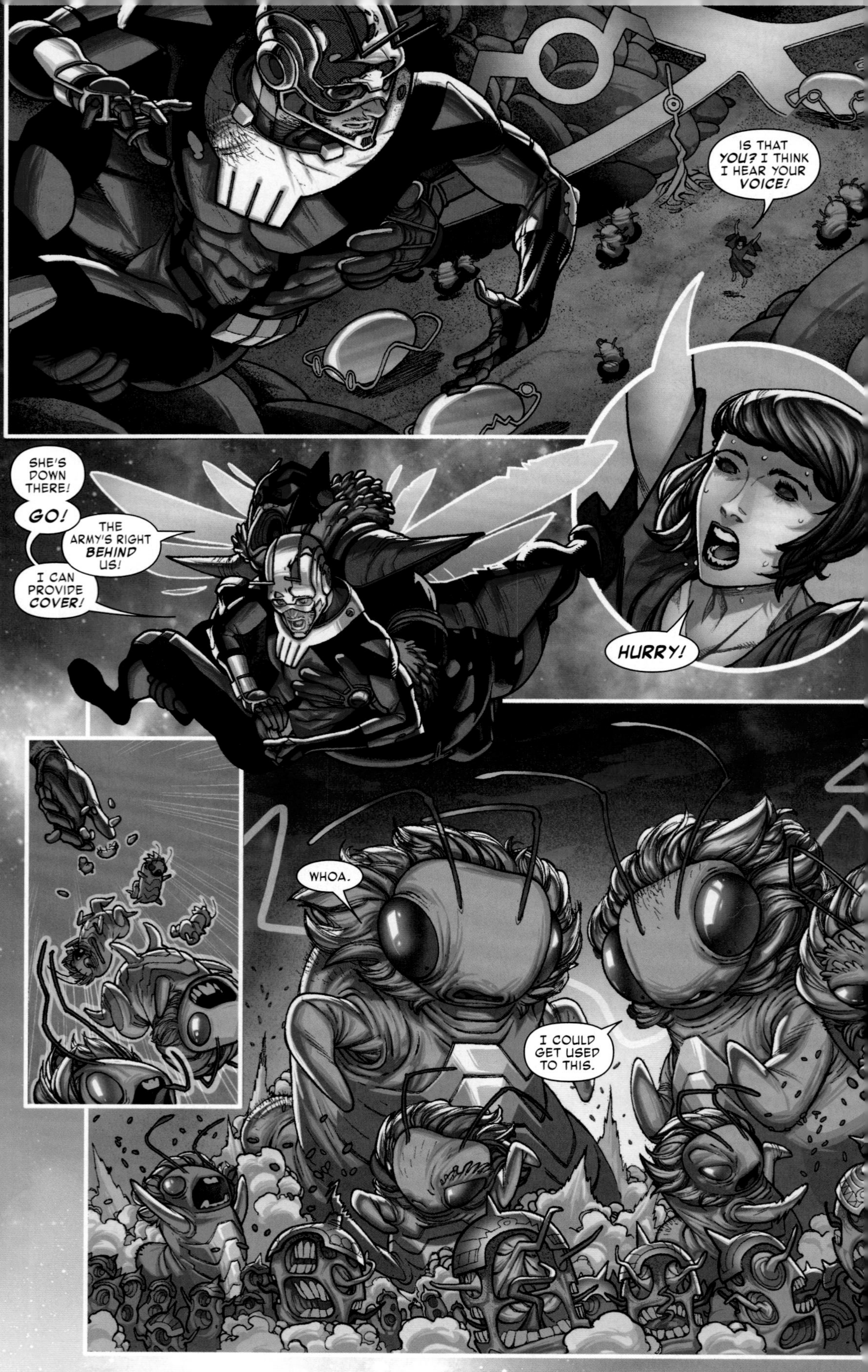
IS THAT YOU? I THINK I HEAR YOUR VOICE!
SHE'S DOWN THERE!
GO!
THE ARMY'S RIGHT BEHIND US!
I CAN PROVIDE COVER!
HURRY!
WHOA.
I COULD GET USED TO THIS.

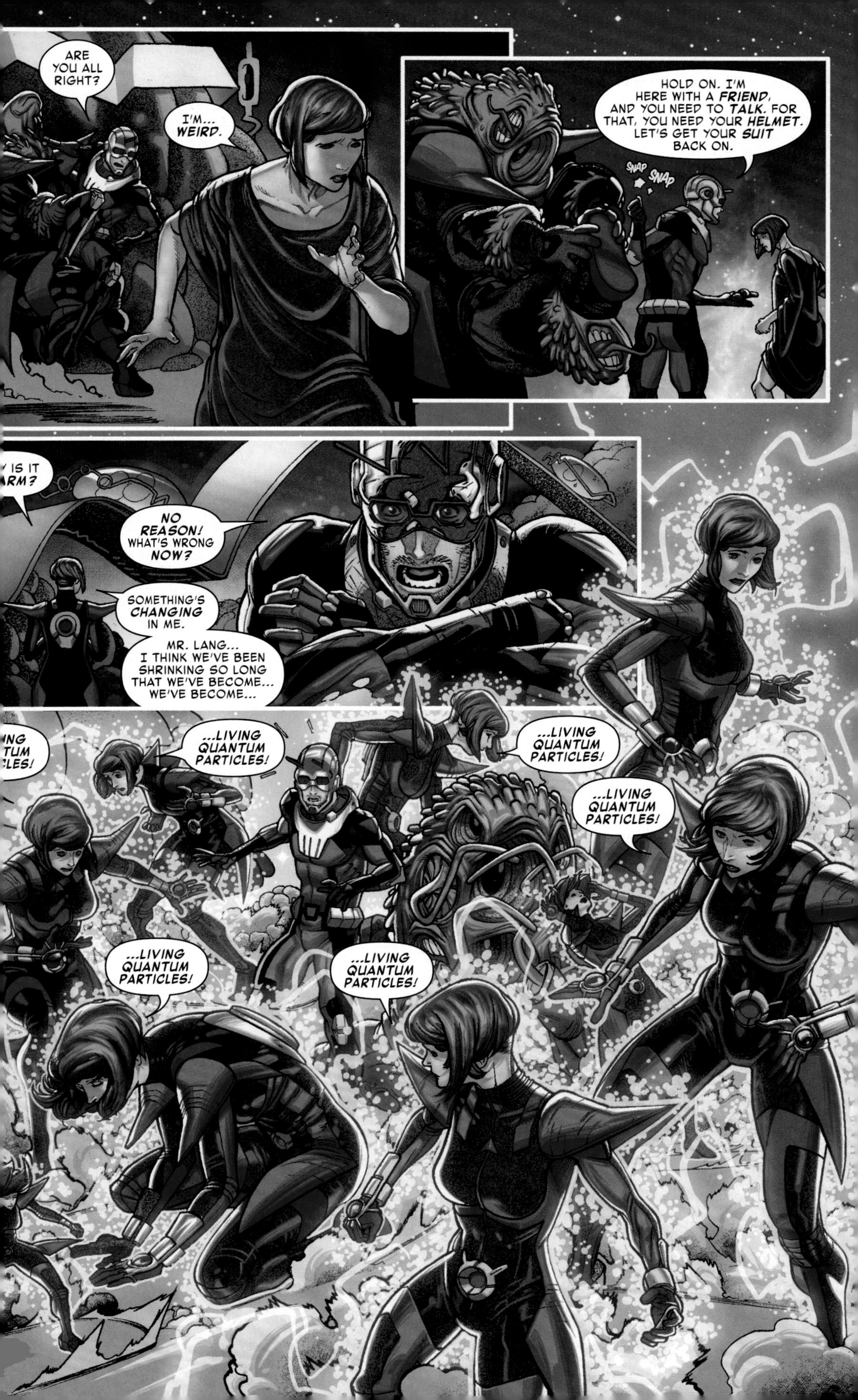
ARE YOU ALL RIGHT?
I'M... WEIRD.
HOLD ON. I'M HERE WITH A FRIEND, AND YOU NEED TO TALK. FOR THAT, YOU NEED YOUR HELMET. LET'S GET YOUR SUIT BACK ON.
SNAP SNAP
NO REASON! WHAT'S WRONG NOW?
SOMETHING'S CHANGING IN ME.
MR. LANG... I THINK WE'VE BEEN SHRINKING SO LONG THAT WE'VE BECOME... WE'VE BECOME...
...LIVING QUANTUM PARTICLES!
...LIVING QUANTUM PARTICLES!
...LIVING QUANTUM PARTICLES!
...LIVING QUANTUM PARTICLES!
...LIVING QUANTUM PARTICLES!

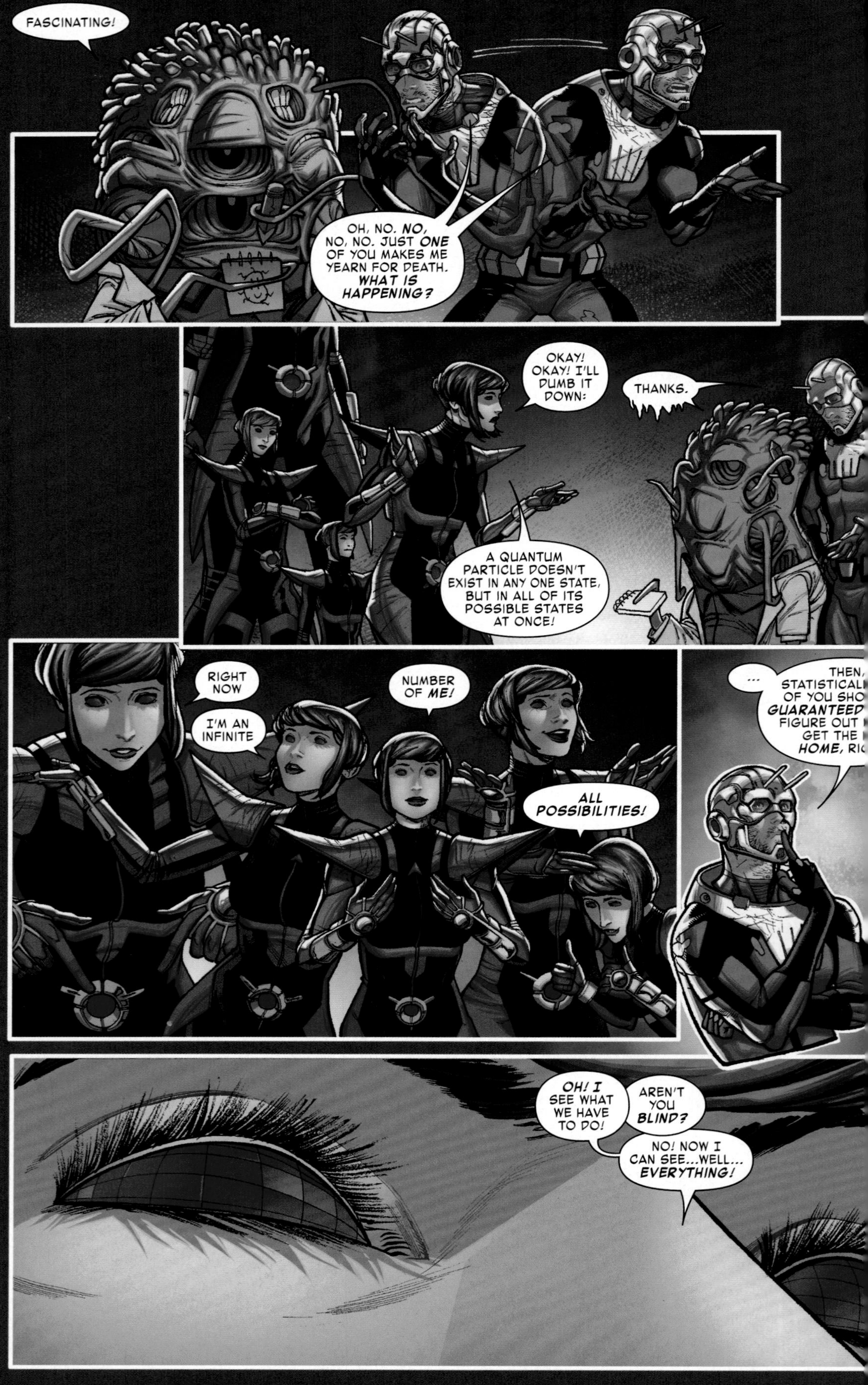
FASCINATING!
OH, NO. NO, NO, NO. JUST ONE OF YOU MAKES ME YEARN FOR DEATH. WHAT IS HAPPENING?
OKAY! OKAY! I'LL DUMB IT DOWN:
THANKS.
A QUANTUM PARTICLE DOESN'T EXIST IN ANY ONE STATE, BUT IN ALL OF ITS POSSIBLE STATES AT ONCE!
RIGHT NOW
I'M AN INFINITE
NUMBER OF ME!
ALL POSSIBILITIES!
...
THEN, STATISTICAL
OF YOU SHO
GUARANTEED
FIGURE OUT
GET THE
HOME, RI
OH! I SEE WHAT WE HAVE TO DO!
AREN'T YOU BLIND?
NO! NOW I CAN SEE...WELL... EVERYTHING!

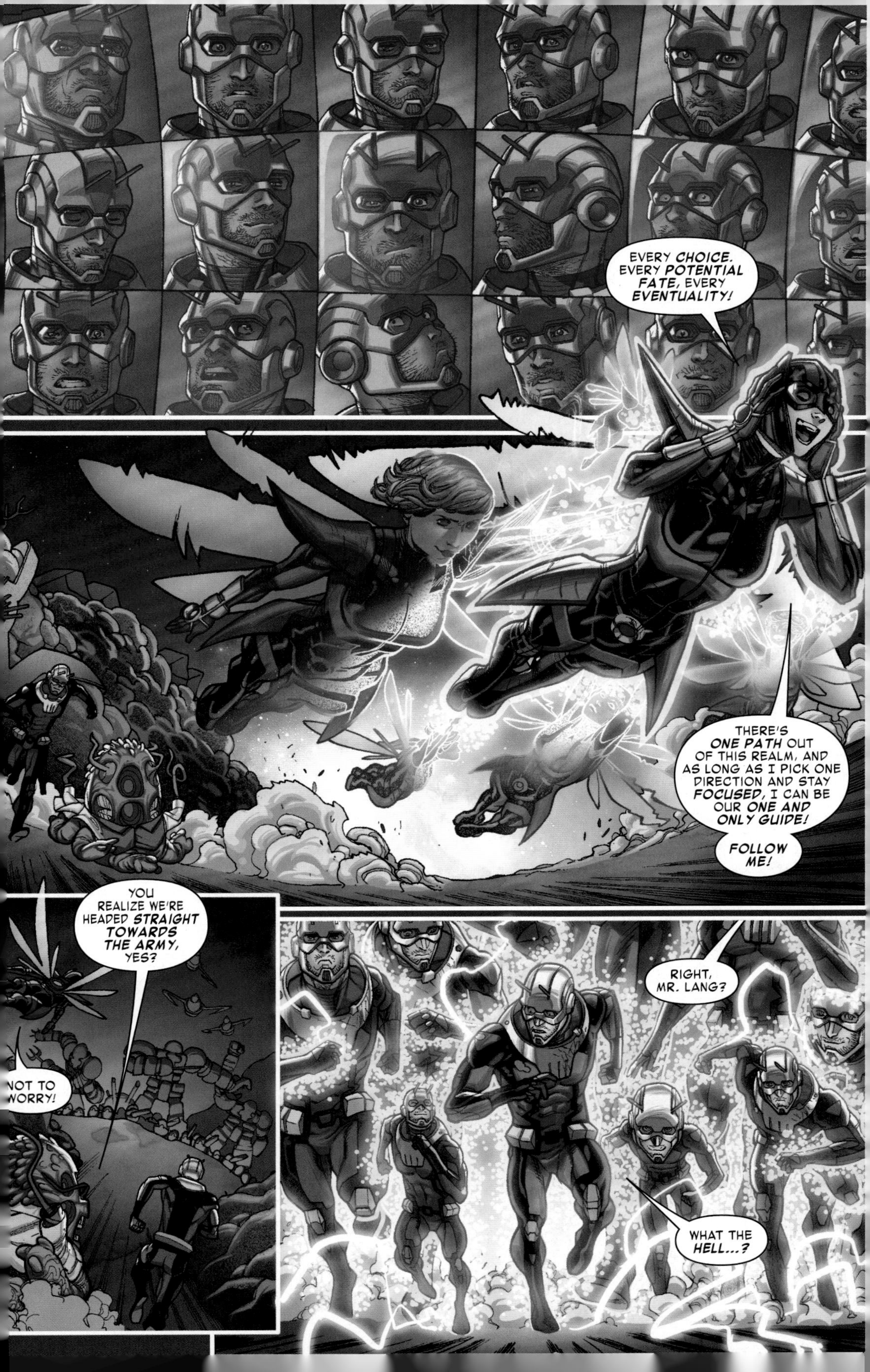
EVERY CHOICE. EVERY POTENTIAL FATE, EVERY EVENTUALITY!
THERE'S ONE PATH OUT OF THIS REALM, AND AS LONG AS I PICK ONE DIRECTION AND STAY FOCUSED, I CAN BE OUR ONE AND ONLY GUIDE!
FOLLOW ME!
YOU REALIZE WE'RE HEADED STRAIGHT TOWARDS THE ARMY, YES?
NOT TO WORRY!
RIGHT, MR. LANG?
WHAT THE HELL...?

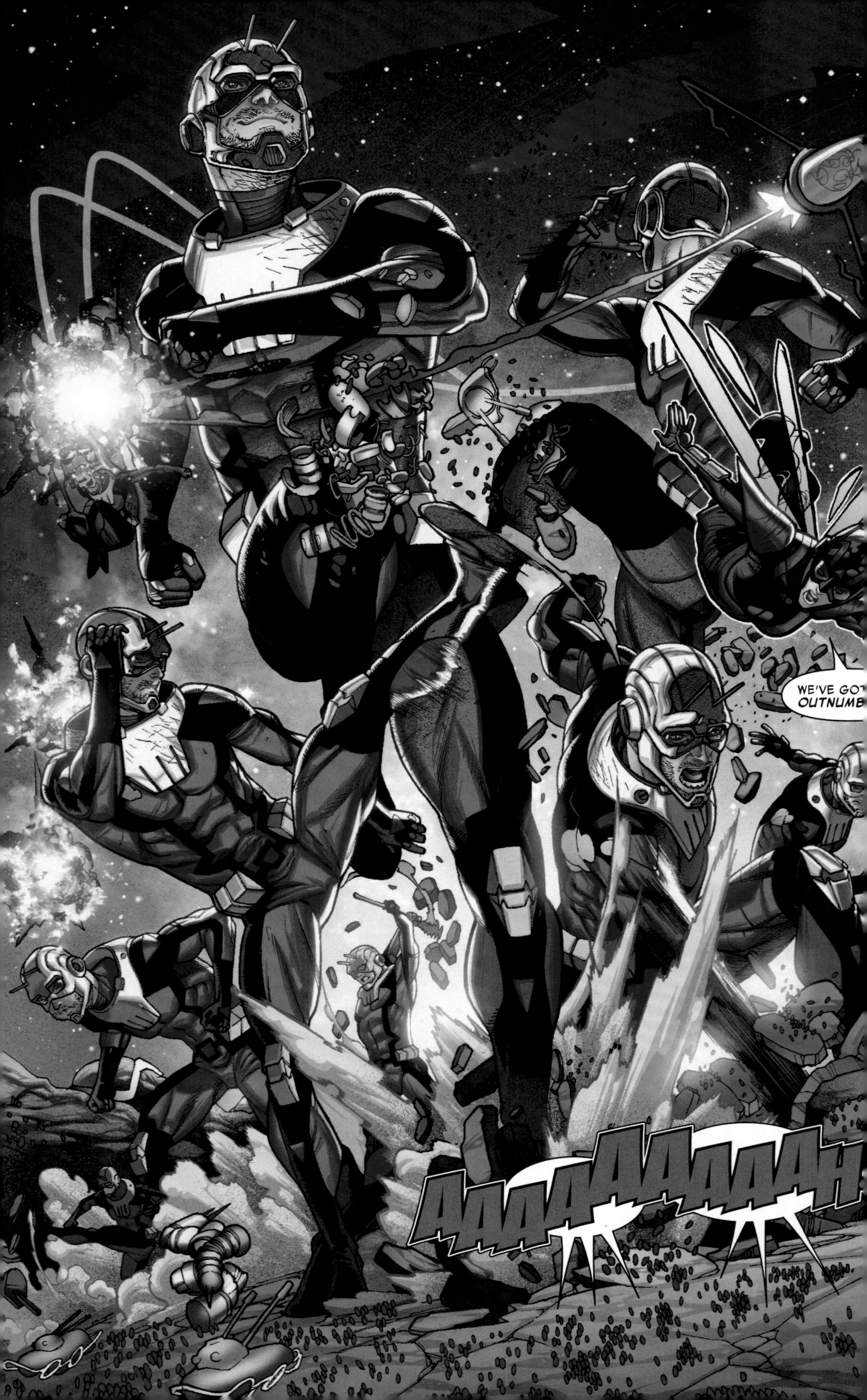
WE'VE GOT
OUTNUMB
AAAAAAAAAH

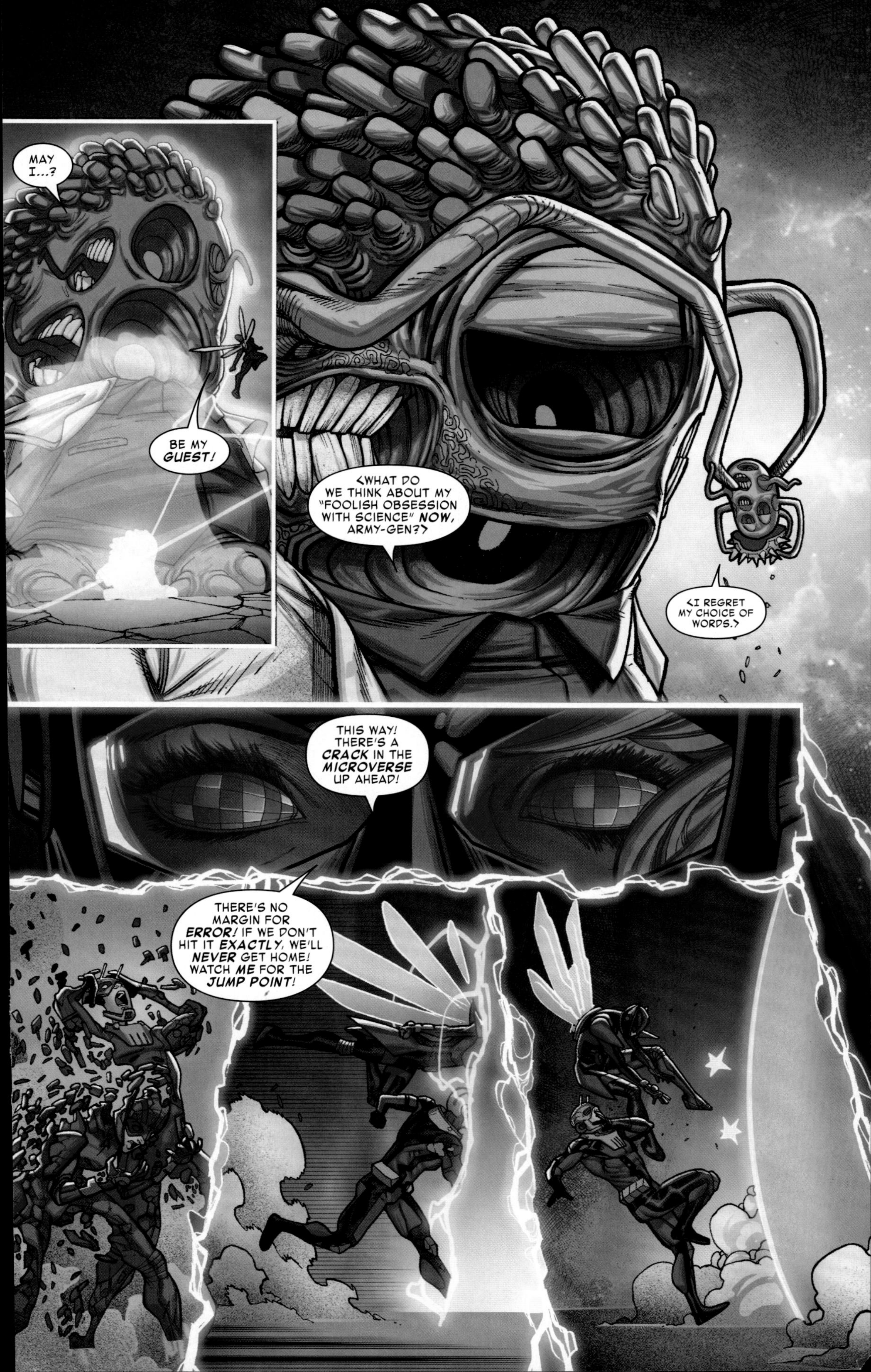
MAY I...?
BE MY GUEST!
<WHAT DO WE THINK ABOUT MY "FOOLISH OBSESSION WITH SCIENCE" NOW, ARMY-GEN?>
<I REGRET MY CHOICE OF WORDS.>
THIS WAY! THERE'S A CRACK IN THE MICROVERSE UP AHEAD!
THERE'S NO MARGIN FOR ERROR! IF WE DON'T HIT IT EXACTLY, WE'LL NEVER GET HOME! WATCH ME FOR THE JUMP POINT!

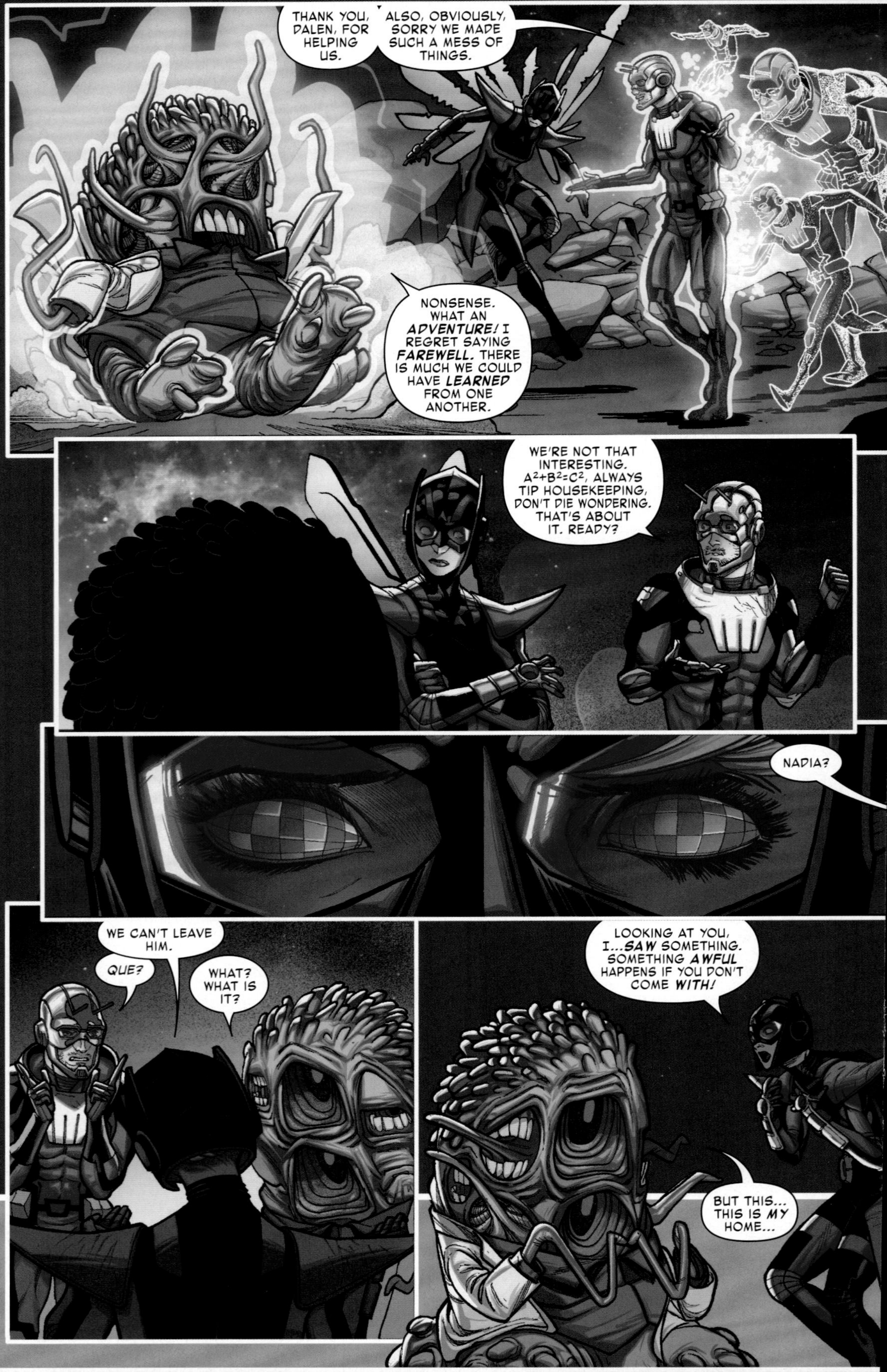

THANK YOU, DALEN, FOR HELPING US.
ALSO, OBVIOUSLY, SORRY WE MADE SUCH A MESS OF THINGS.
NONSENSE. WHAT AN ADVENTURE! I REGRET SAYING FAREWELL. THERE IS MUCH WE COULD HAVE LEARNED FROM ONE ANOTHER.
WE'RE NOT THAT INTERESTING. A²+B²=C², ALWAYS TIP HOUSEKEEPING, DON'T DIE WONDERING. THAT'S ABOUT IT. READY?
NADIA?
WE CAN'T LEAVE HIM.
QUE?
WHAT? WHAT IS IT?
LOOKING AT YOU, I...SAW SOMETHING. SOMETHING AWFUL HAPPENS IF YOU DON'T COME WITH!
BUT THIS... THIS IS MY HOME...

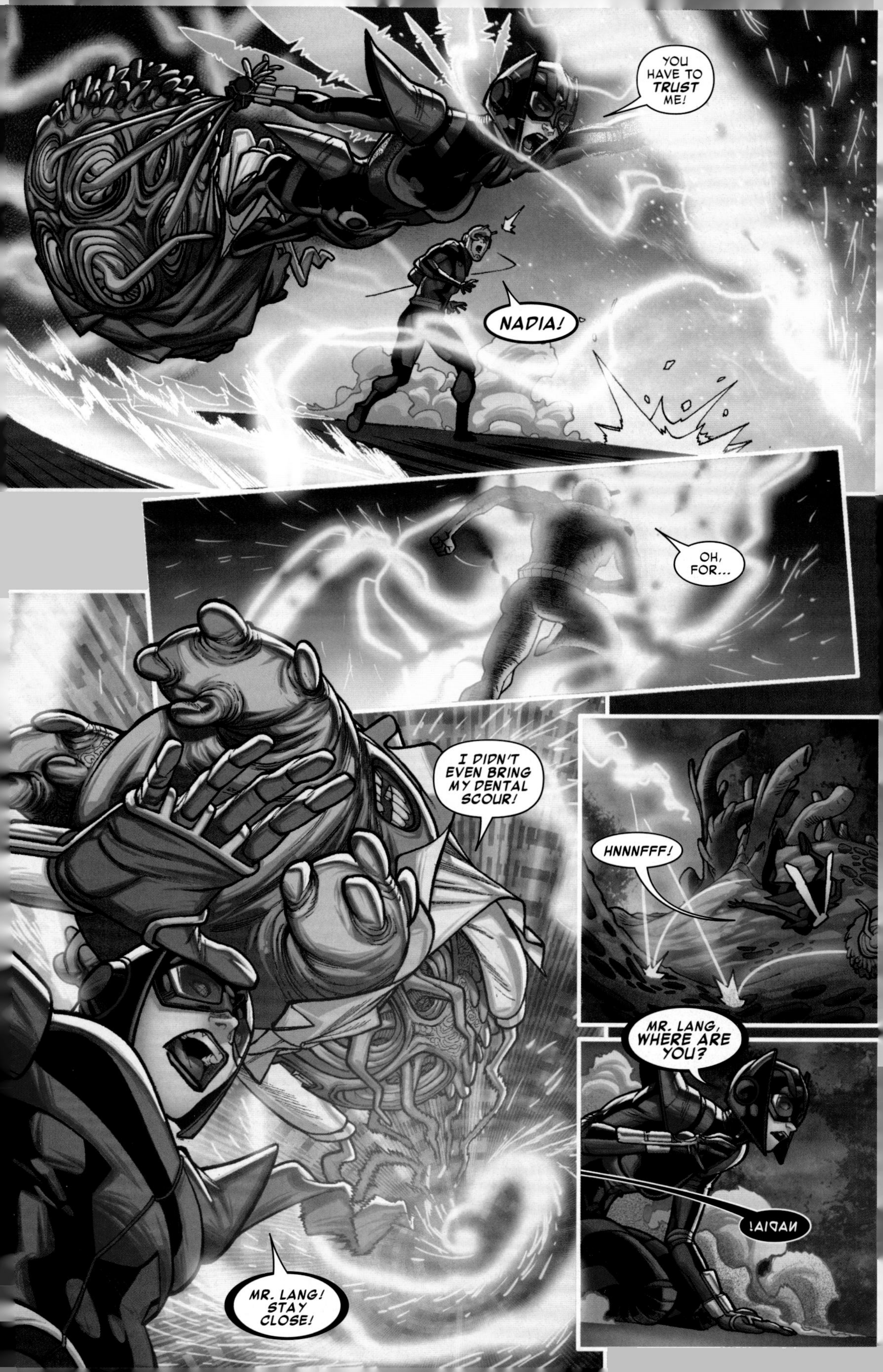
YOU HAVE TO TRUST ME!
NADIA!
OH, FOR...
I DIDN'T EVEN BRING MY DENTAL SCOUR!
MR. LANG! STAY CLOSE!
HNNNFFF!
MR. LANG, WHERE ARE YOU?
NADIA!

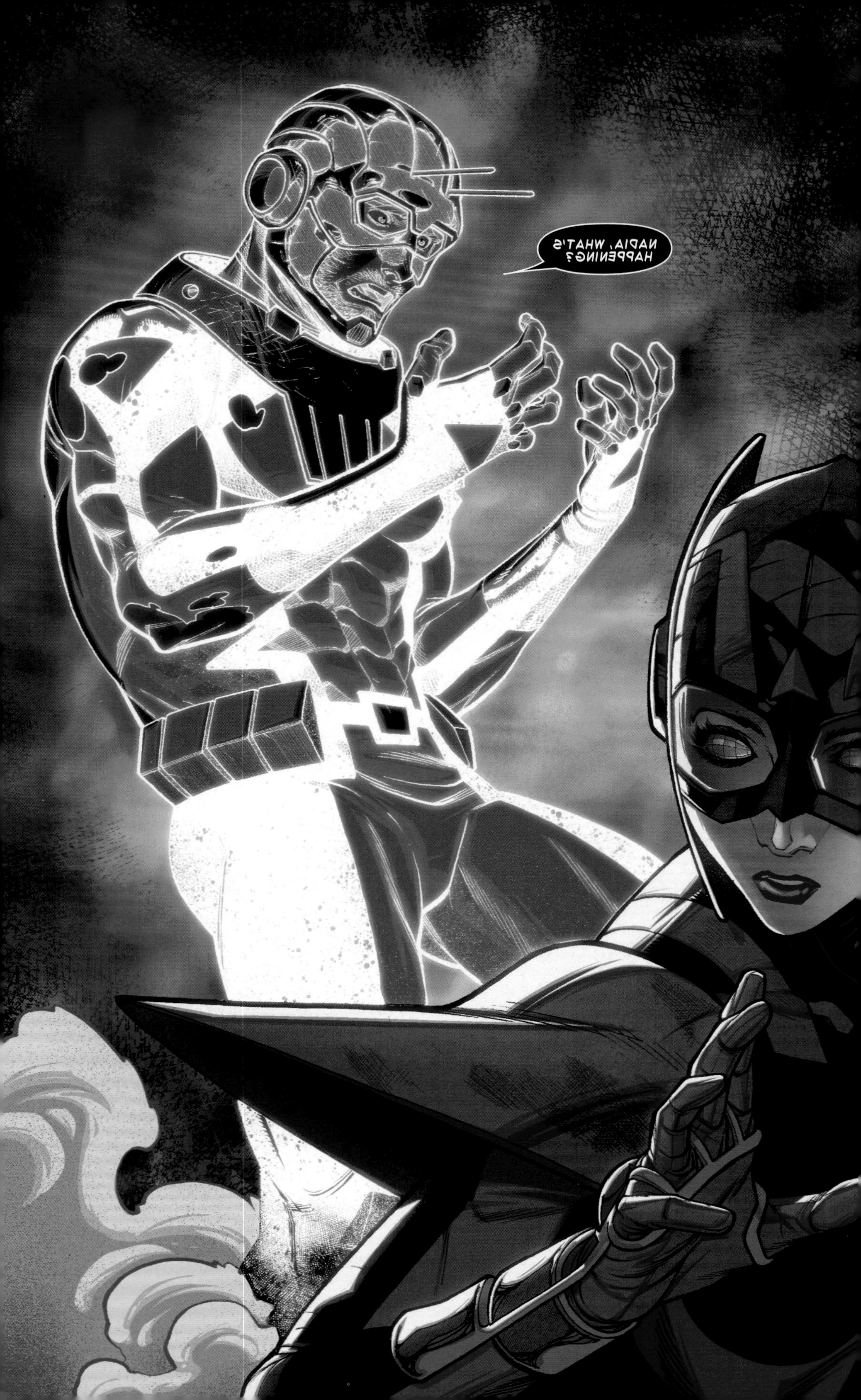
NADIA, WHAT'S HAPPENING?

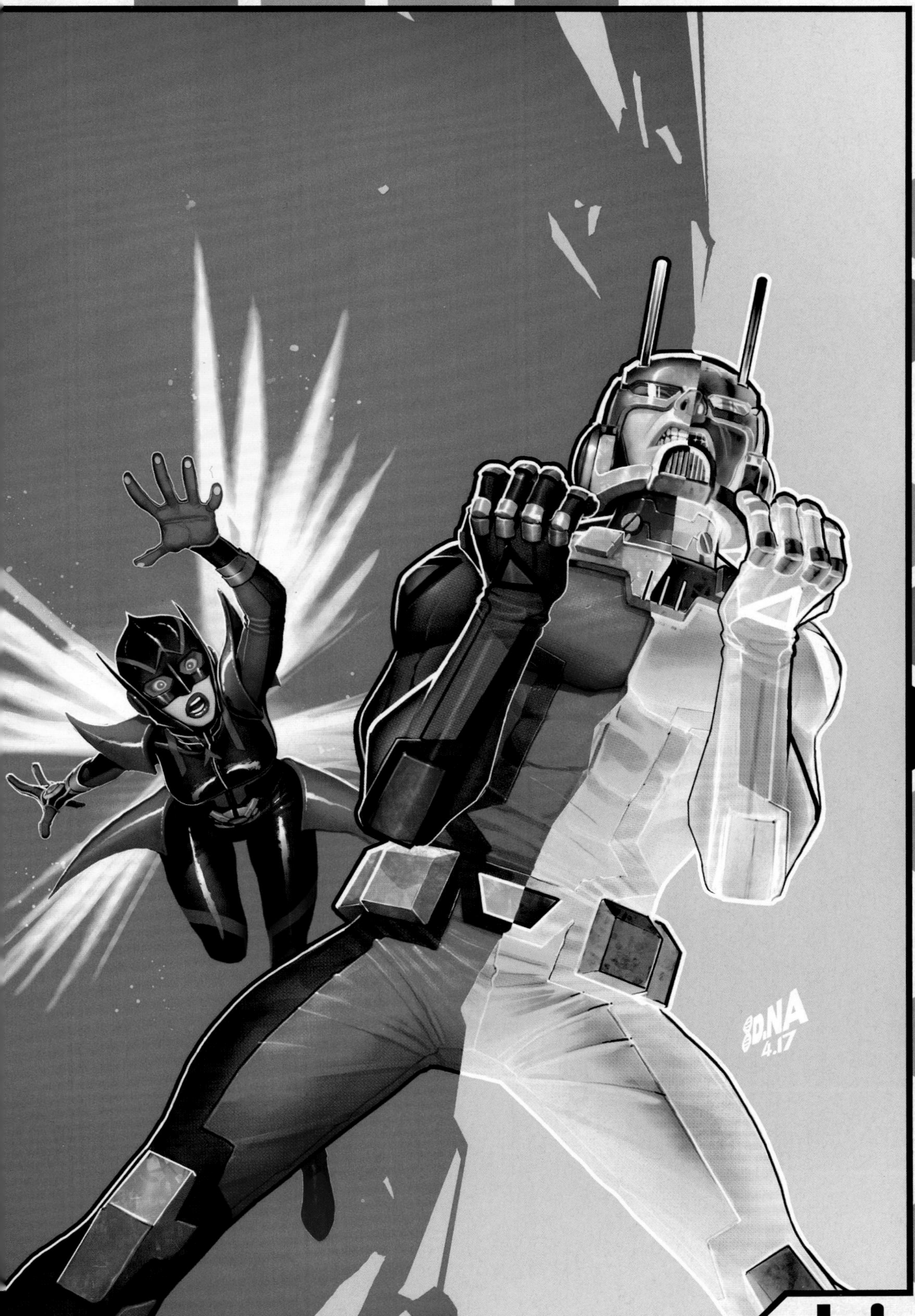
D.NA
4.17

4

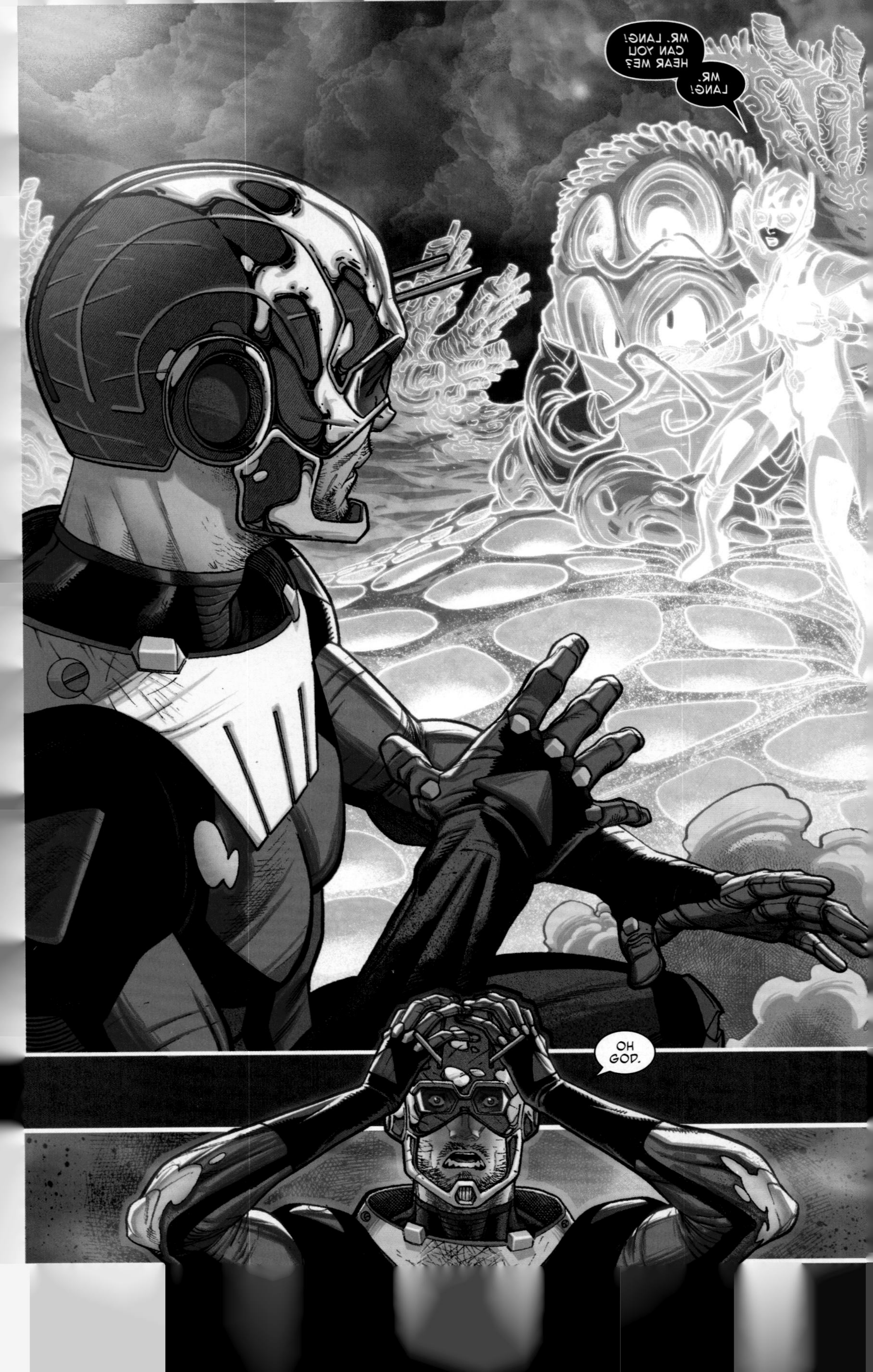
MR. LANG! CAN YOU HEAR ME?
MR. LANG!
OH GOD.

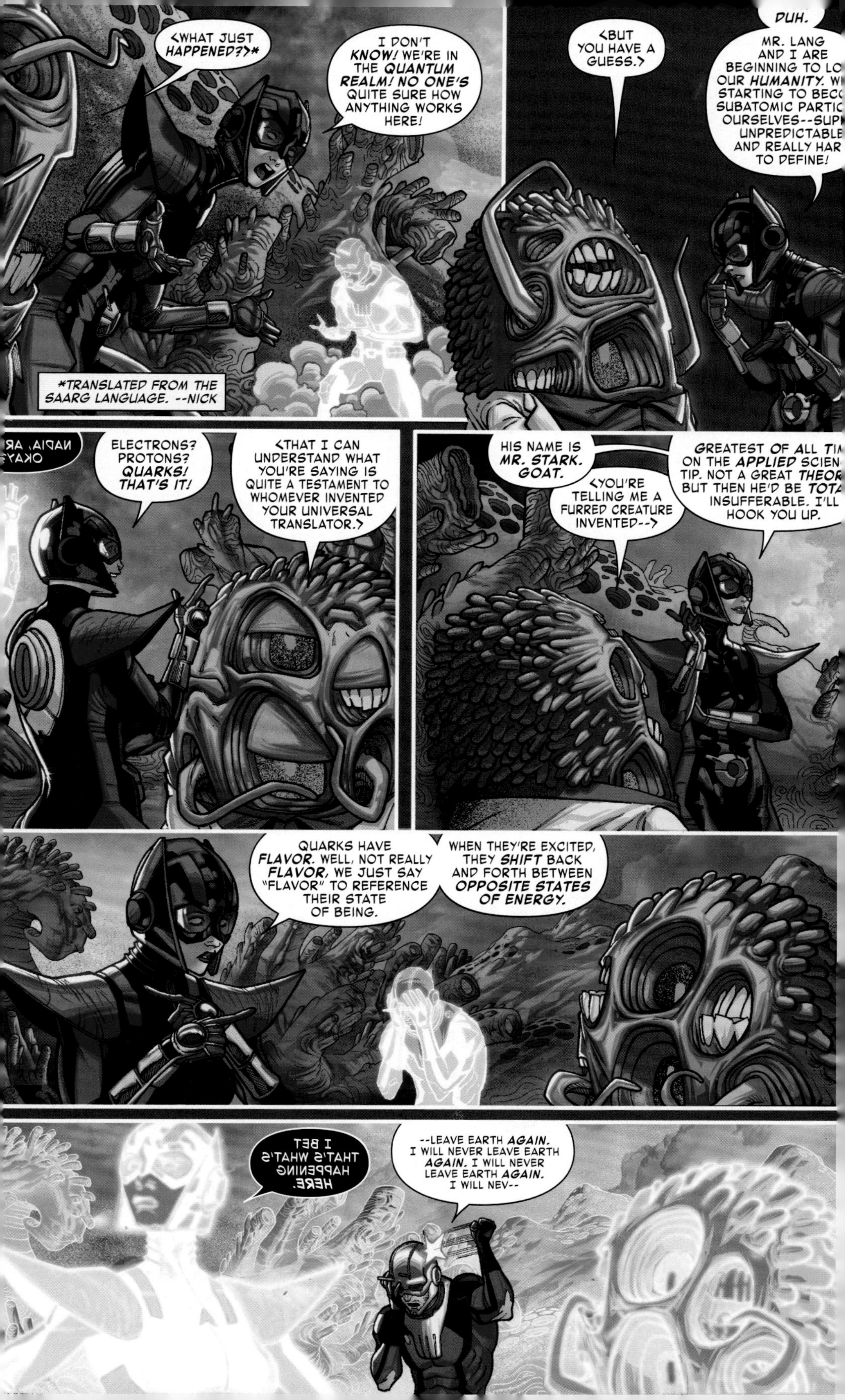
<WHAT JUST HAPPENED?>*
I DON'T KNOW! WE'RE IN THE QUANTUM REALM! NO ONE'S QUITE SURE HOW ANYTHING WORKS HERE!
*TRANSLATED FROM THE SAARG LANGUAGE. --NICK
<BUT YOU HAVE A GUESS.>
DUH.
MR. LANG AND I ARE BEGINNING TO LO OUR HUMANITY. W STARTING TO BEC SUBATOMIC PARTIC OURSELVES--SUP UNPREDICTABLE AND REALLY HAR TO DEFINE!
ELECTRONS? PROTONS? QUARKS! THAT'S IT!
<THAT I CAN UNDERSTAND WHAT YOU'RE SAYING IS QUITE A TESTAMENT TO WHOMEVER INVENTED YOUR UNIVERSAL TRANSLATOR.>
HIS NAME IS MR. STARK. GOAT.
<YOU'RE TELLING ME A FURRED CREATURE INVENTED-->
GREATEST OF ALL TI ON THE APPLIED SCIEN TIP. NOT A GREAT THEOR BUT THEN HE'D BE TOT INSUFFERABLE. I'LL HOOK YOU UP.
QUARKS HAVE FLAVOR. WELL, NOT REALLY FLAVOR, WE JUST SAY "FLAVOR" TO REFERENCE THEIR STATE OF BEING.
WHEN THEY'RE EXCITED, THEY SHIFT BACK AND FORTH BETWEEN OPPOSITE STATES OF ENERGY.
I BET THAT'S WHAT'S HAPPENING HERE.
--LEAVE EARTH AGAIN. I WILL NEVER LEAVE EARTH AGAIN. I WILL NEVER LEAVE EARTH AGAIN. I WILL NEV--

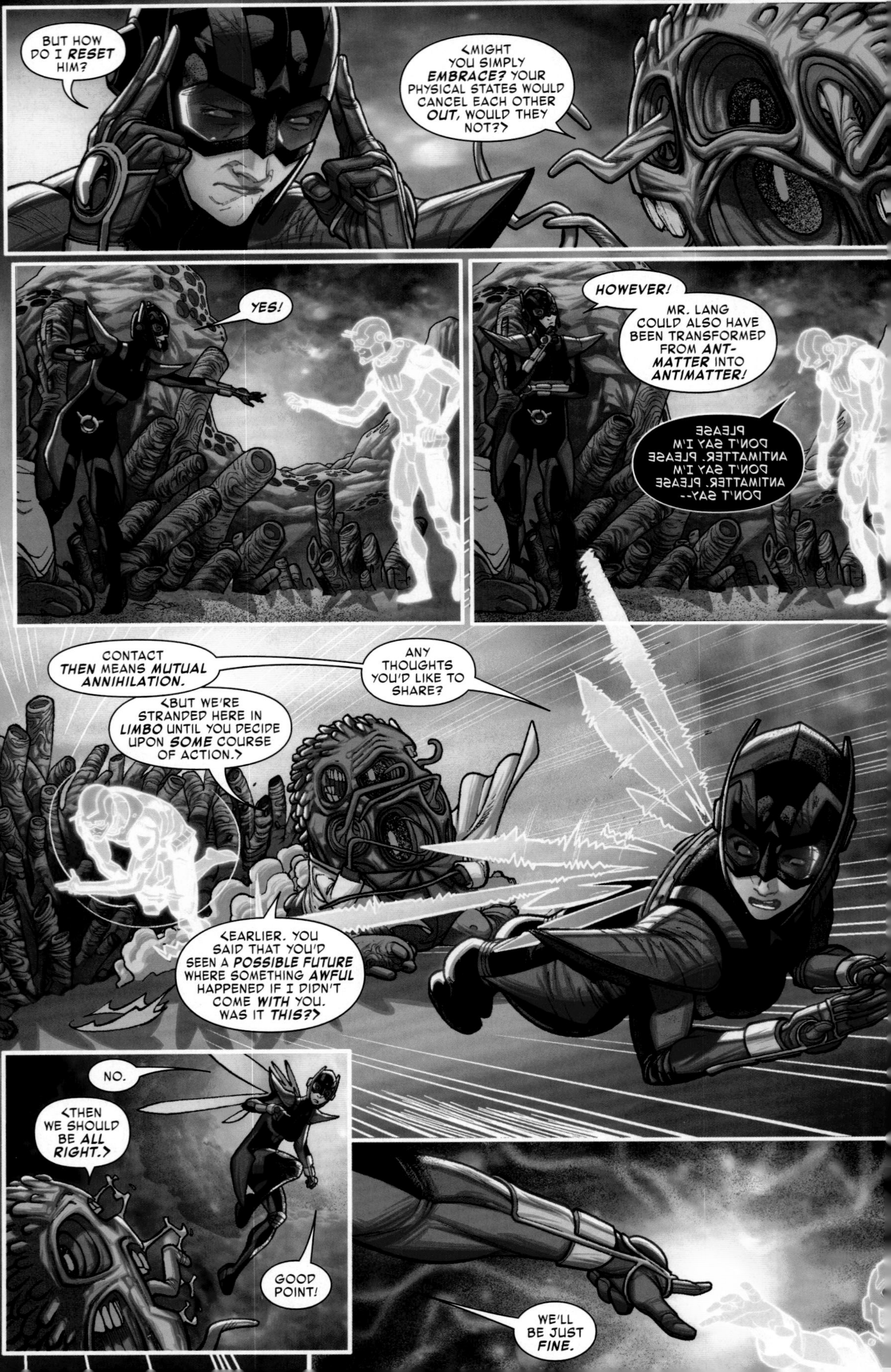

BUT HOW DO I RESET HIM?
<MIGHT YOU SIMPLY EMBRACE? YOUR PHYSICAL STATES WOULD CANCEL EACH OTHER OUT, WOULD THEY NOT?>
YES!
HOWEVER!
MR. LANG COULD ALSO HAVE BEEN TRANSFORMED FROM ANT-MATTER INTO ANTIMATTER!
PLEASE DON'T SAY I'M ANTIMATTER. PLEASE DON'T SAY I'M ANTIMATTER. PLEASE DON'T SAY--
CONTACT THEN MEANS MUTUAL ANNIHILATION.
ANY THOUGHTS YOU'D LIKE TO SHARE?
<BUT WE'RE STRANDED HERE IN LIMBO UNTIL YOU DECIDE UPON SOME COURSE OF ACTION.>
<EARLIER. YOU SAID THAT YOU'D SEEN A POSSIBLE FUTURE WHERE SOMETHING AWFUL HAPPENED IF I DIDN'T COME WITH YOU. WAS IT THIS?>
NO.
<THEN WE SHOULD BE ALL RIGHT.>
GOOD POINT!
WE'LL BE JUST FINE.

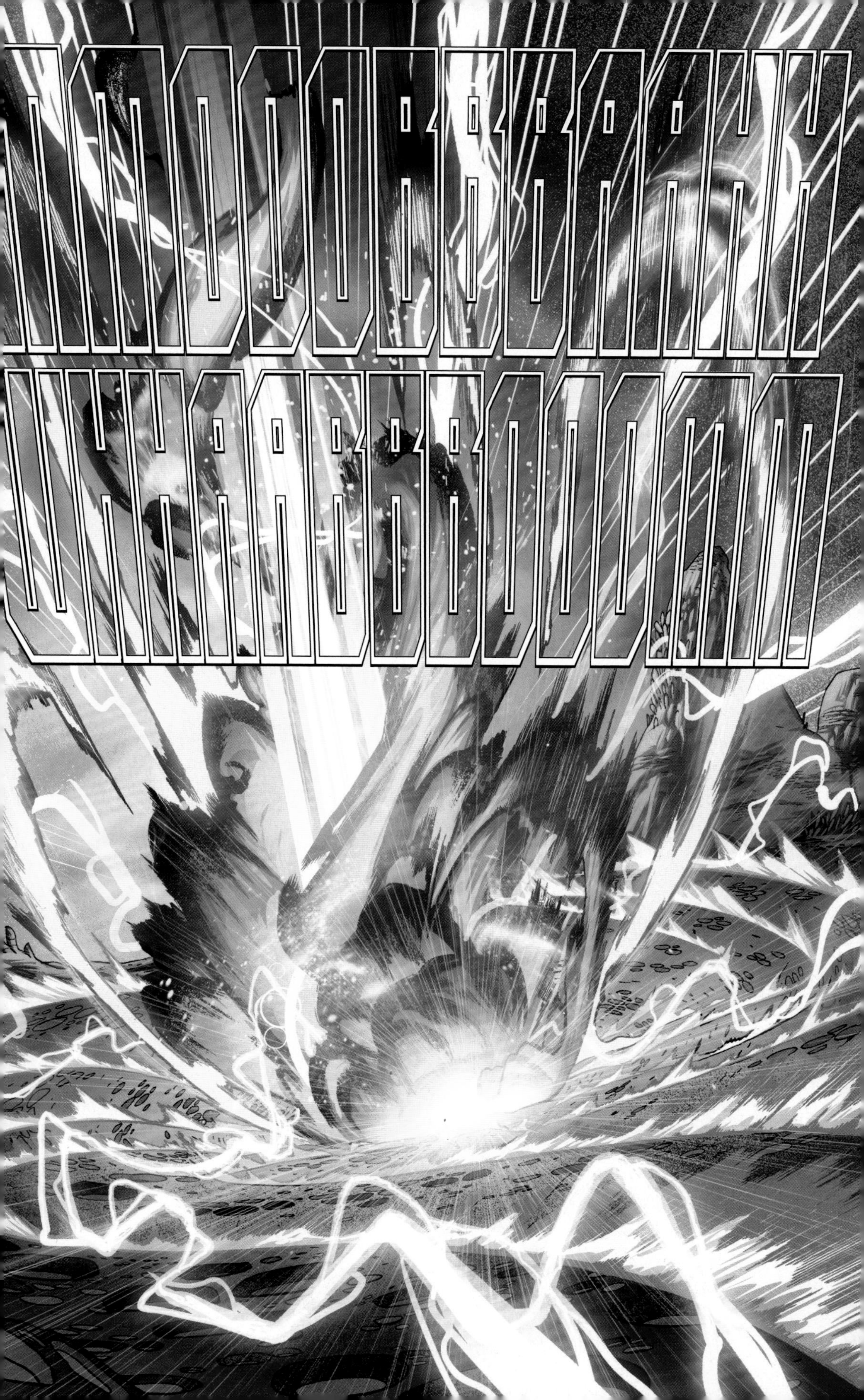

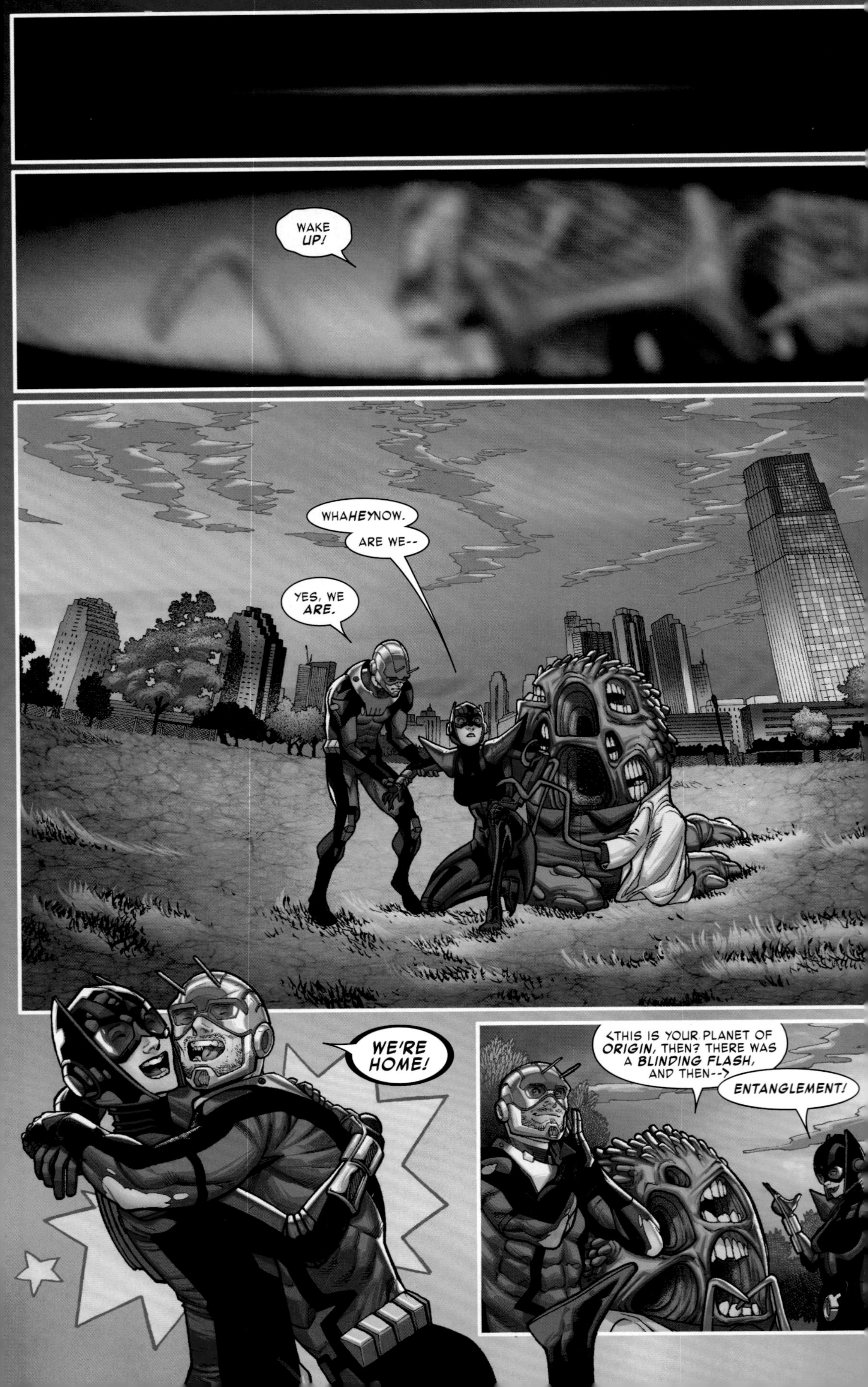
WAKE UP!
WHAHEYNOW.
ARE WE--
YES, WE ARE.
WE'RE HOME!
<THIS IS YOUR PLANET OF ORIGIN, THEN? THERE WAS A BLINDING FLASH, AND THEN-->
ENTANGLEMENT!

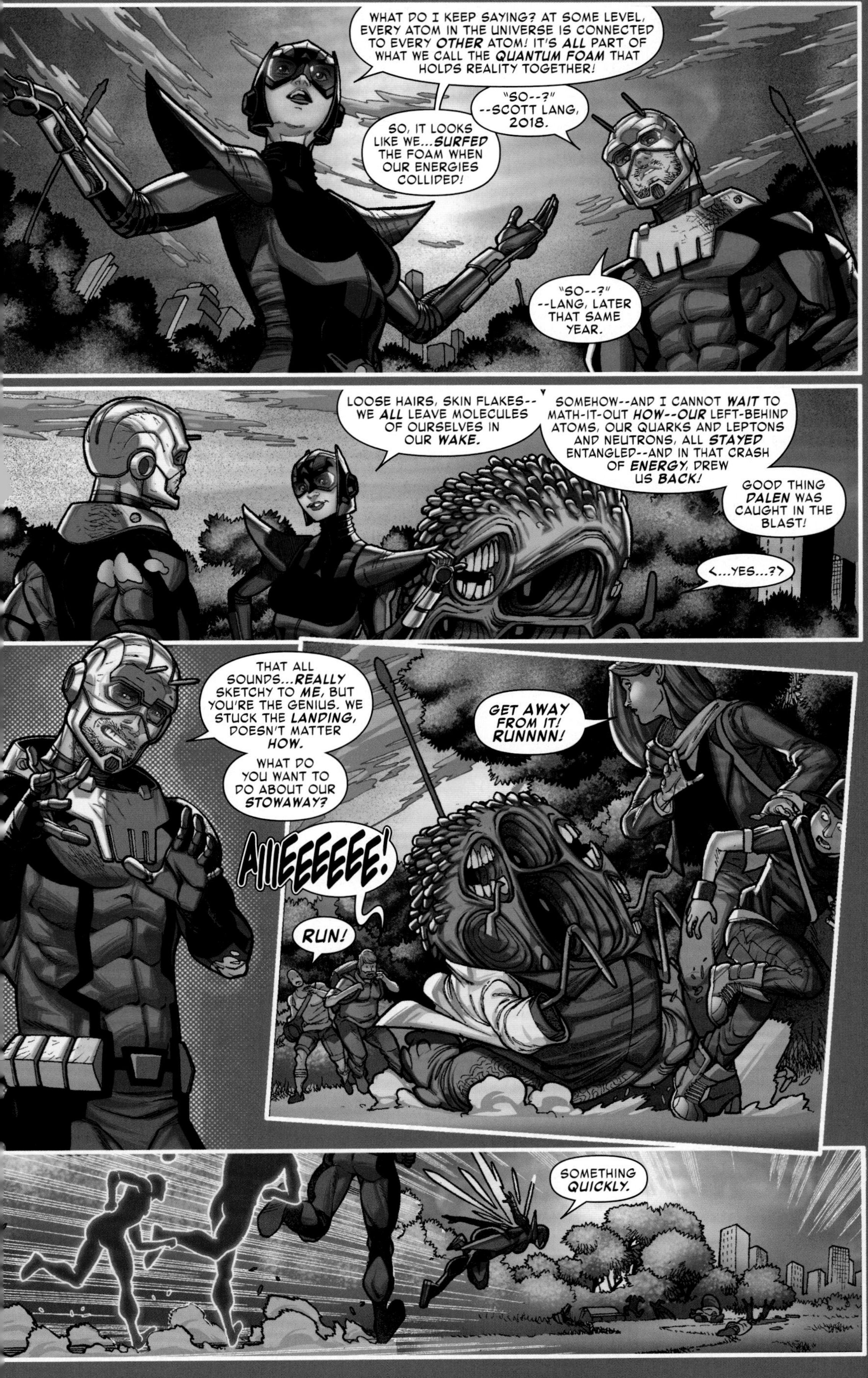
WHAT DO I KEEP SAYING? AT SOME LEVEL, EVERY ATOM IN THE UNIVERSE IS CONNECTED TO EVERY OTHER ATOM! IT'S ALL PART OF WHAT WE CALL THE QUANTUM FOAM THAT HOLDS REALITY TOGETHER!
SO, IT LOOKS LIKE WE...SURFED THE FOAM WHEN OUR ENERGIES COLLIDED!
"SO--?" --SCOTT LANG, 2018.
"SO--?" --LANG, LATER THAT SAME YEAR.
LOOSE HAIRS, SKIN FLAKES-- WE ALL LEAVE MOLECULES OF OURSELVES IN OUR WAKE.
SOMEHOW--AND I CANNOT WAIT TO MATH-IT-OUT HOW--OUR LEFT-BEHIND ATOMS, OUR QUARKS AND LEPTONS AND NEUTRONS, ALL STAYED ENTANGLED--AND IN THAT CRASH OF ENERGY, DREW US BACK!
GOOD THING DALEN WAS CAUGHT IN THE BLAST!
<...YES...?>
THAT ALL SOUNDS...REALLY SKETCHY TO ME, BUT YOU'RE THE GENIUS. WE STUCK THE LANDING, DOESN'T MATTER HOW.
WHAT DO YOU WANT TO DO ABOUT OUR STOWAWAY?
GET AWAY FROM IT! RUNNNN!
AIIIEEEEEEE!
RUN!
SOMETHING QUICKLY.

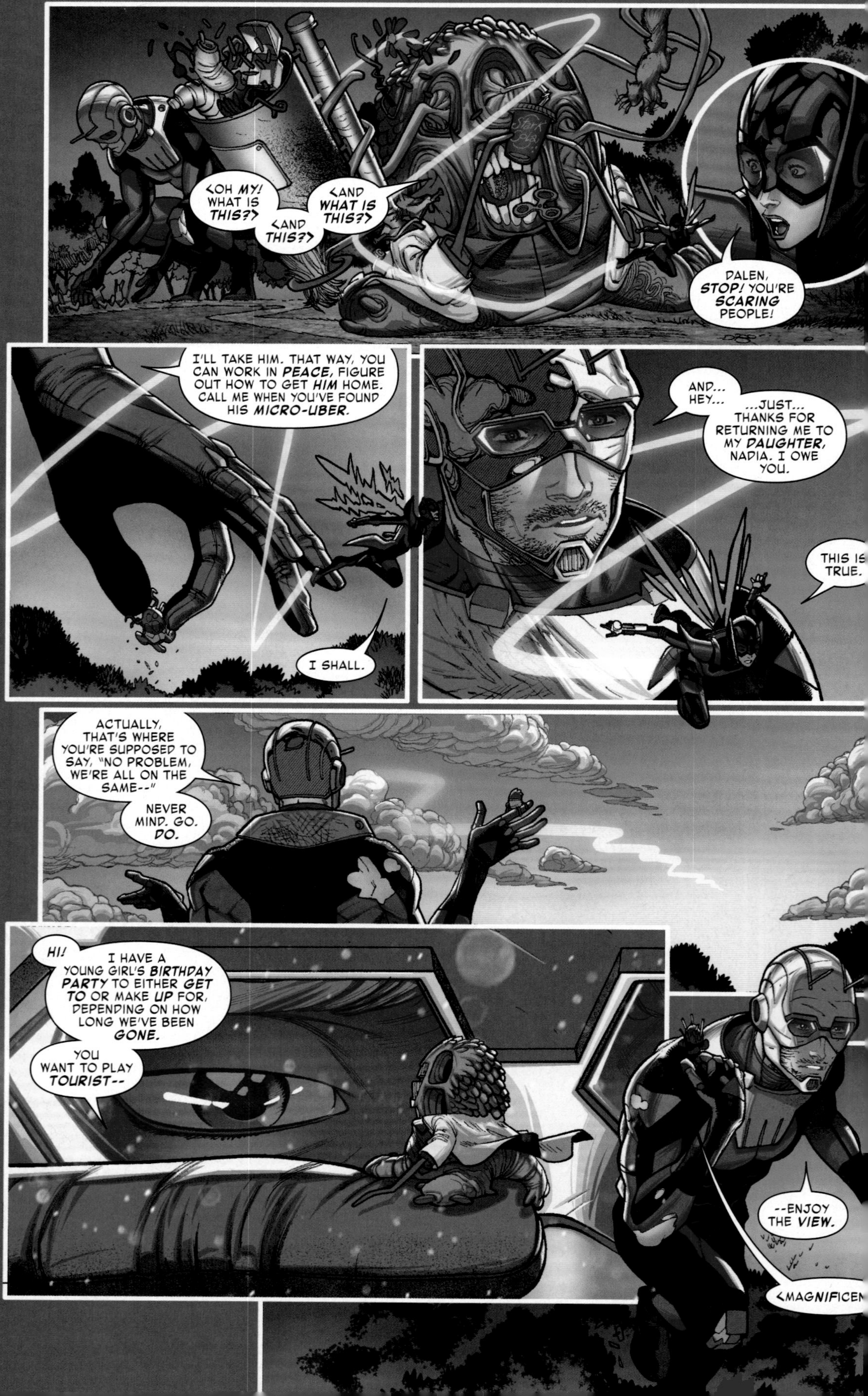
<OH MY! WHAT IS THIS?>
<AND THIS?>
<AND WHAT IS THIS?>
DALEN, STOP! YOU'RE SCARING PEOPLE!
I'LL TAKE HIM. THAT WAY, YOU CAN WORK IN PEACE, FIGURE OUT HOW TO GET HIM HOME. CALL ME WHEN YOU'VE FOUND HIS MICRO-UBER.
I SHALL.
AND... HEY...
...JUST... THANKS FOR RETURNING ME TO MY DAUGHTER, NADIA. I OWE YOU.
THIS IS TRUE.
ACTUALLY, THAT'S WHERE YOU'RE SUPPOSED TO SAY, "NO PROBLEM, WE'RE ALL ON THE SAME--"
NEVER MIND. GO. DO.
HI!
I HAVE A YOUNG GIRL'S BIRTHDAY PARTY TO EITHER GET TO OR MAKE UP FOR, DEPENDING ON HOW LONG WE'VE BEEN GONE.
YOU WANT TO PLAY TOURIST--
--ENJOY THE VIEW.
<MAGNIFICEN

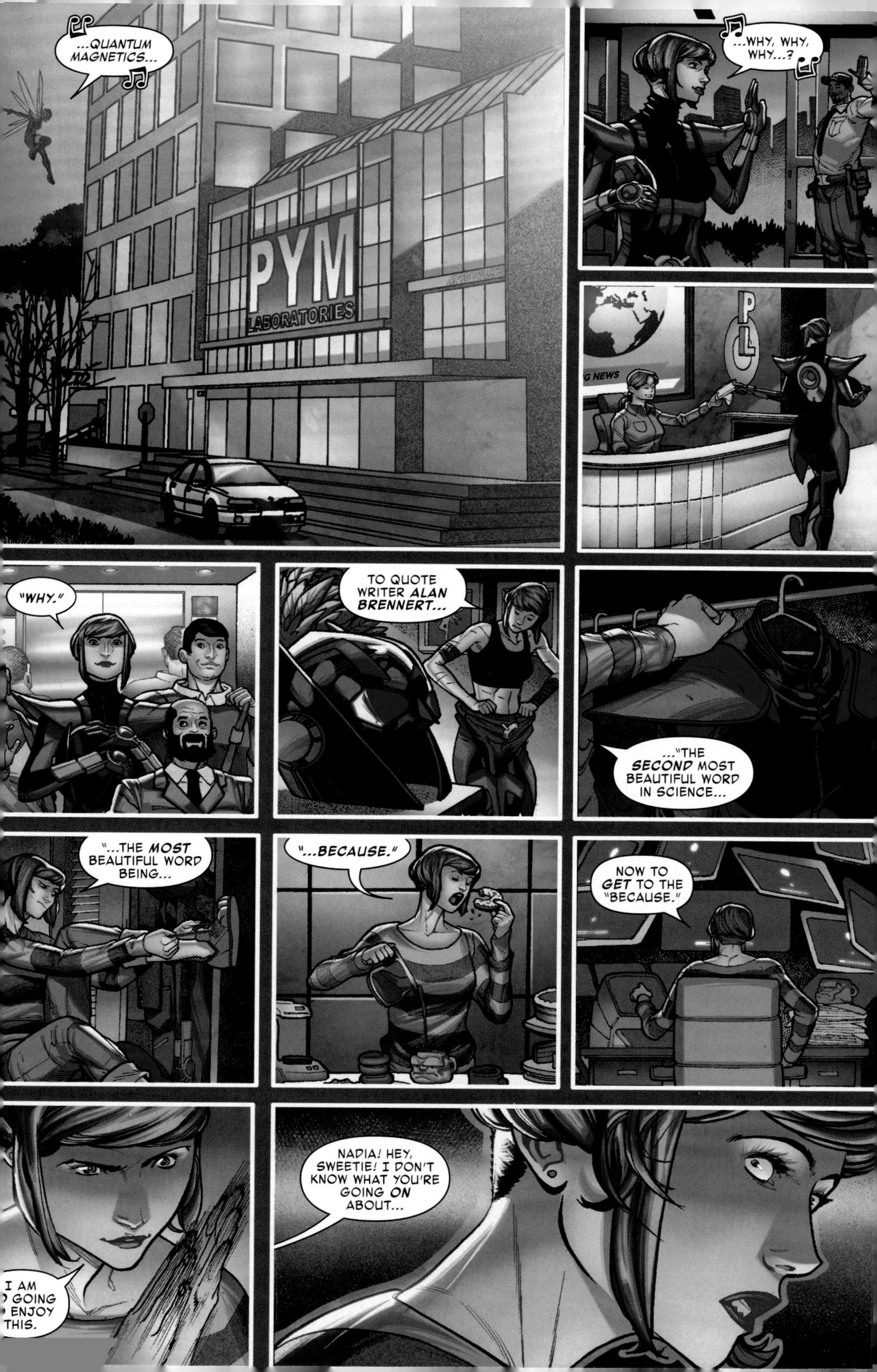
...QUANTUM MAGNETICS...
...WHY, WHY, WHY...?
PYM LABORATORIES
"WHY."
TO QUOTE WRITER ALAN BRENNERT...
..."THE SECOND MOST BEAUTIFUL WORD IN SCIENCE...
"...THE MOST BEAUTIFUL WORD BEING...
"...BECAUSE."
NOW TO GET TO THE "BECAUSE."
I AM GOING ENJOY THIS.
NADIA! HEY, SWEETIE! I DON'T KNOW WHAT YOU'RE GOING ON ABOUT...

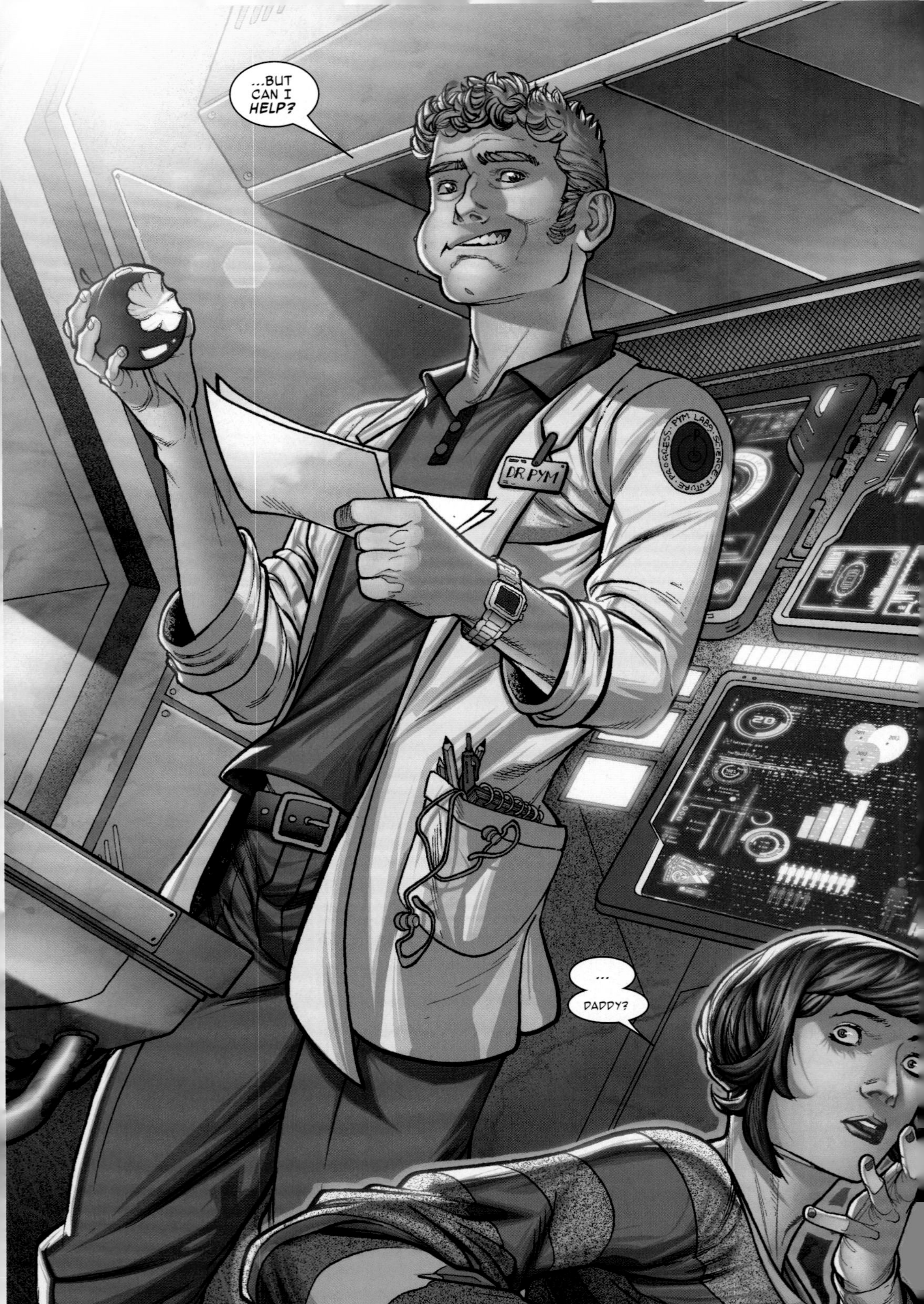
...BUT CAN I HELP?
DR. PYM
PYM LABS · SCIENCE · FUTURE · PROGRESS
...
DADDY?

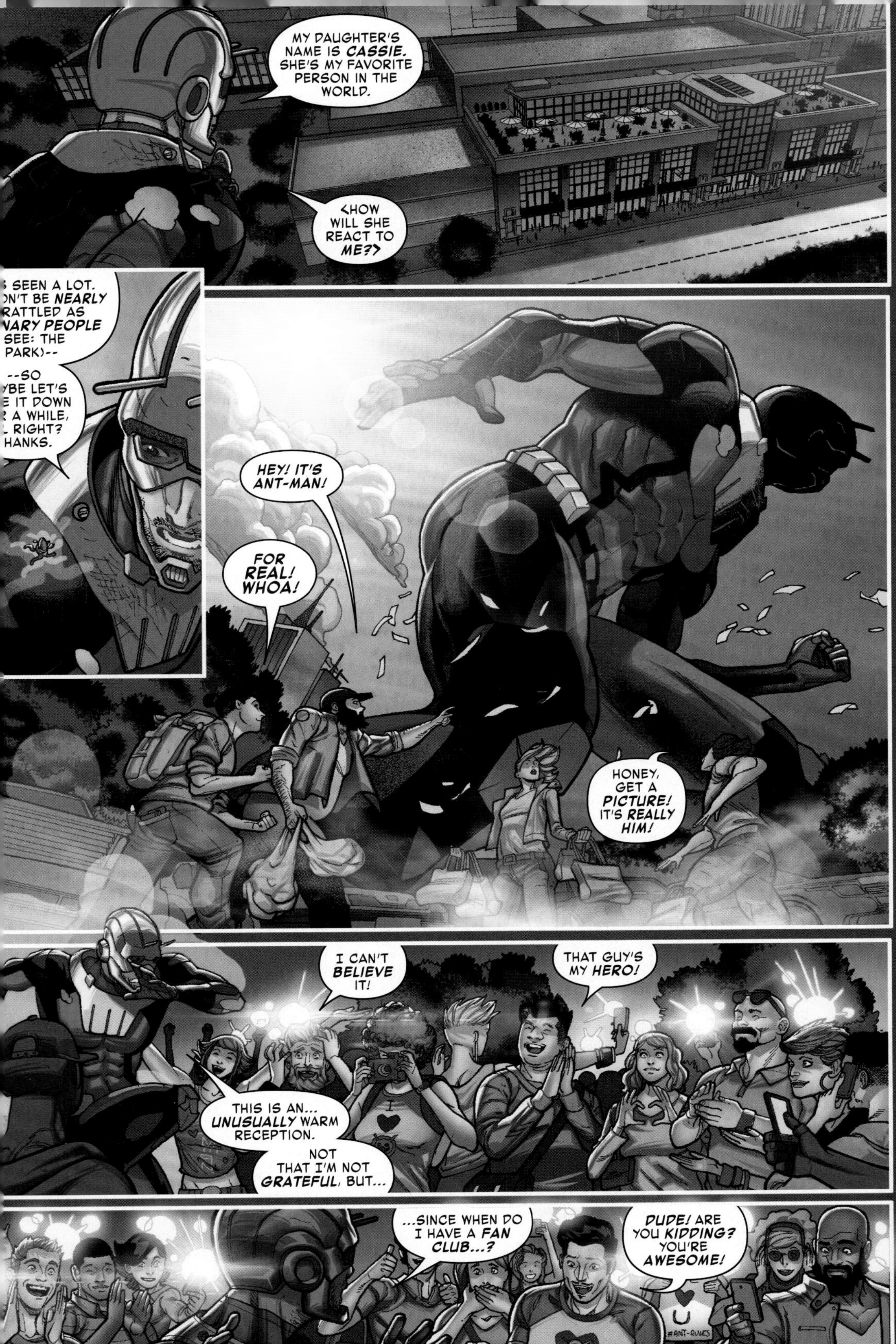
MY DAUGHTER'S NAME IS CASSIE. SHE'S MY FAVORITE PERSON IN THE WORLD.
<HOW WILL SHE REACT TO ME?>
S SEEN A LOT. ON'T BE NEARLY RATTLED AS NARY PEOPLE SEE: THE PARK)--
--SO YBE LET'S E IT DOWN R A WHILE, L RIGHT? HANKS.
HEY! IT'S ANT-MAN!
FOR REAL! WHOA!
HONEY, GET A PICTURE! IT'S REALLY HIM!
I CAN'T BELIEVE IT!
THAT GUY'S MY HERO!
THIS IS AN... UNUSUALLY WARM RECEPTION.
NOT THAT I'M NOT GRATEFUL, BUT...
...SINCE WHEN DO I HAVE A FAN CLUB...?
DUDE! ARE YOU KIDDING? YOU'RE AWESOME!

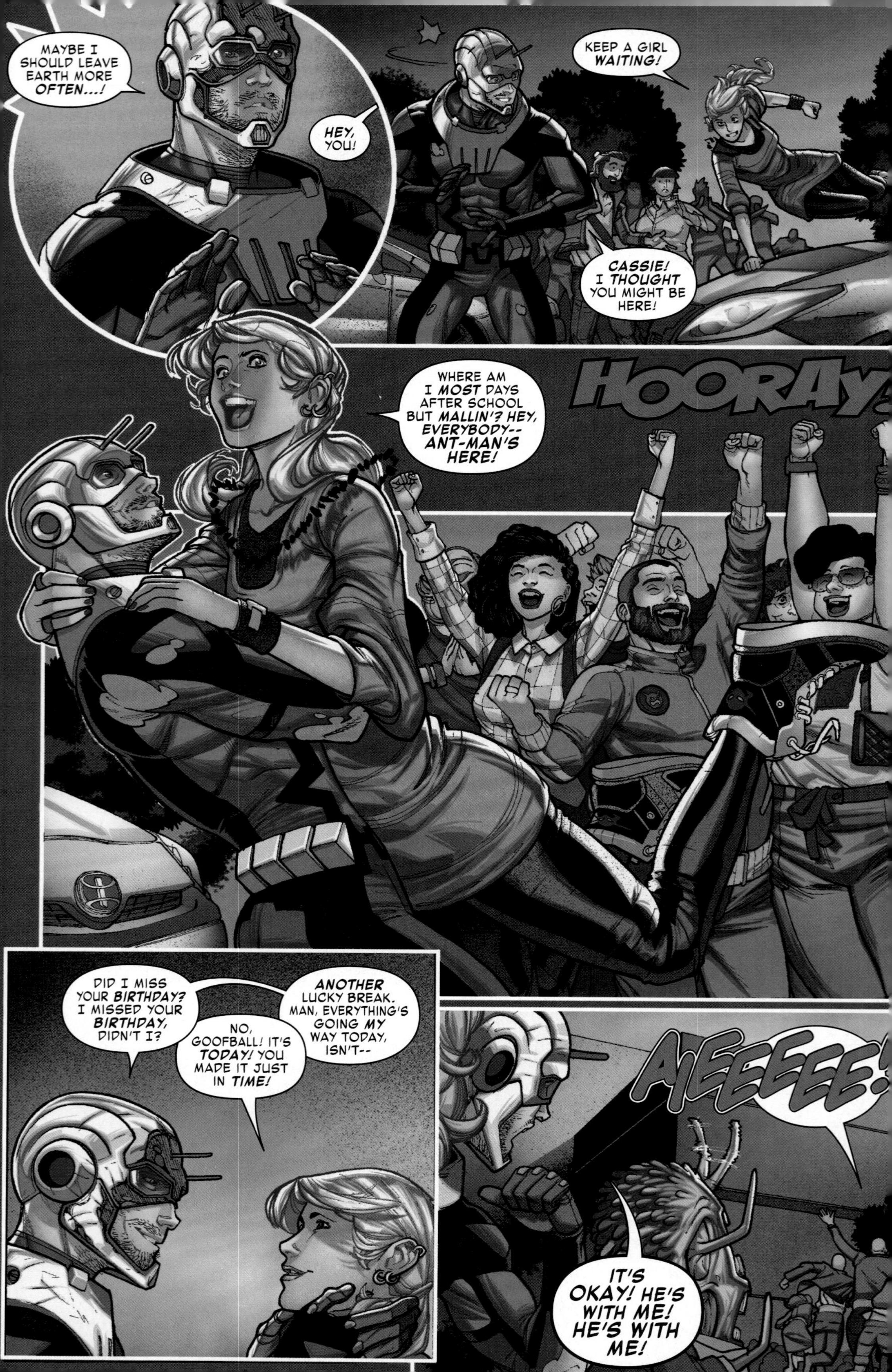

MAYBE I SHOULD LEAVE EARTH MORE OFTEN...!
HEY, YOU!
KEEP A GIRL WAITING!
CASSIE! I THOUGHT YOU MIGHT BE HERE!
WHERE AM I MOST DAYS AFTER SCHOOL BUT MALLIN'? HEY, EVERYBODY-- ANT-MAN'S HERE!
HOORAY!
DID I MISS YOUR BIRTHDAY? I MISSED YOUR BIRTHDAY, DIDN'T I?
NO, GOOFBALL! IT'S TODAY! YOU MADE IT JUST IN TIME!
ANOTHER LUCKY BREAK. MAN, EVERYTHING'S GOING MY WAY TODAY, ISN'T--
AIEEEEE!
IT'S OKAY! HE'S WITH ME! HE'S WITH ME!

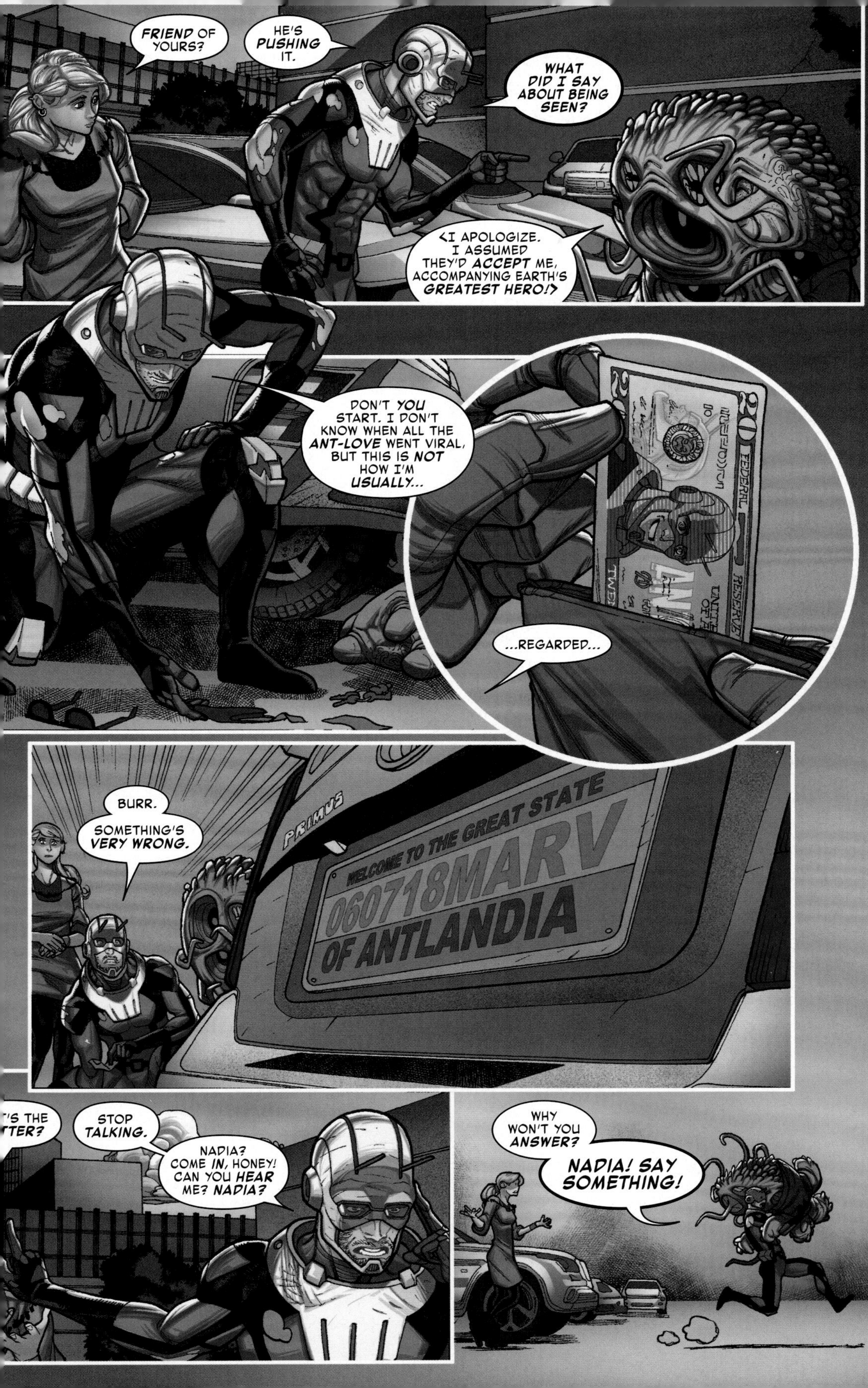

FRIEND OF YOURS?
HE'S PUSHING IT.
WHAT DID I SAY ABOUT BEING SEEN?
<I APOLOGIZE. I ASSUMED THEY'D ACCEPT ME, ACCOMPANYING EARTH'S GREATEST HERO!>
DON'T YOU START. I DON'T KNOW WHEN ALL THE ANT-LOVE WENT VIRAL, BUT THIS IS NOT HOW I'M USUALLY...
...REGARDED...
BURR.
SOMETHING'S VERY WRONG.
PRIMUS
WELCOME TO THE GREAT STATE
060718MARV
OF ANTLANDIA
STOP TALKING.
NADIA? COME IN, HONEY! CAN YOU HEAR ME? NADIA?
WHY WON'T YOU ANSWER?
NADIA! SAY SOMETHING!

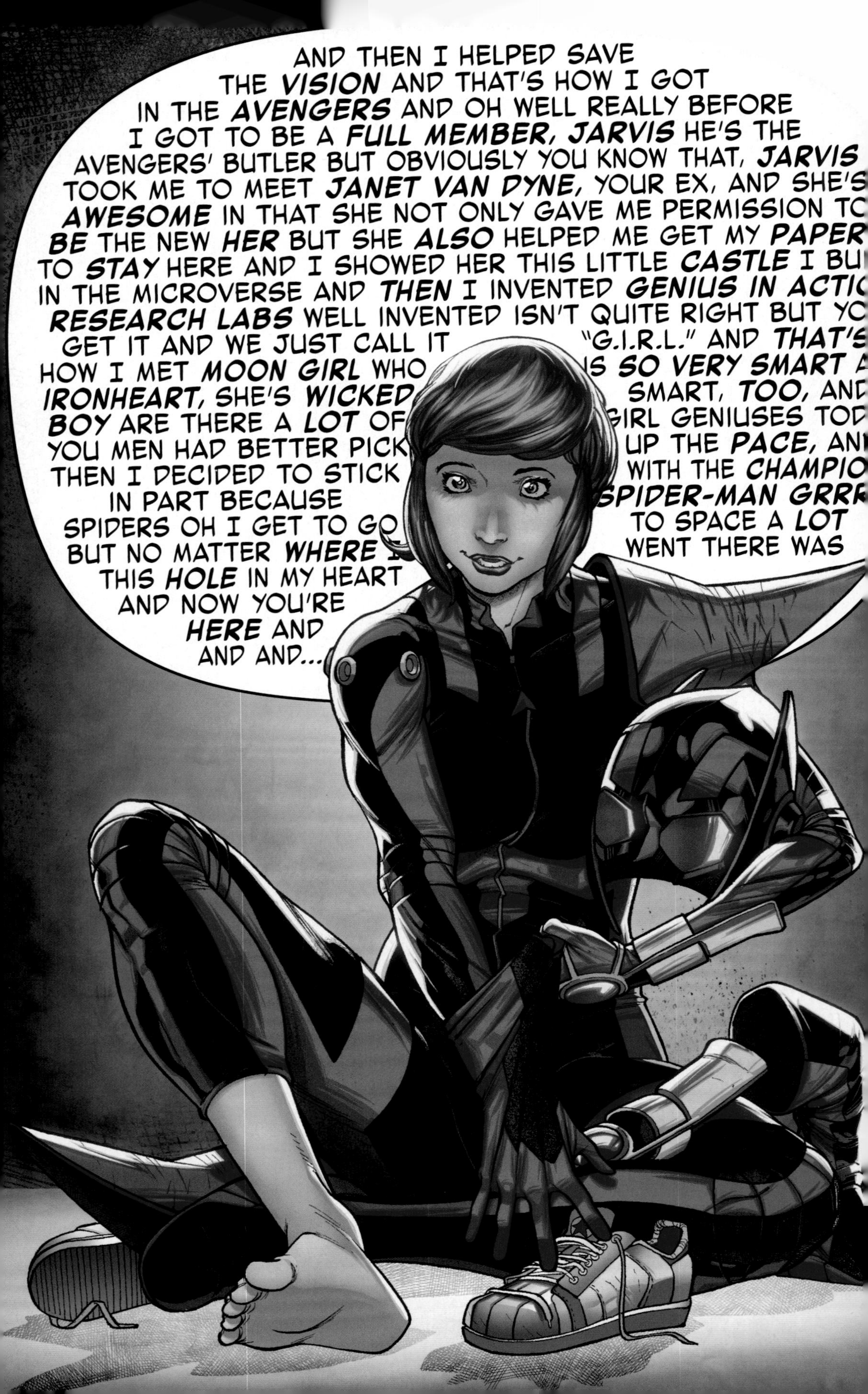
AND THEN I HELPED SAVE THE VISION AND THAT'S HOW I GOT IN THE AVENGERS AND OH WELL REALLY BEFORE I GOT TO BE A FULL MEMBER, JARVIS HE'S THE AVENGERS' BUTLER BUT OBVIOUSLY YOU KNOW THAT, JARVIS TOOK ME TO MEET JANET VAN DYNE, YOUR EX, AND SHE'S AWESOME IN THAT SHE NOT ONLY GAVE ME PERMISSION TO BE THE NEW HER BUT SHE ALSO HELPED ME GET MY PAPER TO STAY HERE AND I SHOWED HER THIS LITTLE CASTLE I BU IN THE MICROVERSE AND THEN I INVENTED GENIUS IN ACTIO RESEARCH LABS WELL INVENTED ISN'T QUITE RIGHT BUT YO GET IT AND WE JUST CALL IT "G.I.R.L." AND THAT'S HOW I MET MOON GIRL WHO IS SO VERY SMART A IRONHEART, SHE'S WICKED SMART, TOO, AND BOY ARE THERE A LOT OF GIRL GENIUSES TOD YOU MEN HAD BETTER PICK UP THE PACE, AN THEN I DECIDED TO STICK WITH THE CHAMPIO IN PART BECAUSE SPIDER-MAN GRRR SPIDERS OH I GET TO GO TO SPACE A LOT BUT NO MATTER WHERE I WENT THERE WAS THIS HOLE IN MY HEART AND NOW YOU'RE HERE AND AND AND...

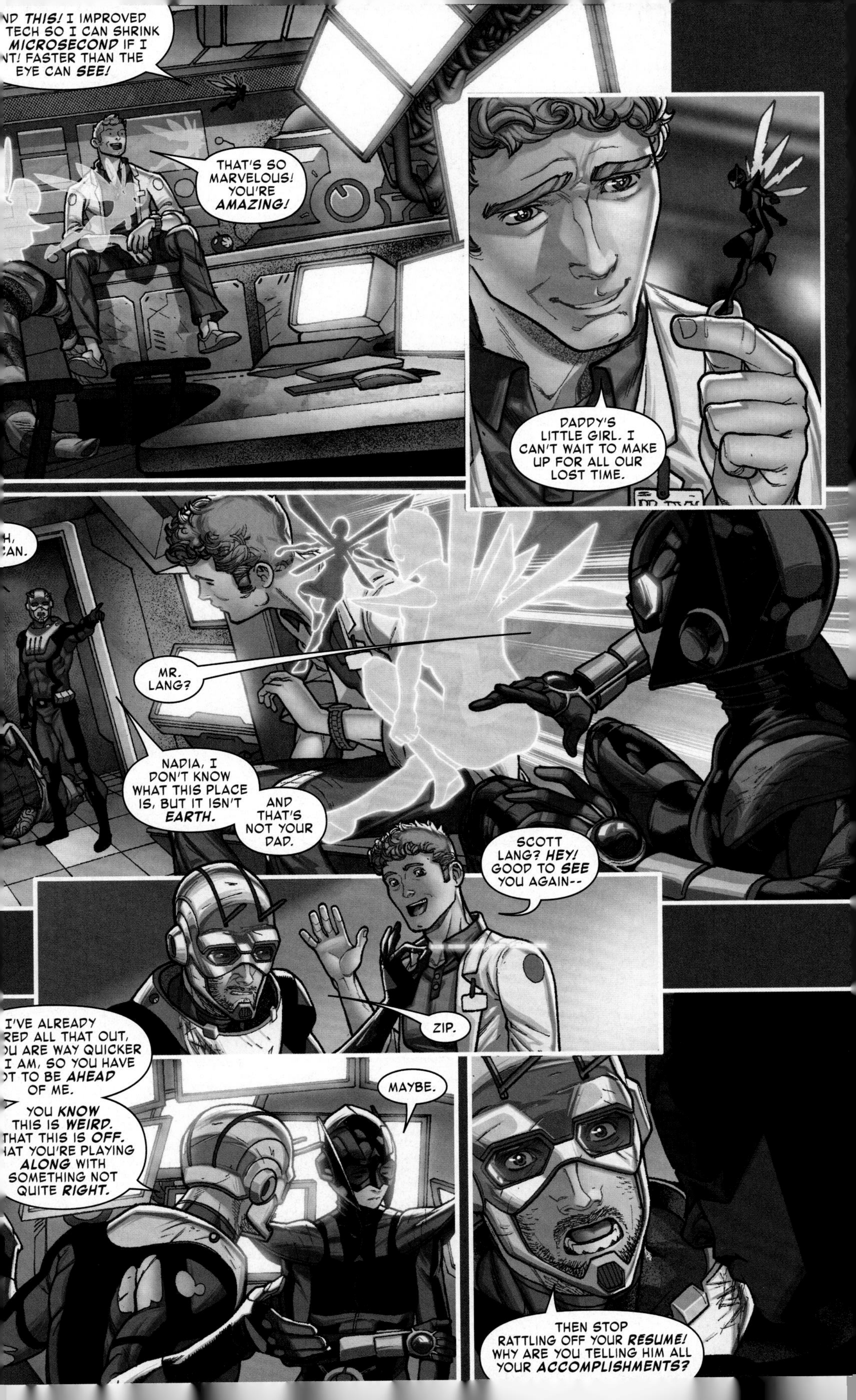
ND THIS! I IMPROVED TECH SO I CAN SHRINK MICROSECOND IF I NT! FASTER THAN THE EYE CAN SEE!
THAT'S SO MARVELOUS! YOU'RE AMAZING!
DADDY'S LITTLE GIRL. I CAN'T WAIT TO MAKE UP FOR ALL OUR LOST TIME.
H, CAN.
MR. LANG?
NADIA, I DON'T KNOW WHAT THIS PLACE IS, BUT IT ISN'T EARTH.
AND THAT'S NOT YOUR DAD.
SCOTT LANG? HEY! GOOD TO SEE YOU AGAIN--
ZIP.
I'VE ALREADY RED ALL THAT OUT, U ARE WAY QUICKER I AM, SO YOU HAVE OT TO BE AHEAD OF ME.
YOU KNOW THIS IS WEIRD. THAT THIS IS OFF. HAT YOU'RE PLAYING ALONG WITH SOMETHING NOT QUITE RIGHT.
MAYBE.
THEN STOP RATTLING OFF YOUR RESUME! WHY ARE YOU TELLING HIM ALL YOUR ACCOMPLISHMENTS?

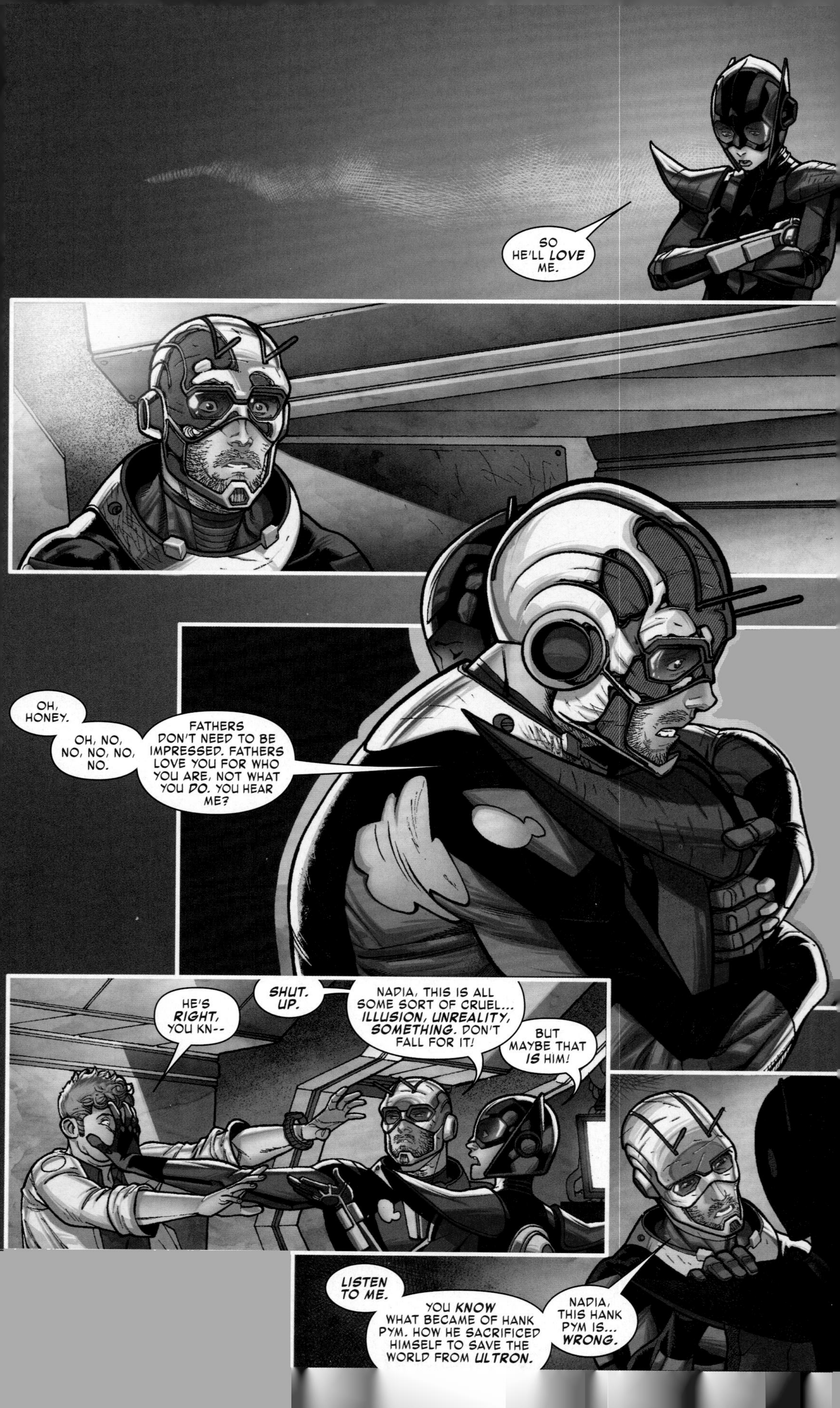
SO HE'LL LOVE ME.
OH, HONEY.
OH, NO, NO, NO, NO, NO.
FATHERS DON'T NEED TO BE IMPRESSED. FATHERS LOVE YOU FOR WHO YOU ARE, NOT WHAT YOU DO. YOU HEAR ME?
HE'S RIGHT, YOU KN--
SHUT. UP.
NADIA, THIS IS ALL SOME SORT OF CRUEL... ILLUSION, UNREALITY, SOMETHING. DON'T FALL FOR IT!
BUT MAYBE THAT IS HIM!
LISTEN TO ME.
YOU KNOW WHAT BECAME OF HANK PYM. HOW HE SACRIFICED HIMSELF TO SAVE THE WORLD FROM ULTRON.
NADIA, THIS HANK PYM IS... WRONG.

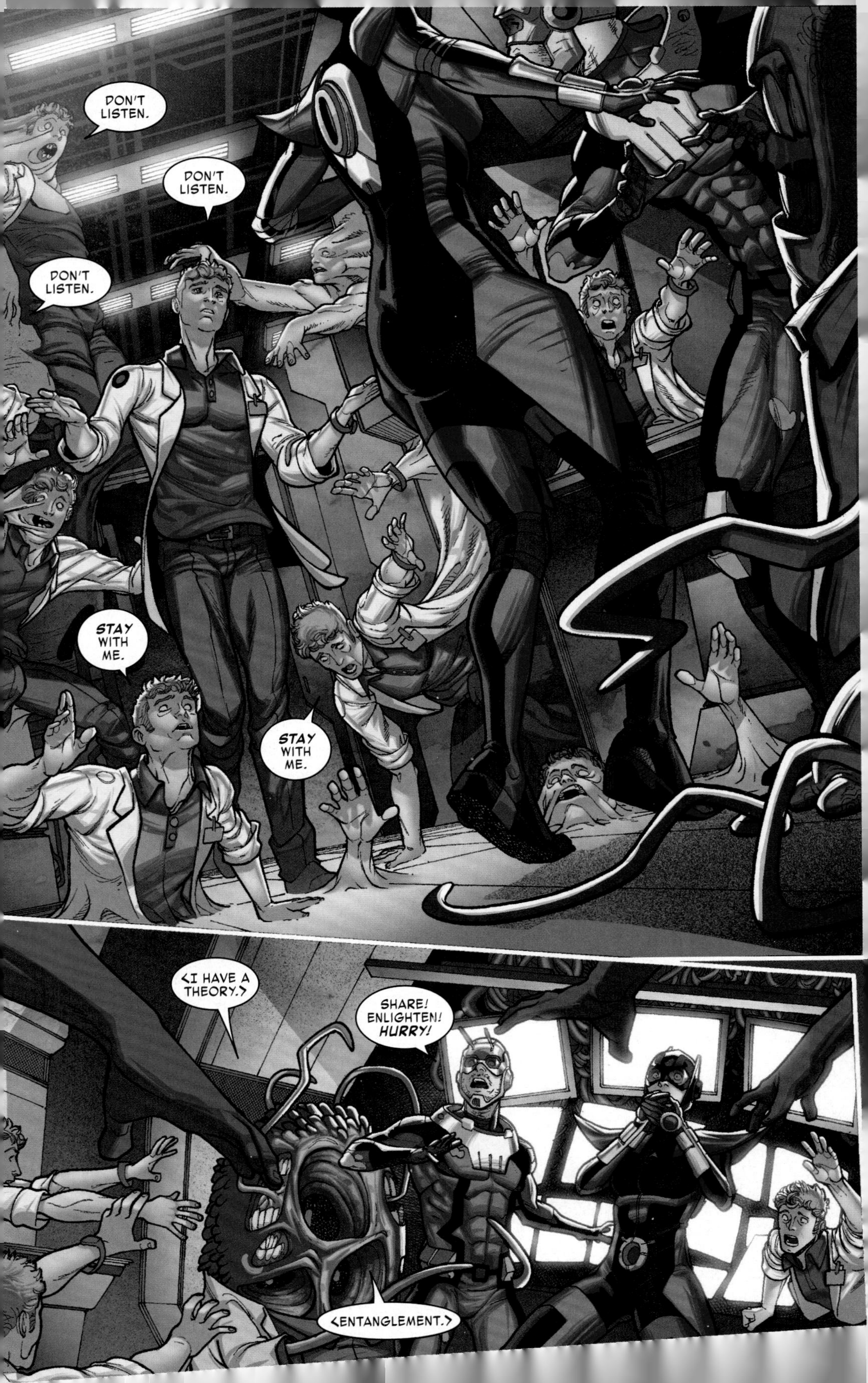
DON'T LISTEN.
DON'T LISTEN.
DON'T LISTEN.
STAY WITH ME.
STAY WITH ME.
<I HAVE A THEORY.>
SHARE! ENLIGHTEN! HURRY!
<ENTANGLEMENT.>

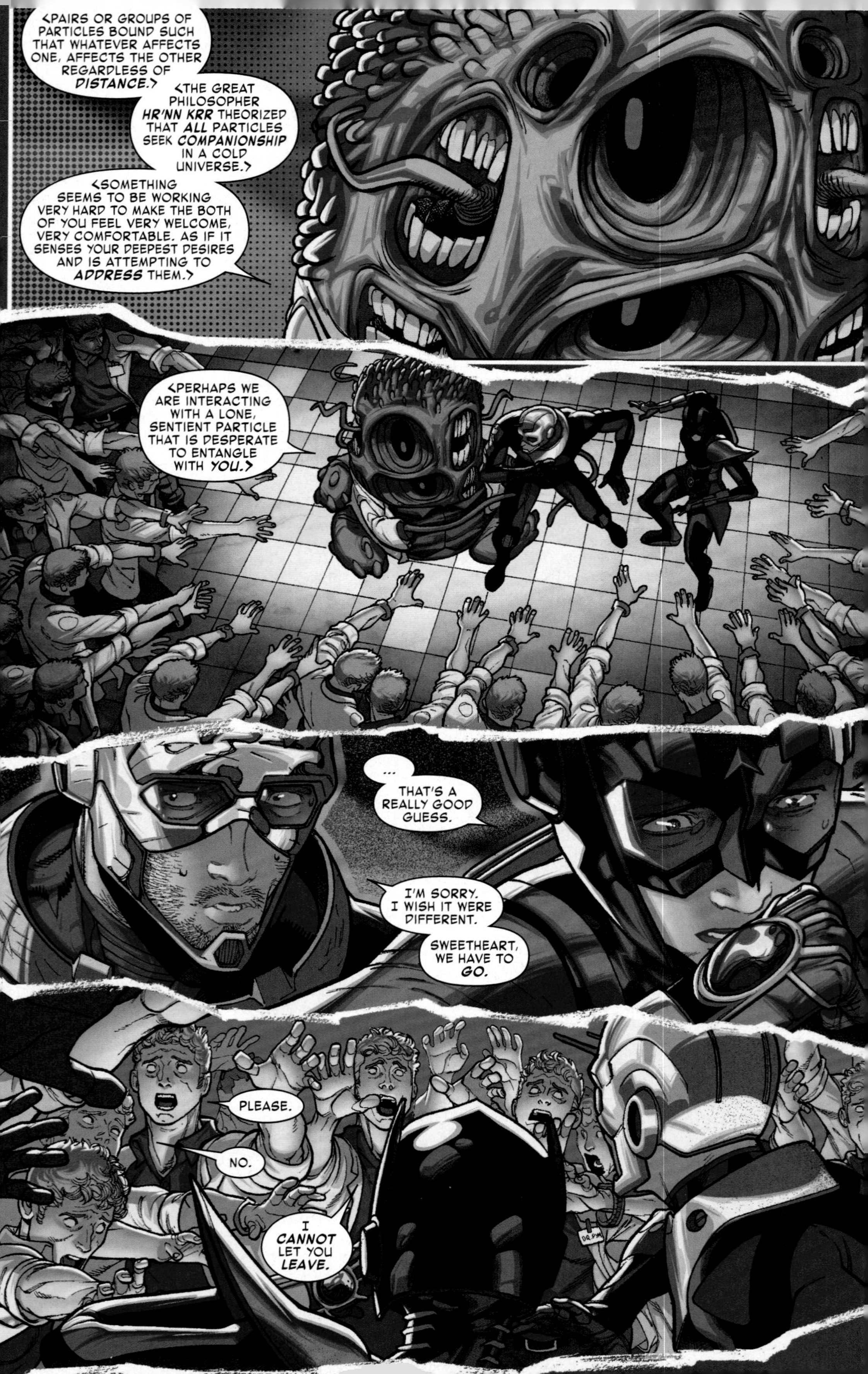
<PAIRS OR GROUPS OF PARTICLES BOUND SUCH THAT WHATEVER AFFECTS ONE, AFFECTS THE OTHER REGARDLESS OF DISTANCE.>
<THE GREAT PHILOSOPHER HR'NN KRR THEORIZED THAT ALL PARTICLES SEEK COMPANIONSHIP IN A COLD UNIVERSE.>
<SOMETHING SEEMS TO BE WORKING VERY HARD TO MAKE THE BOTH OF YOU FEEL VERY WELCOME, VERY COMFORTABLE. AS IF IT SENSES YOUR DEEPEST DESIRES AND IS ATTEMPTING TO ADDRESS THEM.>
<PERHAPS WE ARE INTERACTING WITH A LONE, SENTIENT PARTICLE THAT IS DESPERATE TO ENTANGLE WITH YOU.>
...
THAT'S A REALLY GOOD GUESS.
I'M SORRY. I WISH IT WERE DIFFERENT.
SWEETHEART, WE HAVE TO GO.
PLEASE.
NO.
I CANNOT LET YOU LEAVE.

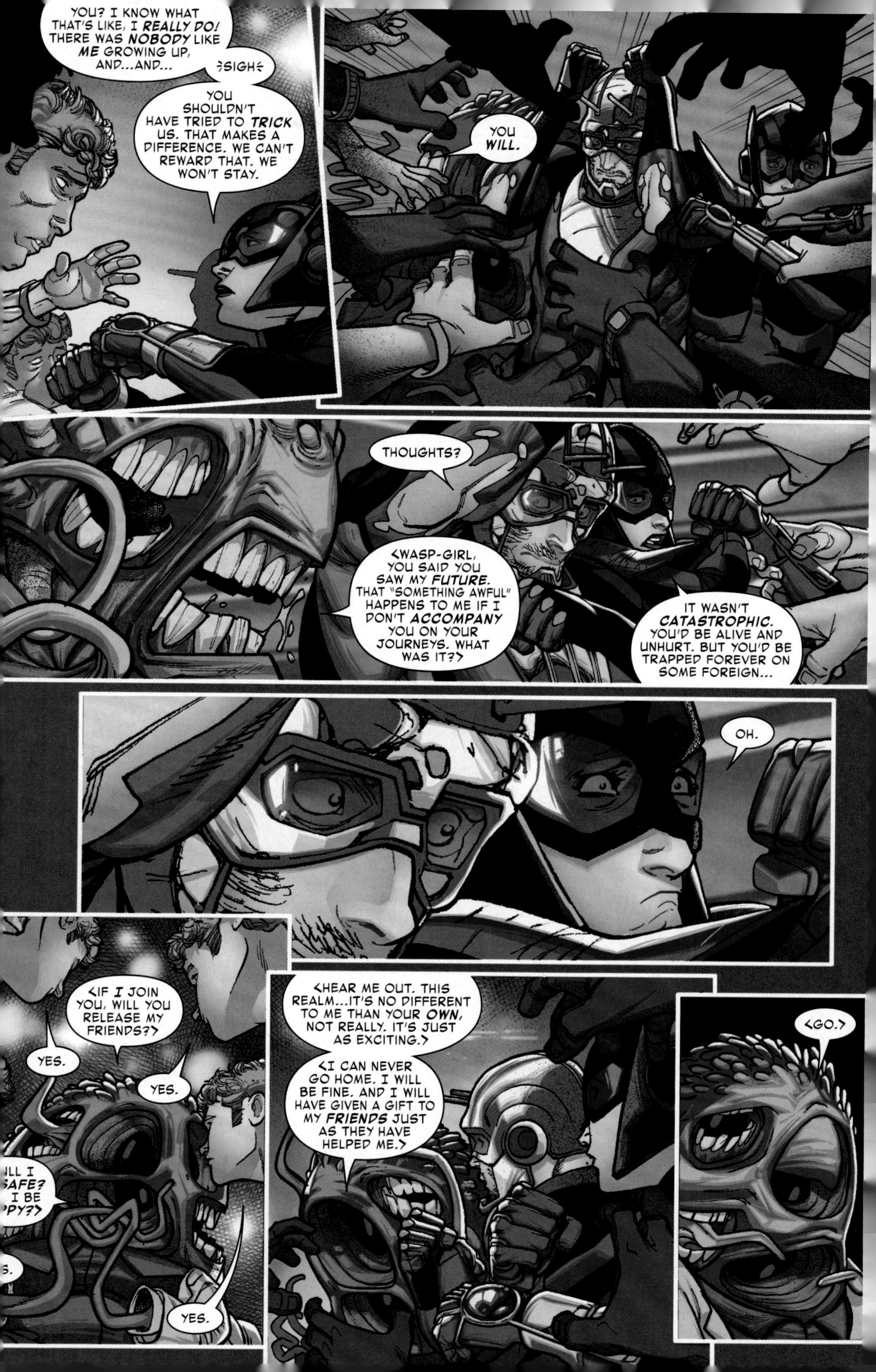

YOU? I KNOW WHAT THAT'S LIKE, I *REALLY DO!* THERE WAS *NOBODY* LIKE *ME* GROWING UP, AND...AND...
⋠SIGH⋡
YOU SHOULDN'T HAVE TRIED TO *TRICK* US. THAT MAKES A DIFFERENCE. WE CAN'T REWARD THAT. WE WON'T STAY.
YOU *WILL.*
THOUGHTS?
<WASP-GIRL, YOU SAID YOU SAW MY *FUTURE.* THAT "SOMETHING AWFUL" HAPPENS TO ME IF I DON'T *ACCOMPANY* YOU ON YOUR JOURNEYS. WHAT WAS IT?>
IT WASN'T *CATASTROPHIC.* YOU'D BE ALIVE AND UNHURT. BUT YOU'D BE TRAPPED FOREVER ON SOME FOREIGN...
OH.
<IF *I* JOIN YOU, WILL YOU RELEASE MY FRIENDS?>
YES.
YES.
YES.
<HEAR ME OUT. THIS REALM...IT'S NO DIFFERENT TO ME THAN YOUR *OWN,* NOT REALLY. IT'S JUST AS EXCITING.>
<I CAN NEVER GO HOME. I WILL BE FINE. AND I WILL HAVE GIVEN A GIFT TO MY *FRIENDS* JUST AS THEY HAVE HELPED ME.>
<GO.>

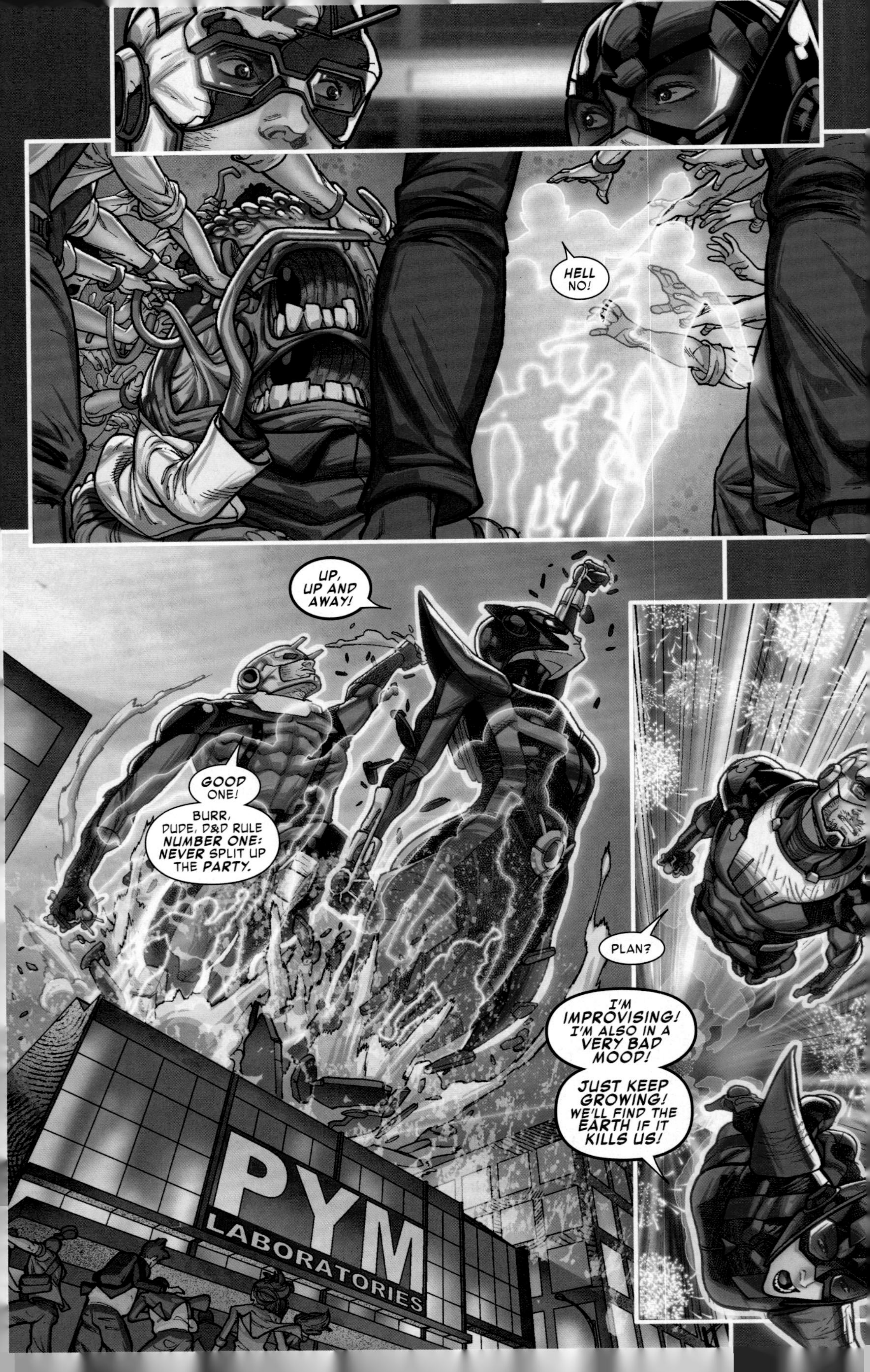
HELL NO!
UP, UP AND AWAY!
GOOD ONE!
BURR, DUDE, D&D RULE NUMBER ONE: NEVER SPLIT UP THE PARTY.
PYM LABORATORIES
PLAN?
I'M IMPROVISING! I'M ALSO IN A VERY BAD MOOD!
JUST KEEP GROWING! WE'LL FIND THE EARTH IF IT KILLS US!

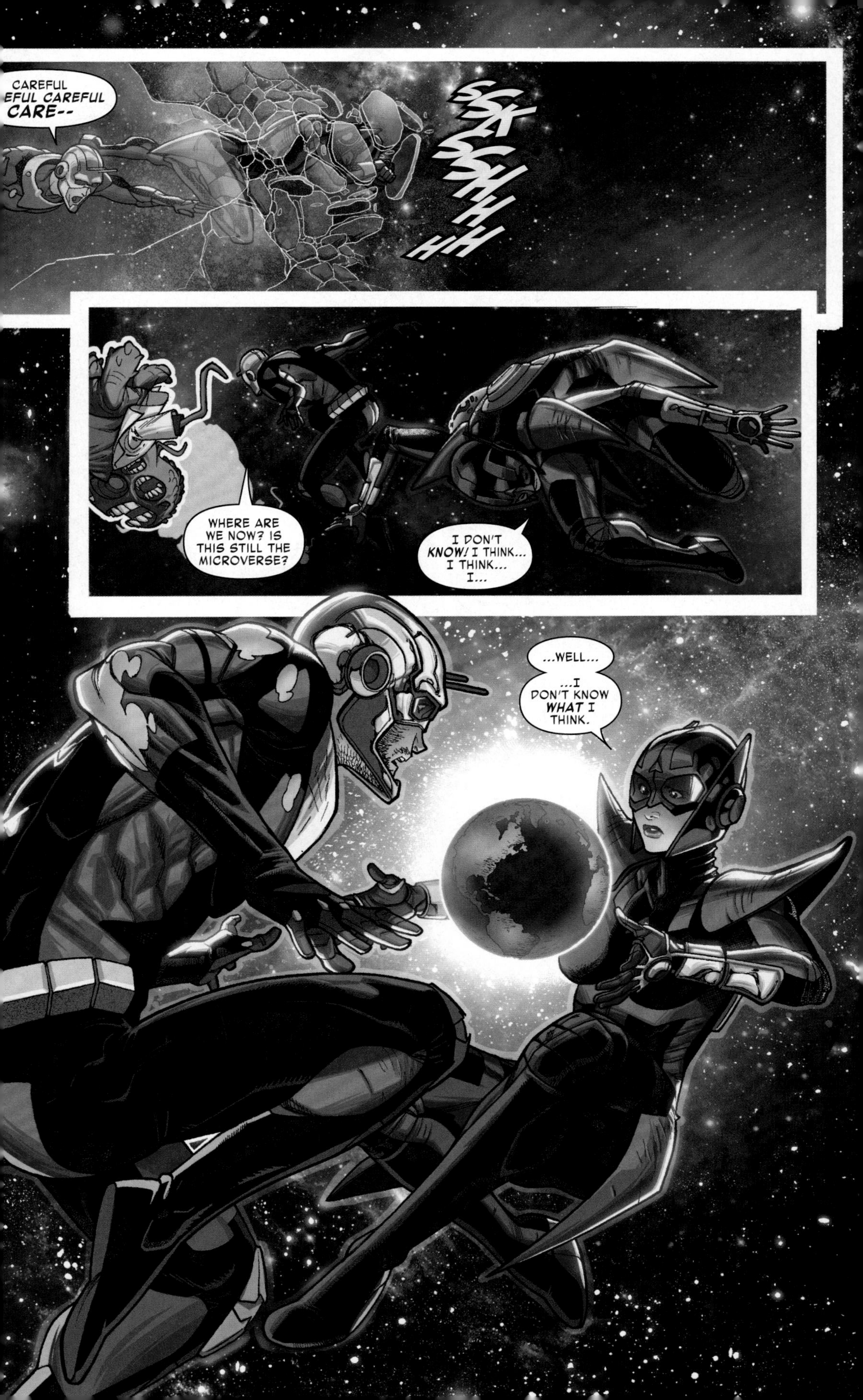
CAREFUL
EFUL CAREFUL
CARE--
SSKSSHHHHH
WHERE ARE WE NOW? IS THIS STILL THE MICROVERSE?
I DON'T *KNOW!* I THINK... I THINK... I...
...WELL...
...I DON'T KNOW *WHAT* I THINK.

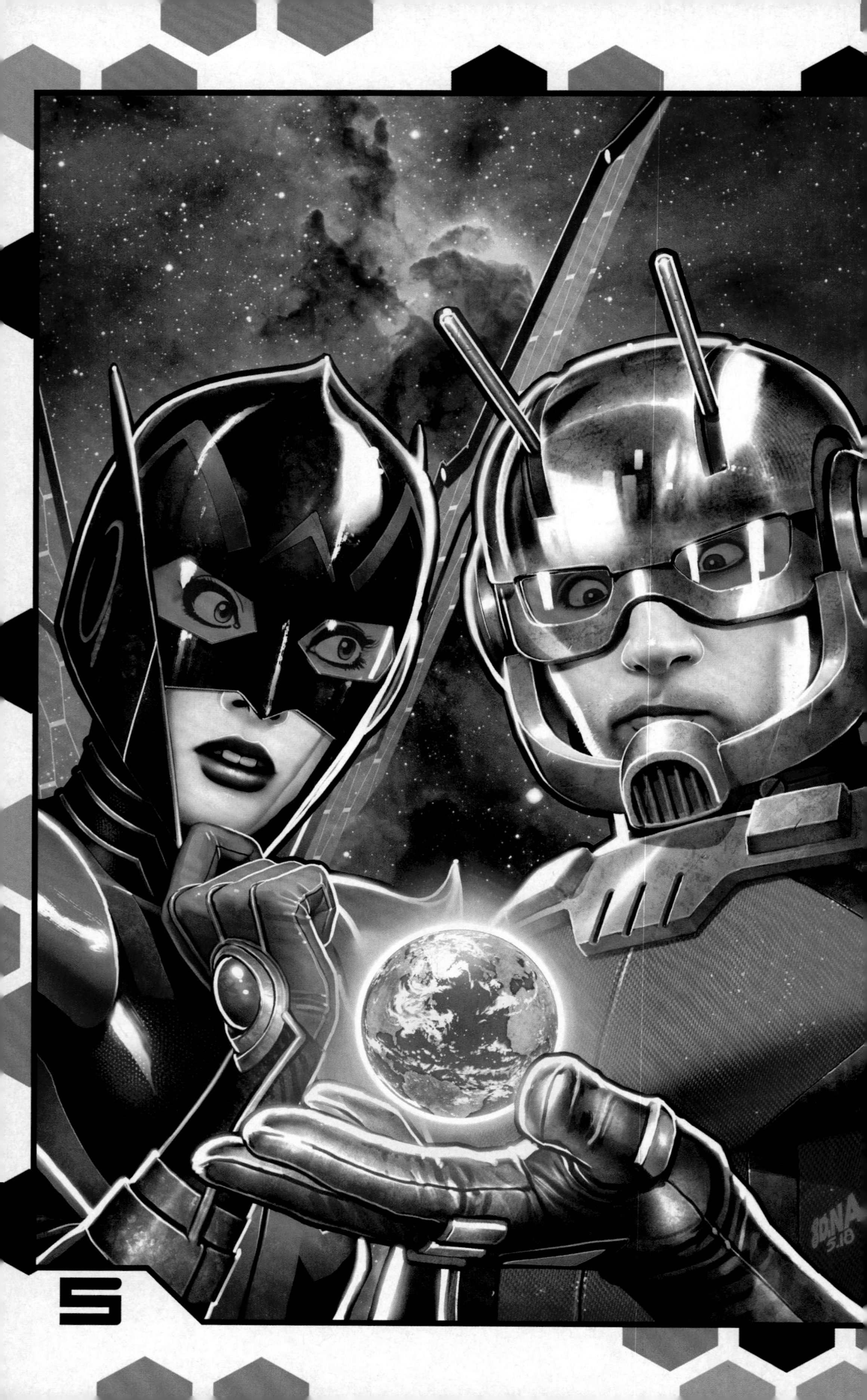
5

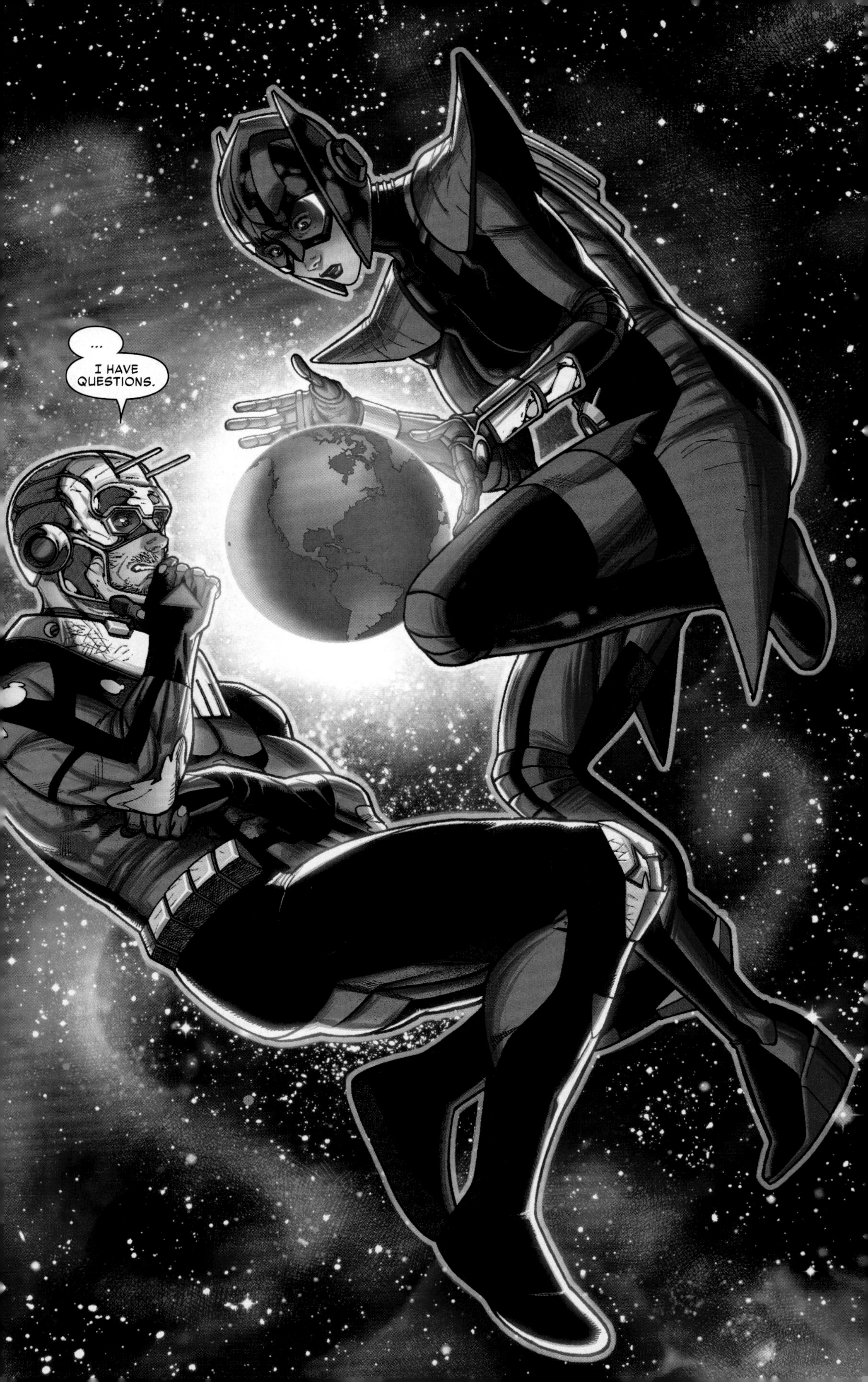
...
I HAVE QUESTIONS.

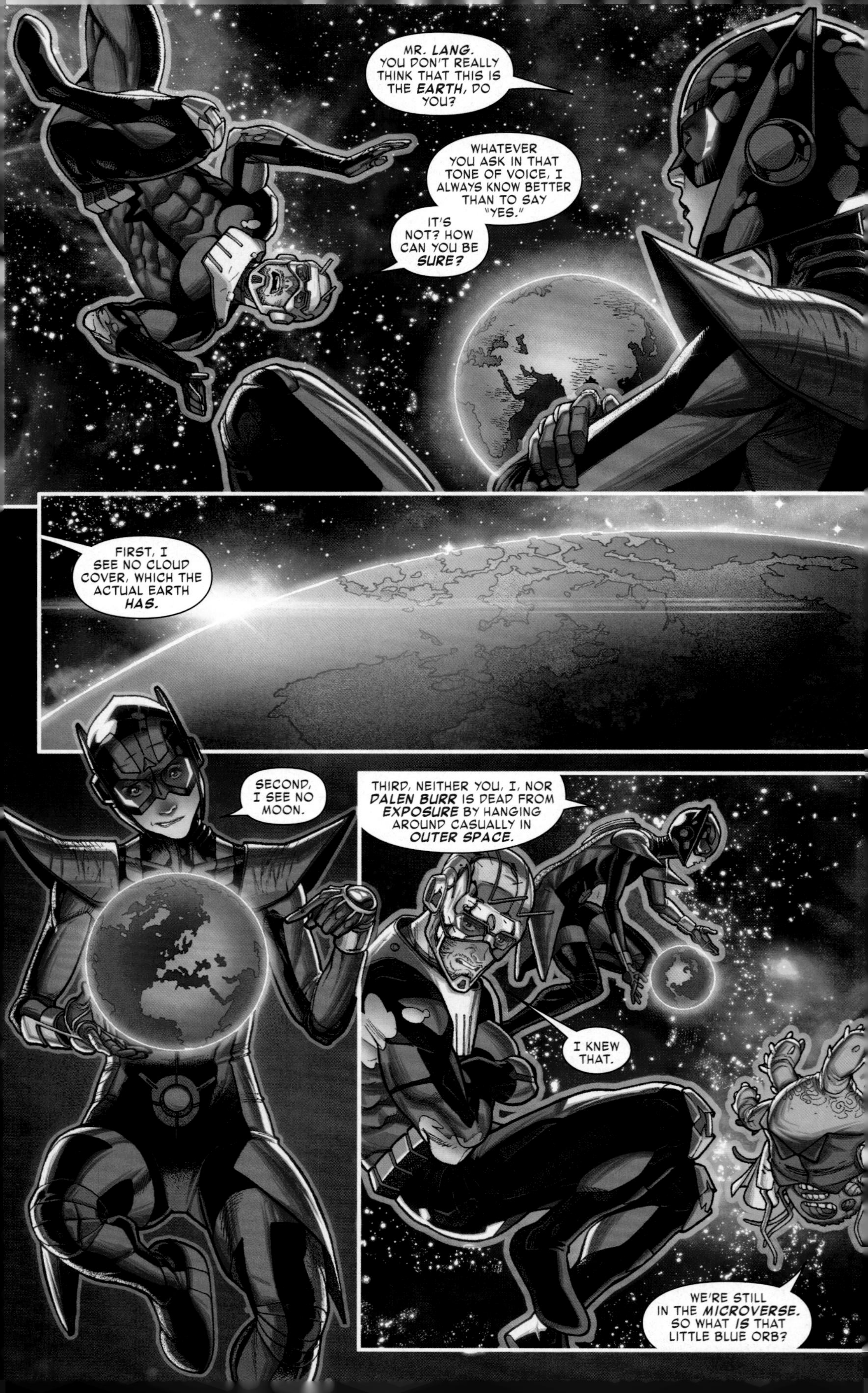
MR. LANG. YOU DON'T REALLY THINK THAT THIS IS THE EARTH, DO YOU?
WHATEVER YOU ASK IN THAT TONE OF VOICE, I ALWAYS KNOW BETTER THAN TO SAY "YES."
IT'S NOT? HOW CAN YOU BE SURE?
FIRST, I SEE NO CLOUD COVER, WHICH THE ACTUAL EARTH HAS.
SECOND, I SEE NO MOON.
THIRD, NEITHER YOU, I, NOR DALEN BURR IS DEAD FROM EXPOSURE BY HANGING AROUND CASUALLY IN OUTER SPACE.
I KNEW THAT.
WE'RE STILL IN THE MICROVERSE. SO WHAT IS THAT LITTLE BLUE ORB?

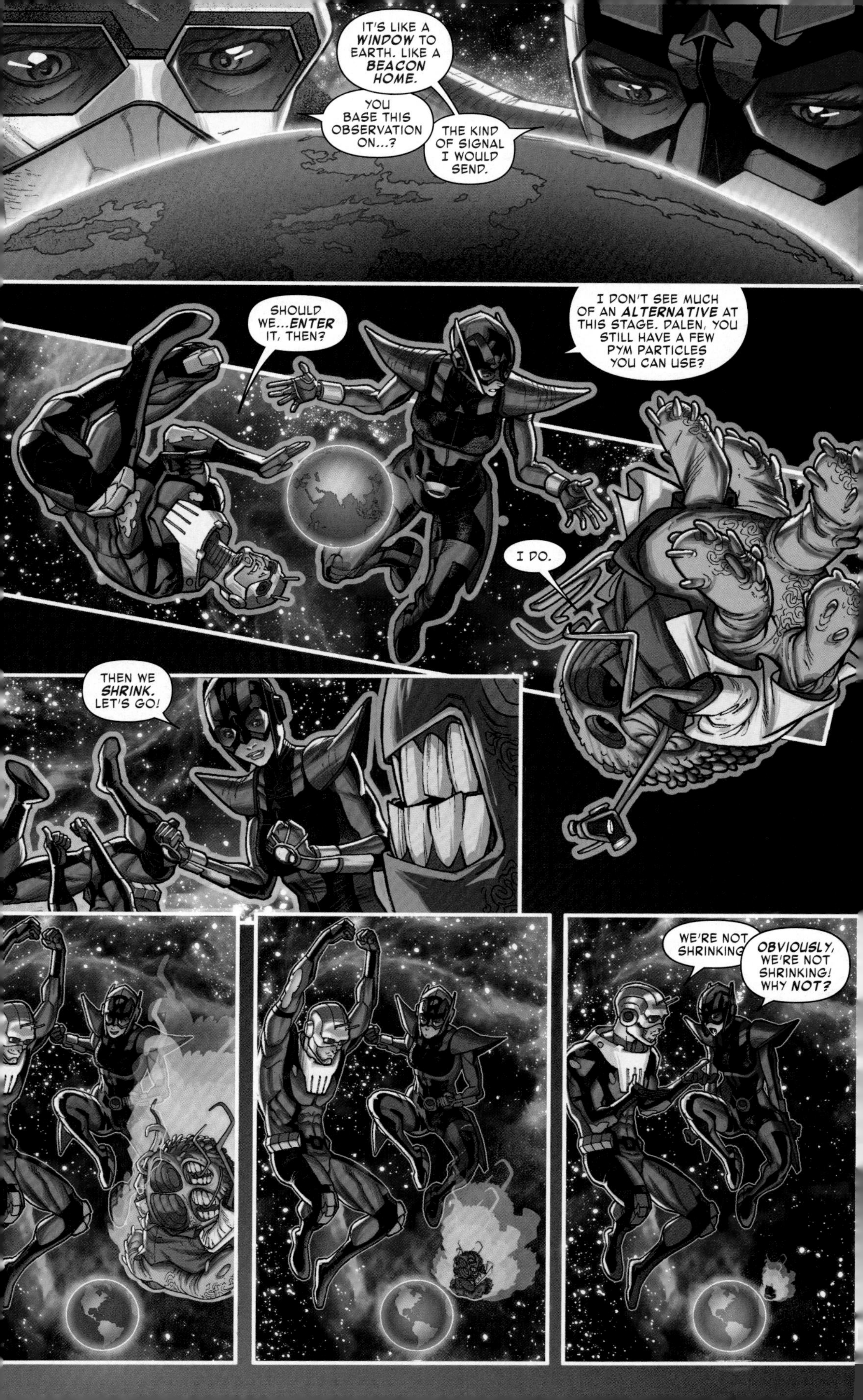

IT'S LIKE A *WINDOW* TO EARTH. LIKE A *BEACON HOME.*
YOU BASE THIS OBSERVATION ON...?
THE KIND OF SIGNAL I WOULD SEND.
SHOULD WE...*ENTER* IT, THEN?
I DON'T SEE MUCH OF AN *ALTERNATIVE* AT THIS STAGE. DALEN, YOU STILL HAVE A FEW PYM PARTICLES YOU CAN USE?
I DO.
THEN WE *SHRINK.* LET'S GO!
WE'RE NOT SHRINKING.
OBVIOUSLY, WE'RE NOT SHRINKING! WHY *NOT?*

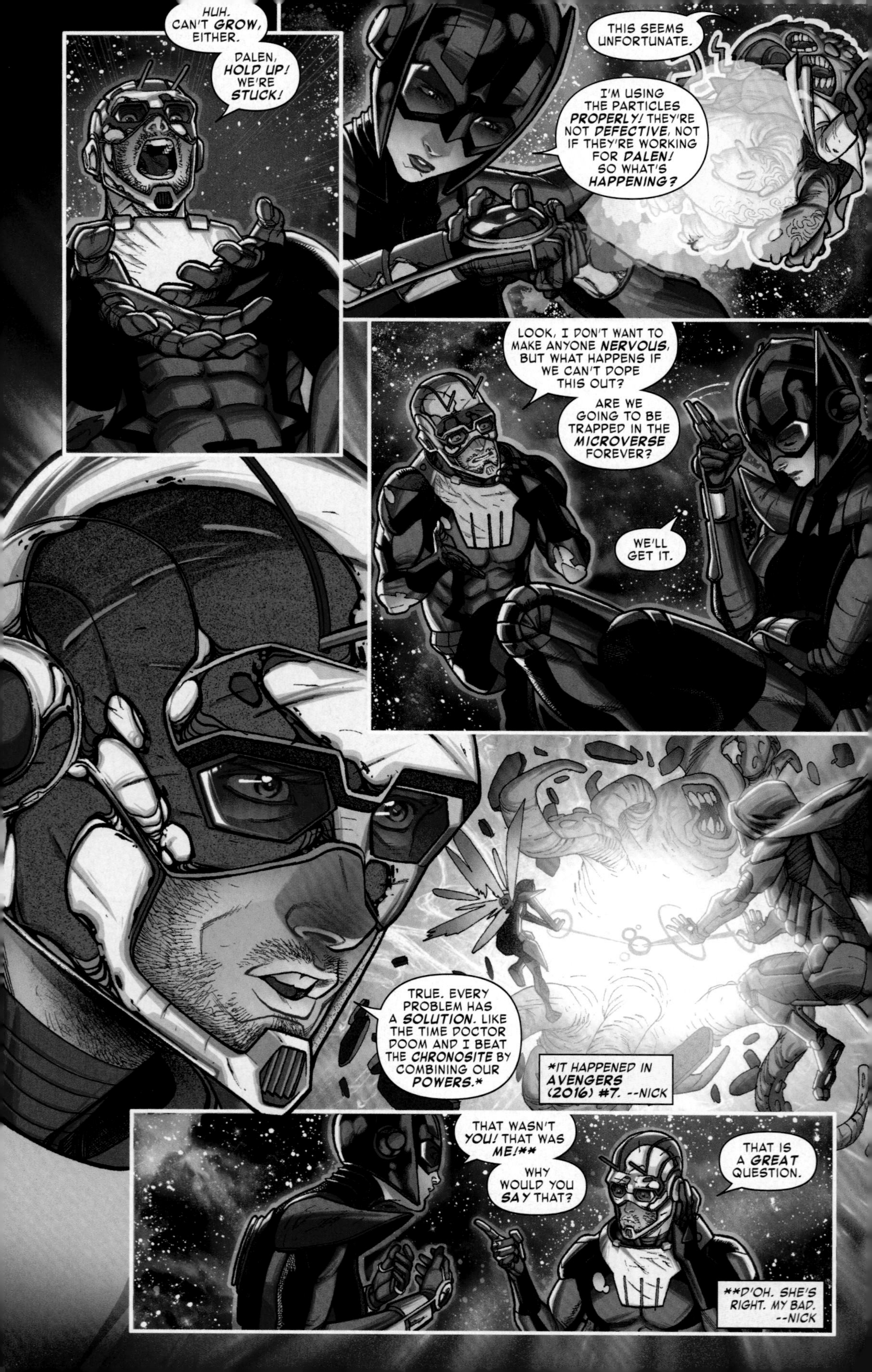
HUH. CAN'T GROW, EITHER.
DALEN, HOLD UP! WE'RE STUCK!
THIS SEEMS UNFORTUNATE.
I'M USING THE PARTICLES PROPERLY! THEY'RE NOT DEFECTIVE, NOT IF THEY'RE WORKING FOR DALEN! SO WHAT'S HAPPENING?
LOOK, I DON'T WANT TO MAKE ANYONE NERVOUS, BUT WHAT HAPPENS IF WE CAN'T DOPE THIS OUT?
ARE WE GOING TO BE TRAPPED IN THE MICROVERSE FOREVER?
WE'LL GET IT.
TRUE. EVERY PROBLEM HAS A SOLUTION. LIKE THE TIME DOCTOR DOOM AND I BEAT THE CHRONOSITE BY COMBINING OUR POWERS.*
*IT HAPPENED IN AVENGERS (2016) #7. --NICK
THAT WASN'T YOU! THAT WAS ME!**
WHY WOULD YOU SAY THAT?
THAT IS A GREAT QUESTION.
**D'OH. SHE'S RIGHT. MY BAD. --NICK

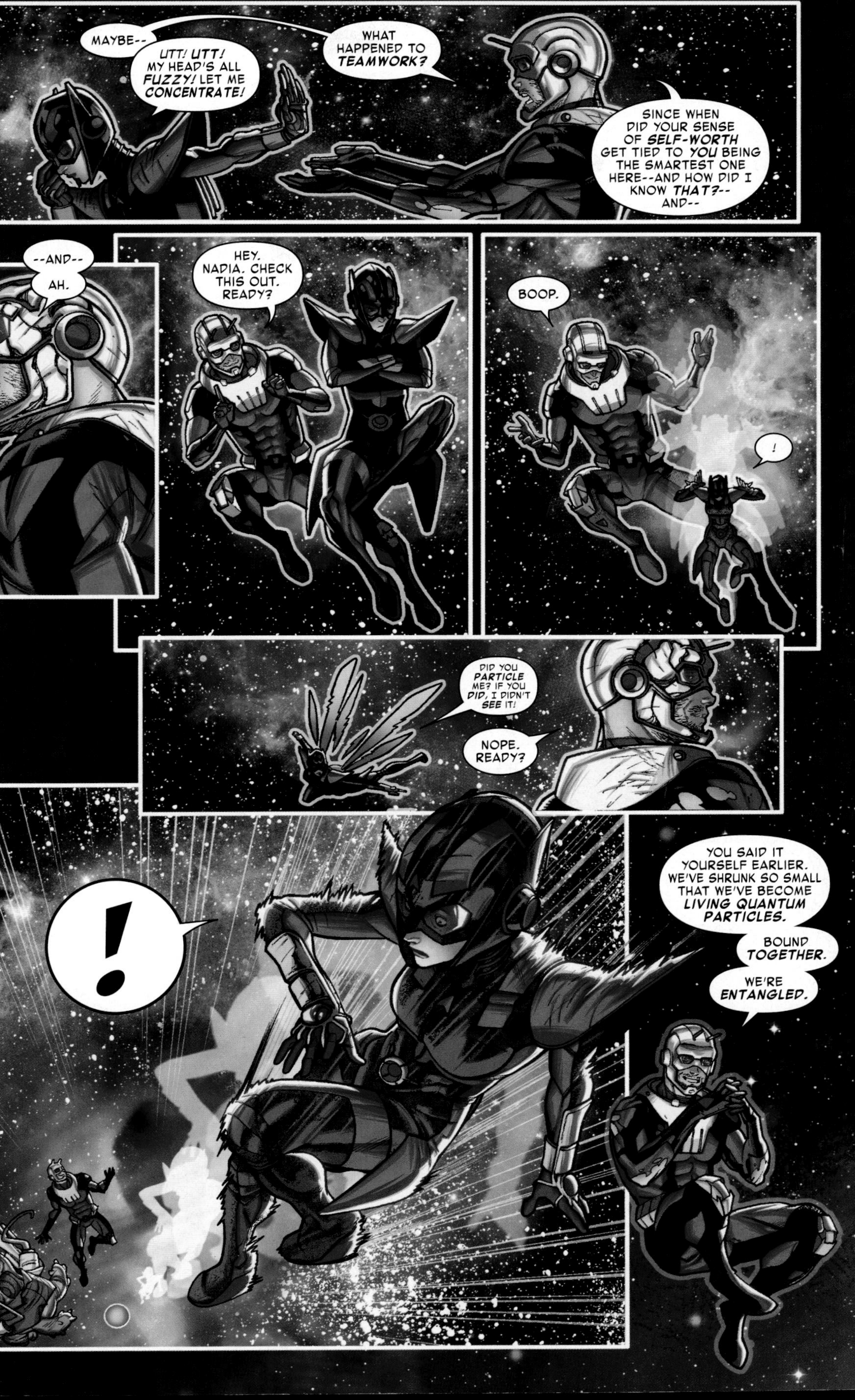
MAYBE--
WHAT HAPPENED TO TEAMWORK?
UTT! UTT! MY HEAD'S ALL FUZZY! LET ME CONCENTRATE!
SINCE WHEN DID YOUR SENSE OF SELF-WORTH GET TIED TO YOU BEING THE SMARTEST ONE HERE--AND HOW DID I KNOW THAT?-- AND--
--AND--
AH.
HEY. NADIA. CHECK THIS OUT. READY?
BOOP.
!
DID YOU PARTICLE ME? IF YOU DID, I DIDN'T SEE IT!
NOPE. READY?
!
YOU SAID IT YOURSELF EARLIER. WE'VE SHRUNK SO SMALL THAT WE'VE BECOME LIVING QUANTUM PARTICLES.
BOUND TOGETHER.
WE'RE ENTANGLED.

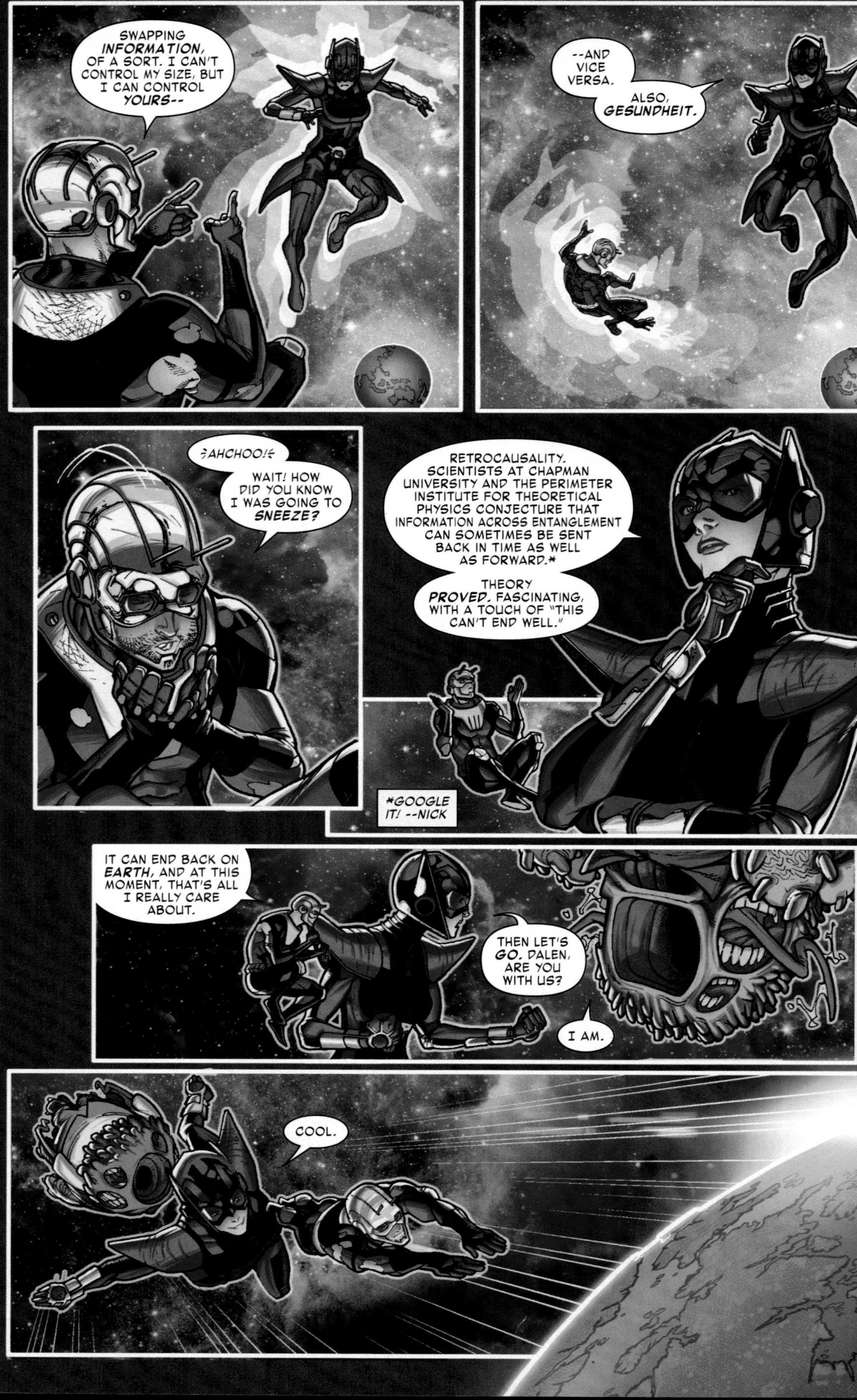
SWAPPING INFORMATION, OF A SORT. I CAN'T CONTROL MY SIZE, BUT I CAN CONTROL YOURS--
--AND VICE VERSA.
ALSO, GESUNDHEIT.
AHCHOO!
WAIT! HOW DID YOU KNOW I WAS GOING TO SNEEZE?
RETROCAUSALITY. SCIENTISTS AT CHAPMAN UNIVERSITY AND THE PERIMETER INSTITUTE FOR THEORETICAL PHYSICS CONJECTURE THAT INFORMATION ACROSS ENTANGLEMENT CAN SOMETIMES BE SENT BACK IN TIME AS WELL AS FORWARD.*
THEORY PROVED. FASCINATING, WITH A TOUCH OF "THIS CAN'T END WELL."
*GOOGLE IT! --NICK
IT CAN END BACK ON EARTH, AND AT THIS MOMENT, THAT'S ALL I REALLY CARE ABOUT.
THEN LET'S GO. DALEN, ARE YOU WITH US?
I AM.
COOL.

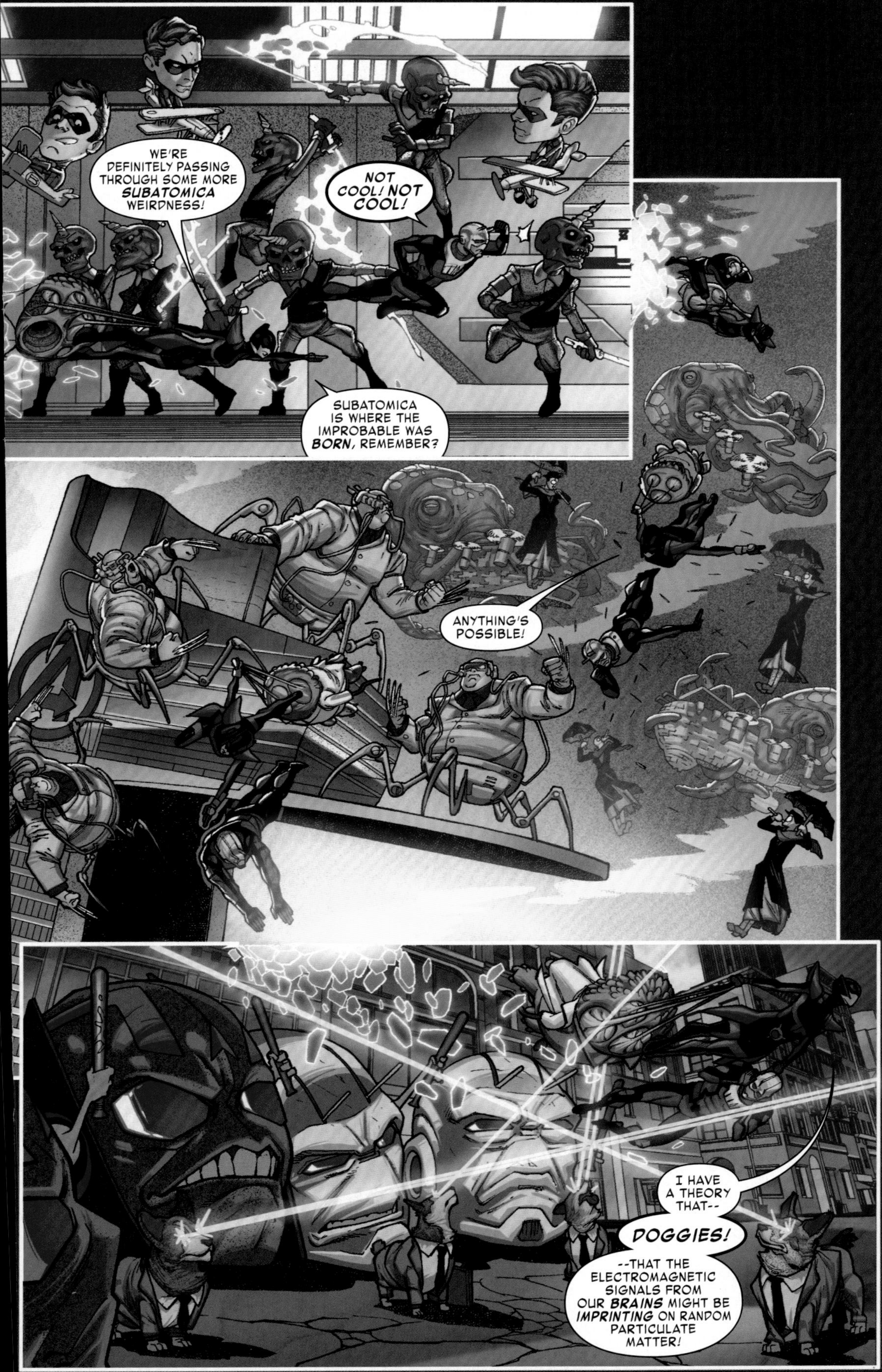
WE'RE DEFINITELY PASSING THROUGH SOME MORE SUBATOMICA WEIRDNESS!
NOT COOL! NOT COOL!
SUBATOMICA IS WHERE THE IMPROBABLE WAS BORN, REMEMBER?
ANYTHING'S POSSIBLE!
I HAVE A THEORY THAT--
DOGGIES!
--THAT THE ELECTROMAGNETIC SIGNALS FROM OUR BRAINS MIGHT BE IMPRINTING ON RANDOM PARTICULATE MATTER!

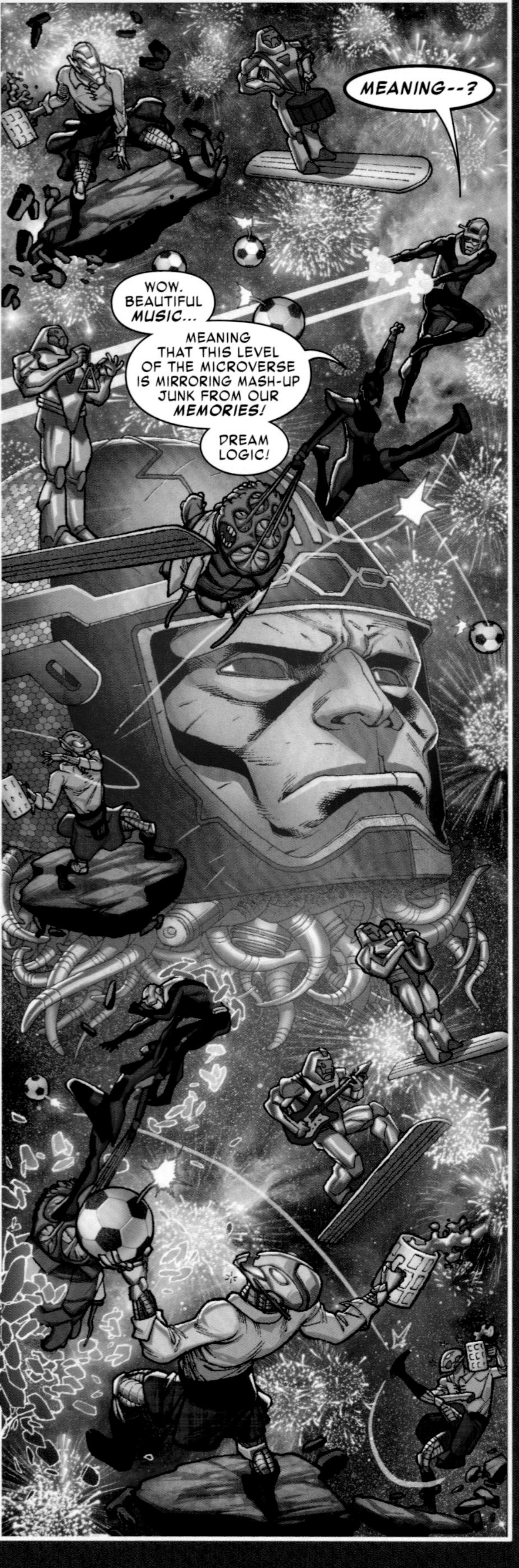
MEANING--?
WOW. BEAUTIFUL MUSIC...
MEANING THAT THIS LEVEL OF THE MICROVERSE IS MIRRORING MASH-UP JUNK FROM OUR MEMORIES!
DREAM LOGIC!

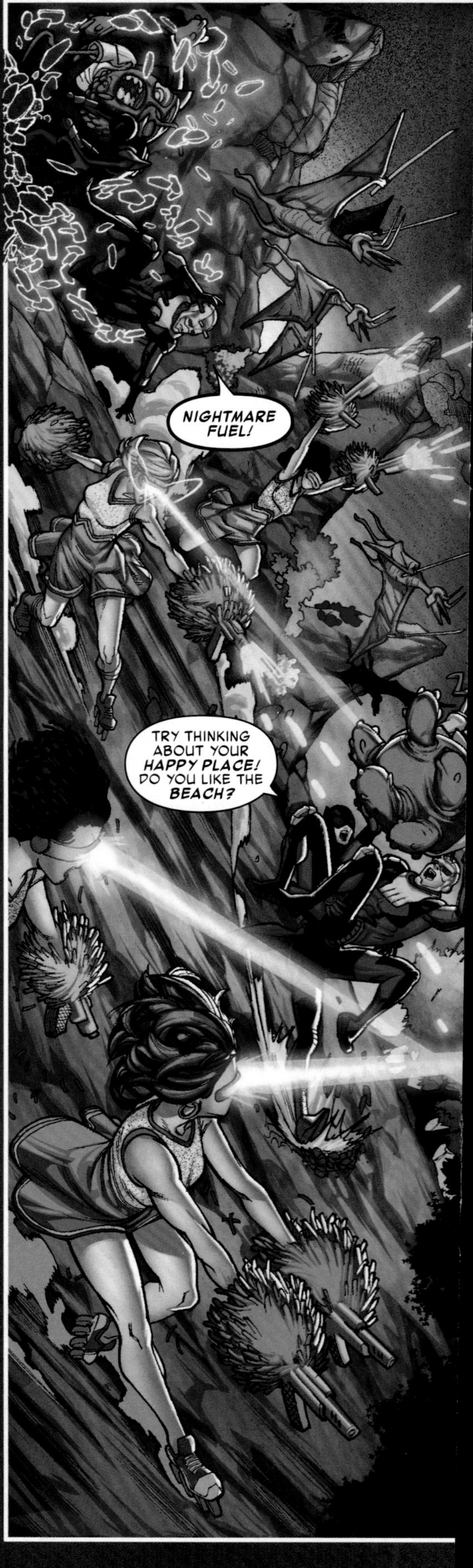
NIGHTMARE FUEL!
TRY THINKING ABOUT YOUR HAPPY PLACE! DO YOU LIKE THE BEACH?

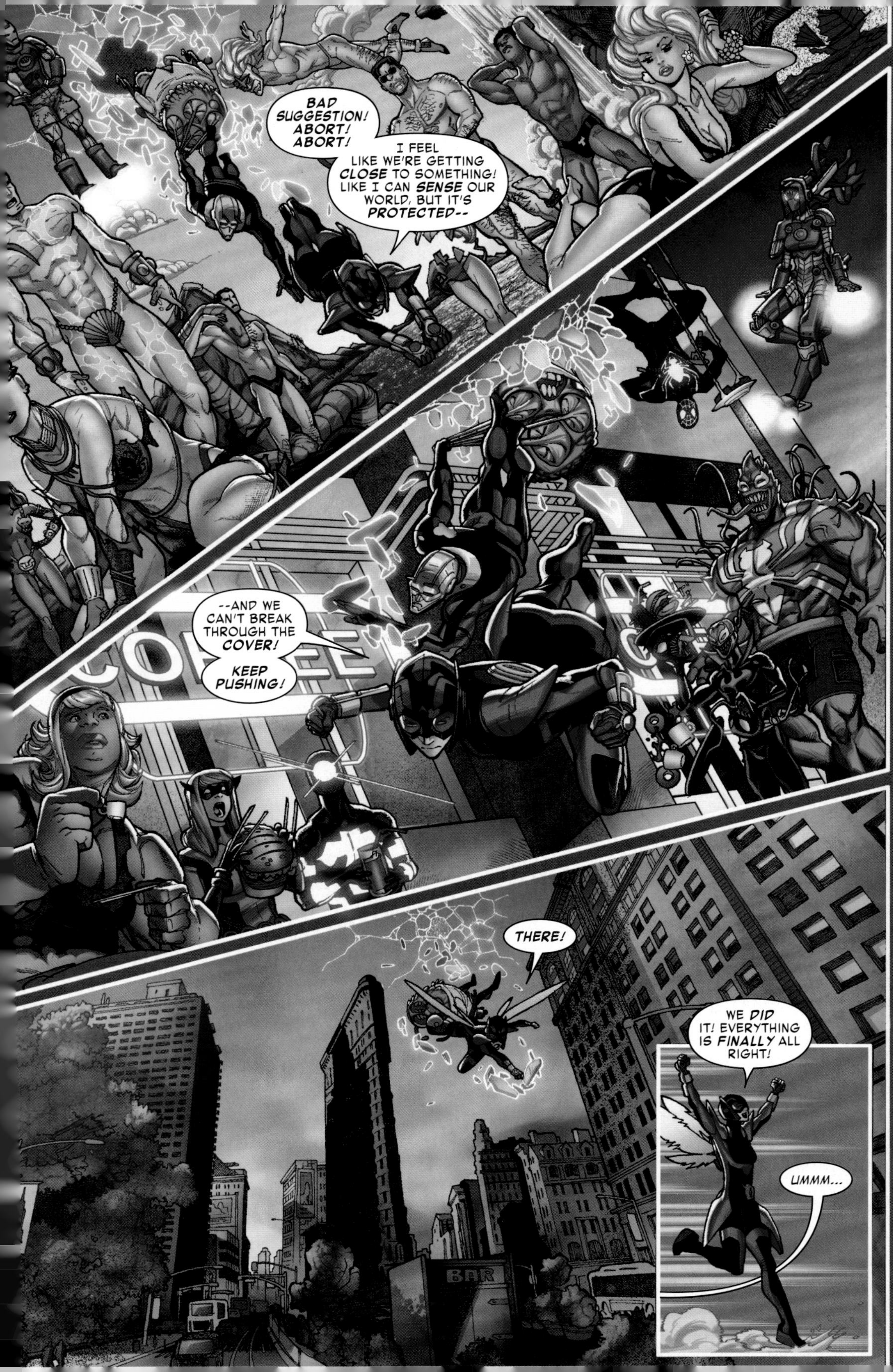
BAD SUGGESTION! ABORT! ABORT!
I FEEL LIKE WE'RE GETTING CLOSE TO SOMETHING! LIKE I CAN SENSE OUR WORLD, BUT IT'S PROTECTED--
--AND WE CAN'T BREAK THROUGH THE COVER!
KEEP PUSHING!
COFFEE
THERE!
WE DID IT! EVERYTHING IS FINALLY ALL RIGHT!
UMMM...
BAR

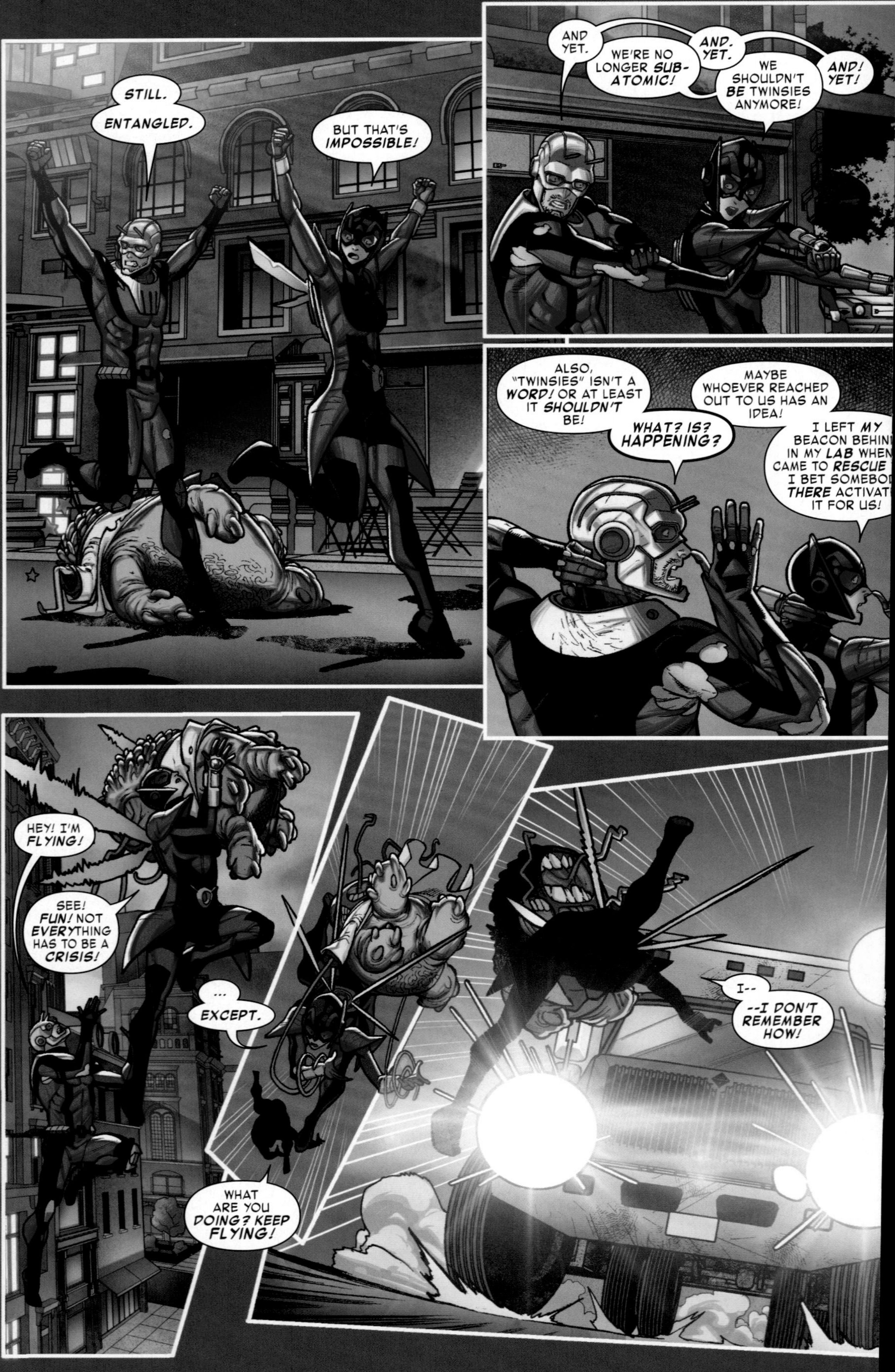

STILL.
ENTANGLED.
BUT THAT'S IMPOSSIBLE!
AND YET.
WE'RE NO LONGER SUB-ATOMIC!
AND. YET.
WE SHOULDN'T BE TWINSIES ANYMORE!
AND! YET!
ALSO, "TWINSIES" ISN'T A WORD! OR AT LEAST IT SHOULDN'T BE!
WHAT? IS? HAPPENING?
MAYBE WHOEVER REACHED OUT TO US HAS AN IDEA!
I LEFT MY BEACON BEHIND IN MY LAB WHEN CAME TO RESCUE I BET SOMEBOD THERE ACTIVAT IT FOR US!
HEY! I'M FLYING!
SEE! FUN! NOT EVERYTHING HAS TO BE A CRISIS!
... EXCEPT.
WHAT ARE YOU DOING? KEEP FLYING!
I--
--I DON'T REMEMBER HOW!

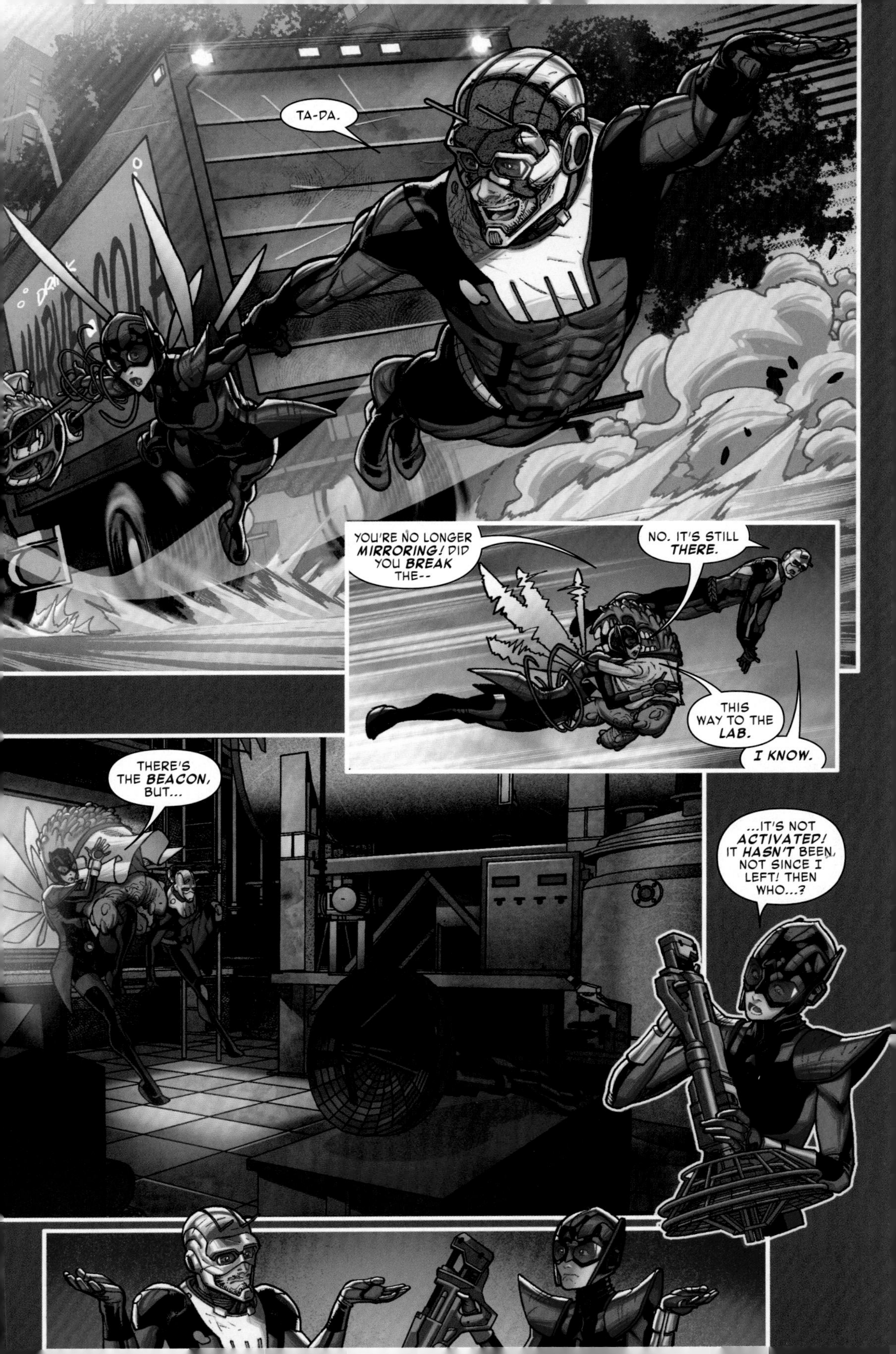
TA-DA.
DRINK MARVEL COLA
YOU'RE NO LONGER MIRRORING! DID YOU BREAK THE--
NO. IT'S STILL THERE.
THIS WAY TO THE LAB.
I KNOW.
THERE'S THE BEACON, BUT...
...IT'S NOT ACTIVATED! IT HASN'T BEEN, NOT SINCE I LEFT! THEN WHO...?

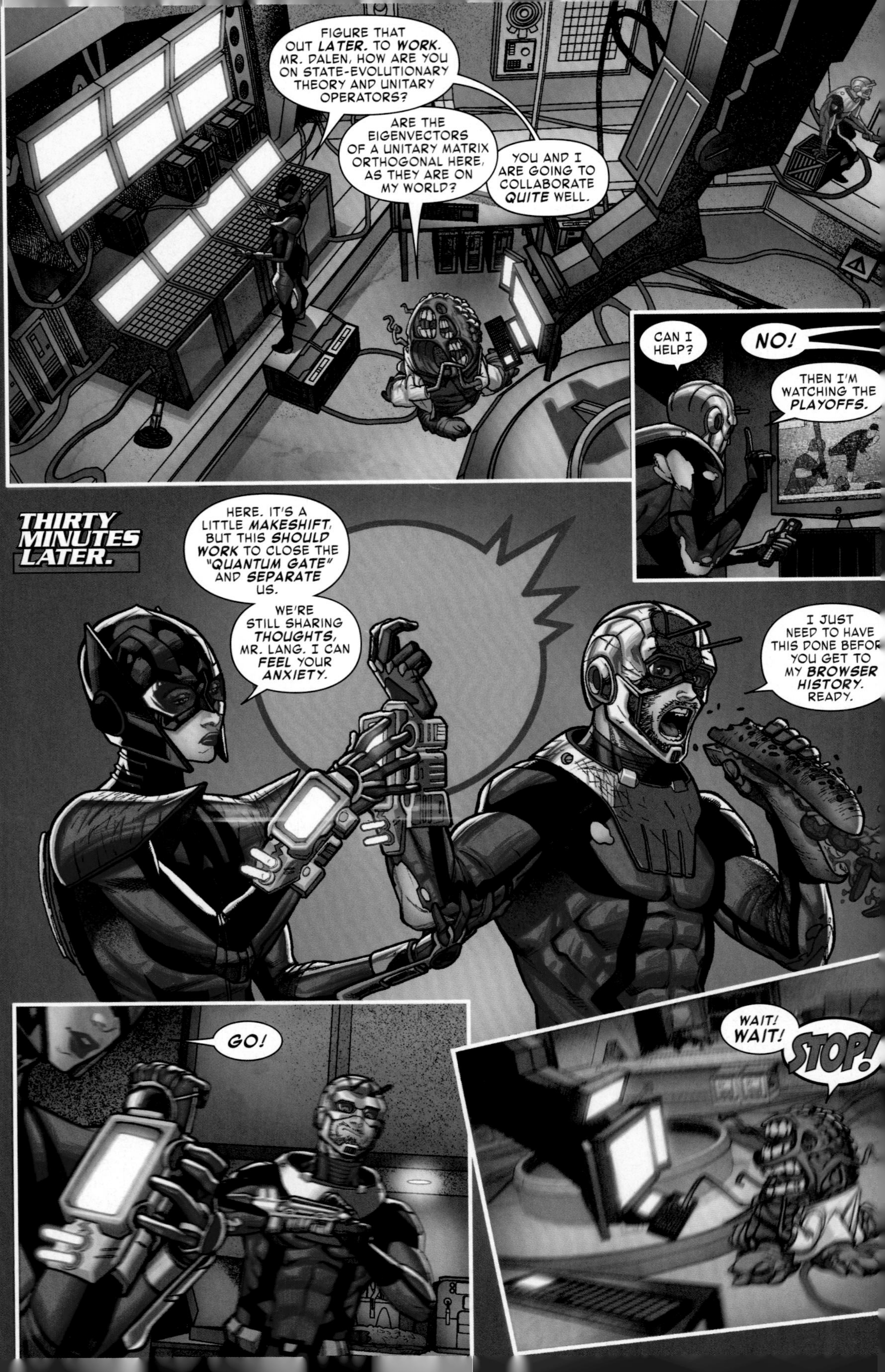

FIGURE THAT OUT LATER. TO WORK. MR. DALEN, HOW ARE YOU ON STATE-EVOLUTIONARY THEORY AND UNITARY OPERATORS?
ARE THE EIGENVECTORS OF A UNITARY MATRIX ORTHOGONAL HERE, AS THEY ARE ON MY WORLD?
YOU AND I ARE GOING TO COLLABORATE QUITE WELL.
CAN I HELP?
NO!
THEN I'M WATCHING THE PLAYOFFS.
THIRTY MINUTES LATER.
HERE. IT'S A LITTLE MAKESHIFT, BUT THIS SHOULD WORK TO CLOSE THE "QUANTUM GATE" AND SEPARATE US.
WE'RE STILL SHARING THOUGHTS, MR. LANG. I CAN FEEL YOUR ANXIETY.
I JUST NEED TO HAVE THIS DONE BEFOR YOU GET TO MY BROWSER HISTORY. READY.
GO!
WAIT! WAIT!
STOP!

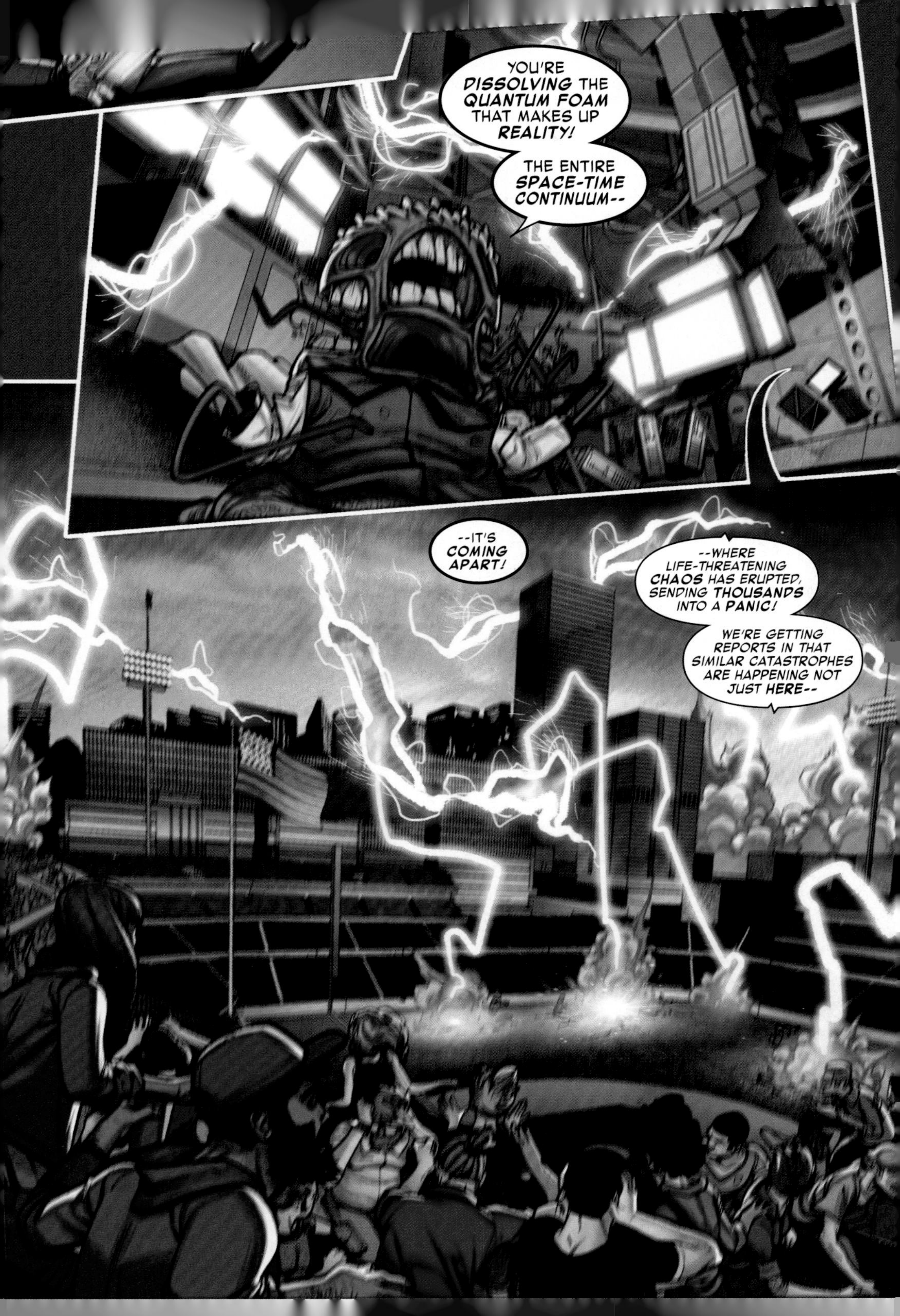
YOU'RE DISSOLVING THE QUANTUM FOAM THAT MAKES UP REALITY!
THE ENTIRE SPACE-TIME CONTINUUM--
--IT'S COMING APART!
--WHERE LIFE-THREATENING CHAOS HAS ERUPTED, SENDING THOUSANDS INTO A PANIC!
WE'RE GETTING REPORTS IN THAT SIMILAR CATASTROPHES ARE HAPPENING NOT JUST HERE--

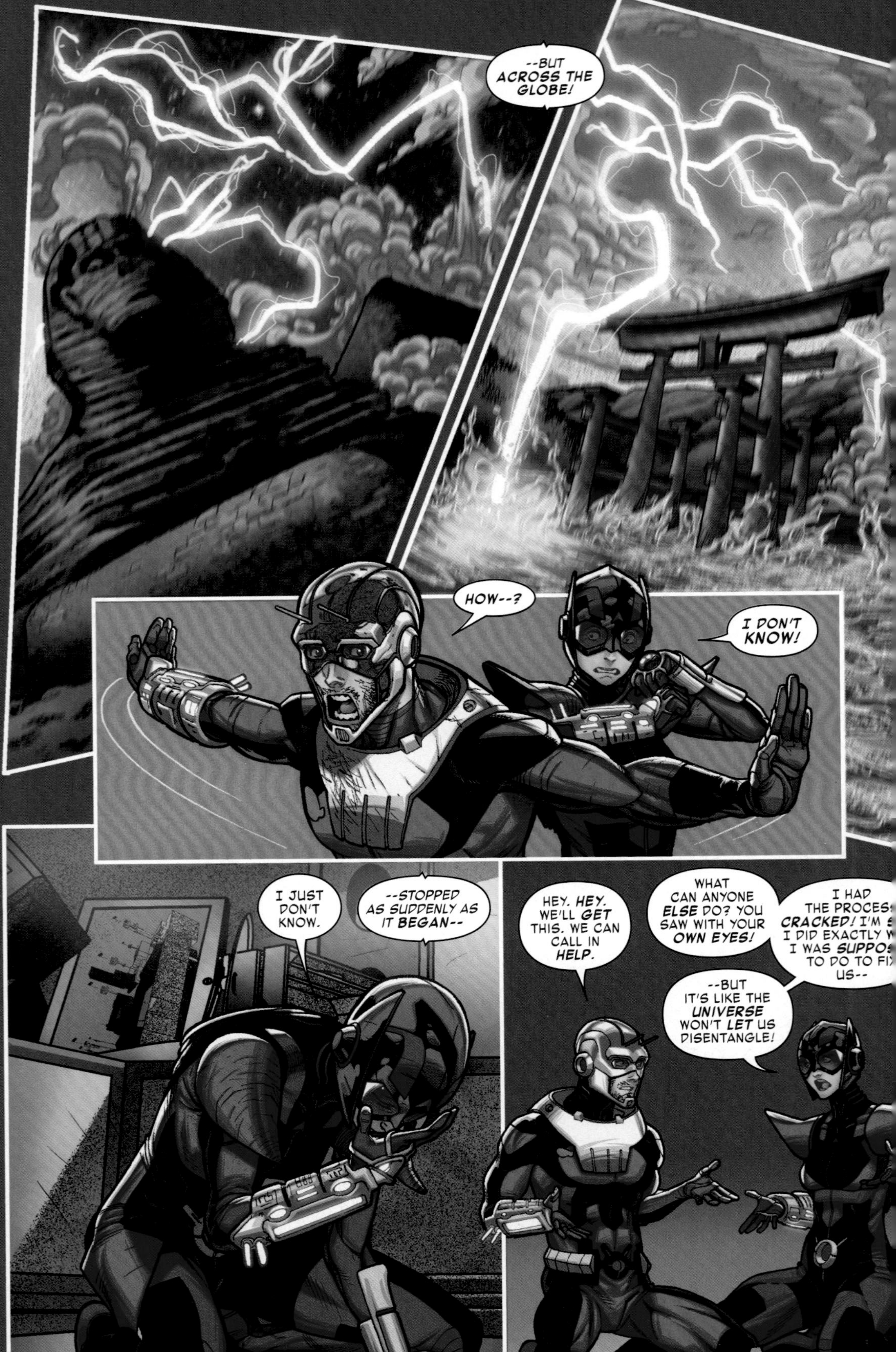
--BUT ACROSS THE GLOBE!
HOW--?
I DON'T KNOW!
I JUST DON'T KNOW.
--STOPPED AS SUDDENLY AS IT BEGAN--
HEY. HEY. WE'LL GET THIS. WE CAN CALL IN HELP.
WHAT CAN ANYONE ELSE DO? YOU SAW WITH YOUR OWN EYES!
I HAD THE PROCES CRACKED! I'M S I DID EXACTLY W I WAS SUPPOS TO DO TO FIX US--
--BUT IT'S LIKE THE UNIVERSE WON'T LET US DISENTANGLE!

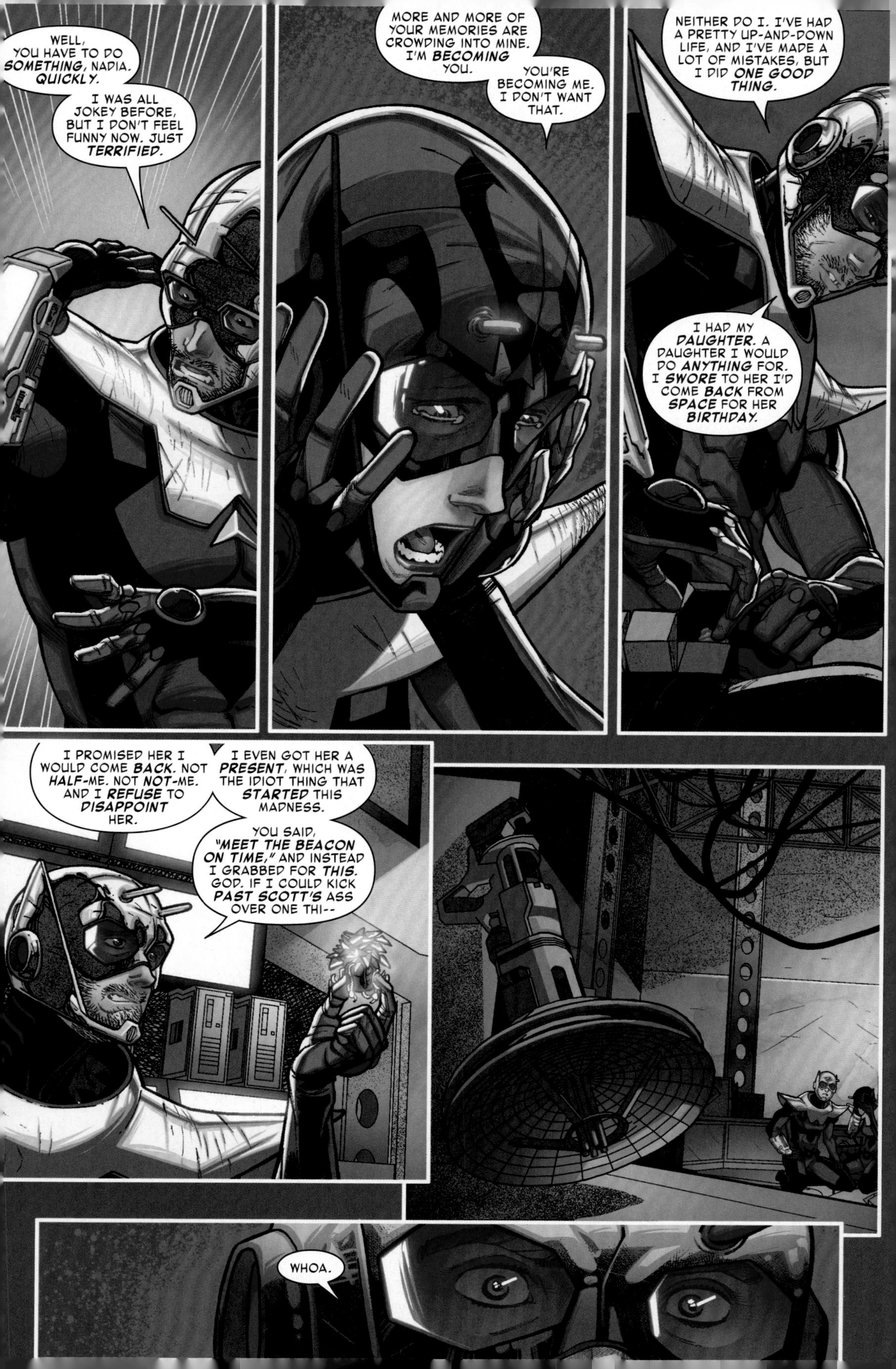
WELL, YOU HAVE TO DO SOMETHING, NADIA. QUICKLY.
I WAS ALL JOKEY BEFORE, BUT I DON'T FEEL FUNNY NOW. JUST TERRIFIED.
MORE AND MORE OF YOUR MEMORIES ARE CROWDING INTO MINE. I'M BECOMING YOU.
YOU'RE BECOMING ME. I DON'T WANT THAT.
NEITHER DO I. I'VE HAD A PRETTY UP-AND-DOWN LIFE, AND I'VE MADE A LOT OF MISTAKES, BUT I DID ONE GOOD THING.
I HAD MY DAUGHTER. A DAUGHTER I WOULD DO ANYTHING FOR. I SWORE TO HER I'D COME BACK FROM SPACE FOR HER BIRTHDAY.
I PROMISED HER I WOULD COME BACK. NOT HALF-ME. NOT NOT-ME. AND I REFUSE TO DISAPPOINT HER.
I EVEN GOT HER A PRESENT, WHICH WAS THE IDIOT THING THAT STARTED THIS MADNESS.
YOU SAID, "MEET THE BEACON ON TIME," AND INSTEAD I GRABBED FOR THIS. GOD. IF I COULD KICK PAST SCOTT'S ASS OVER ONE THI--
WHOA.

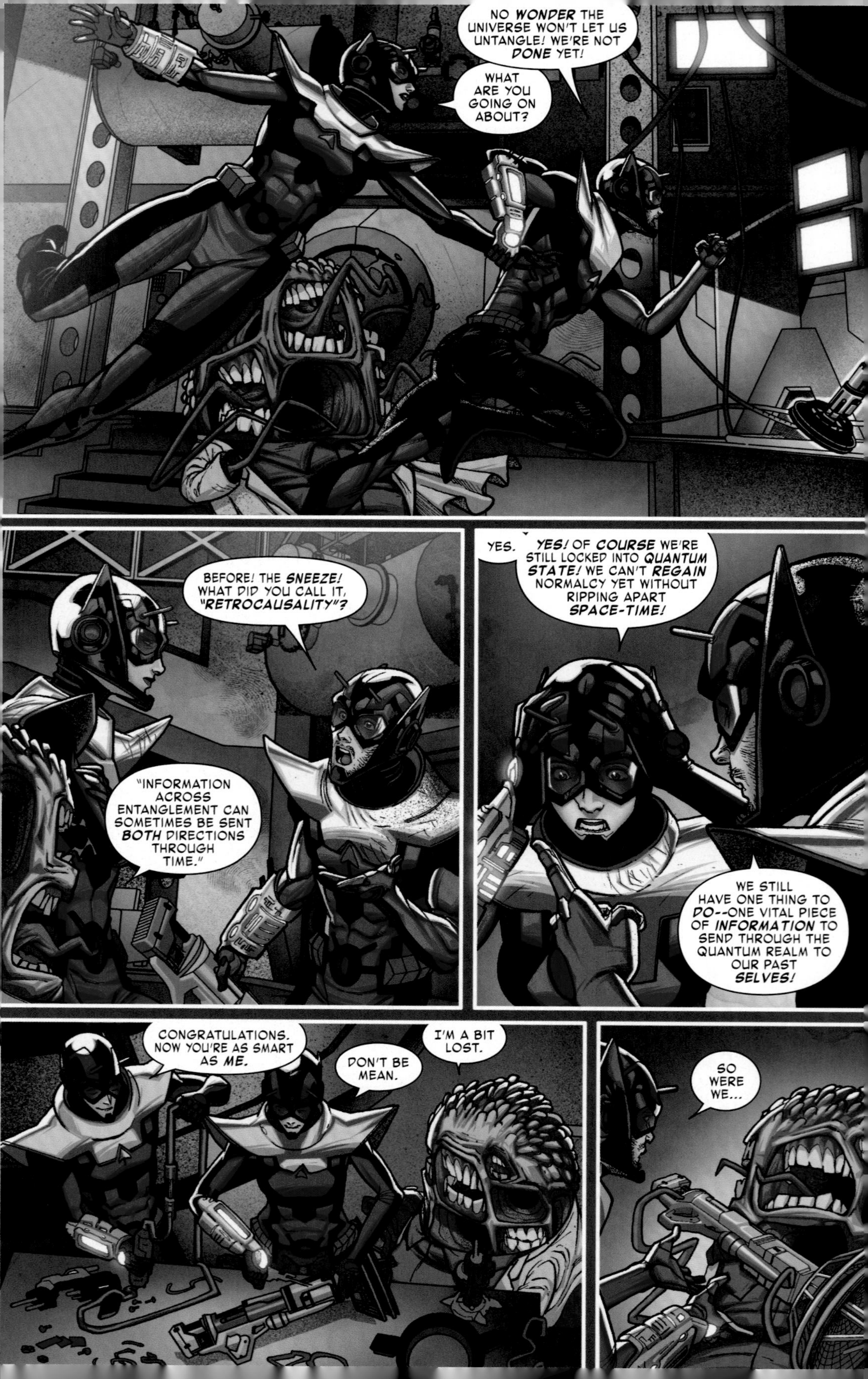
NO WONDER THE UNIVERSE WON'T LET US UNTANGLE! WE'RE NOT DONE YET!
WHAT ARE YOU GOING ON ABOUT?
BEFORE! THE SNEEZE! WHAT DID YOU CALL IT, "RETROCAUSALITY"?
"INFORMATION ACROSS ENTANGLEMENT CAN SOMETIMES BE SENT BOTH DIRECTIONS THROUGH TIME."
YES.
YES! OF COURSE WE'RE STILL LOCKED INTO QUANTUM STATE! WE CAN'T REGAIN NORMALCY YET WITHOUT RIPPING APART SPACE-TIME!
WE STILL HAVE ONE THING TO DO--ONE VITAL PIECE OF INFORMATION TO SEND THROUGH THE QUANTUM REALM TO OUR PAST SELVES!
CONGRATULATIONS. NOW YOU'RE AS SMART AS ME.
DON'T BE MEAN.
I'M A BIT LOST.
SO WERE WE...

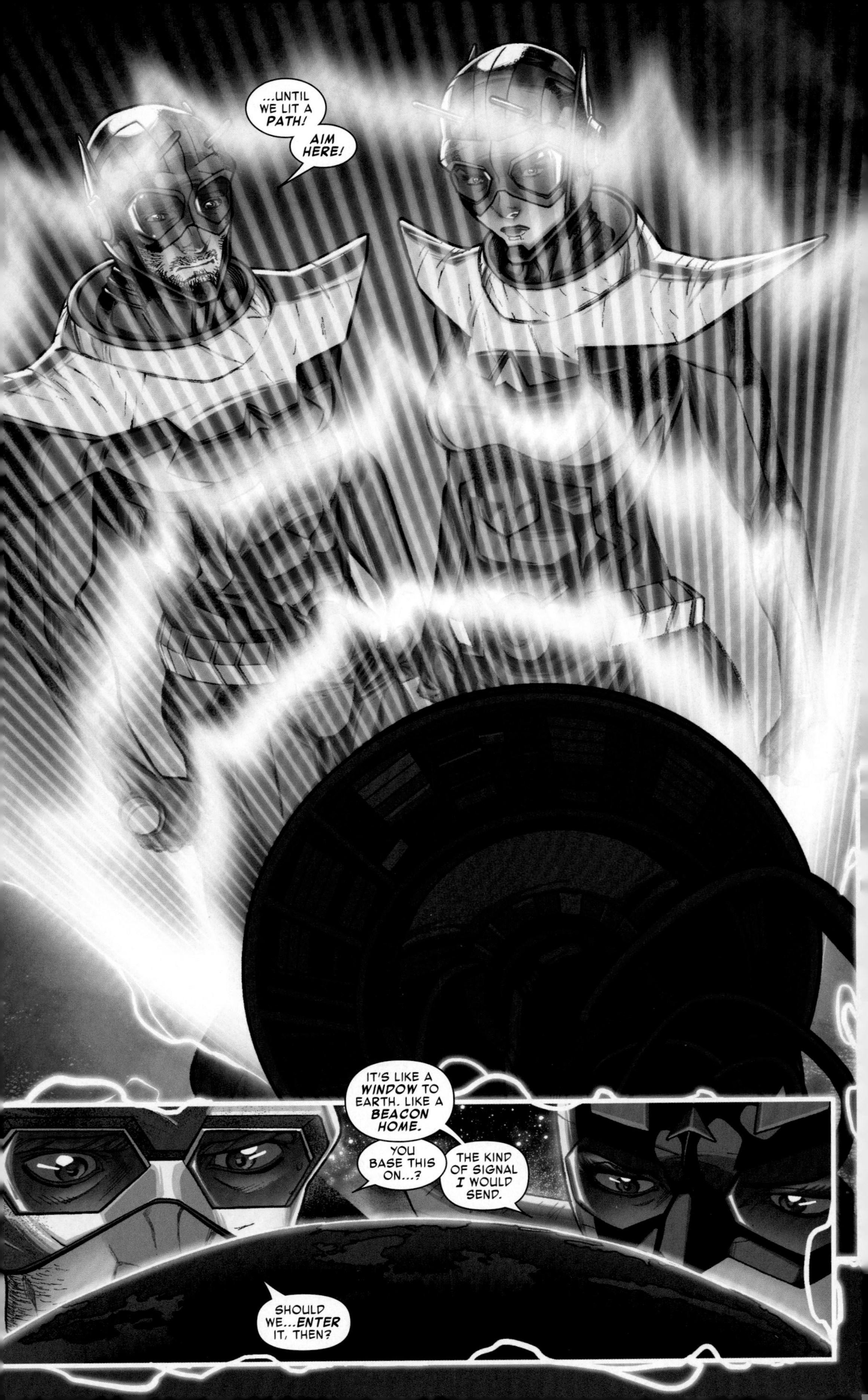

...UNTIL WE LIT A *PATH!*
AIM HERE!
IT'S LIKE A *WINDOW* TO EARTH. LIKE A *BEACON HOME.*
YOU BASE THIS ON...?
THE KIND OF SIGNAL *I* WOULD SEND.
SHOULD WE...*ENTER* IT, THEN?

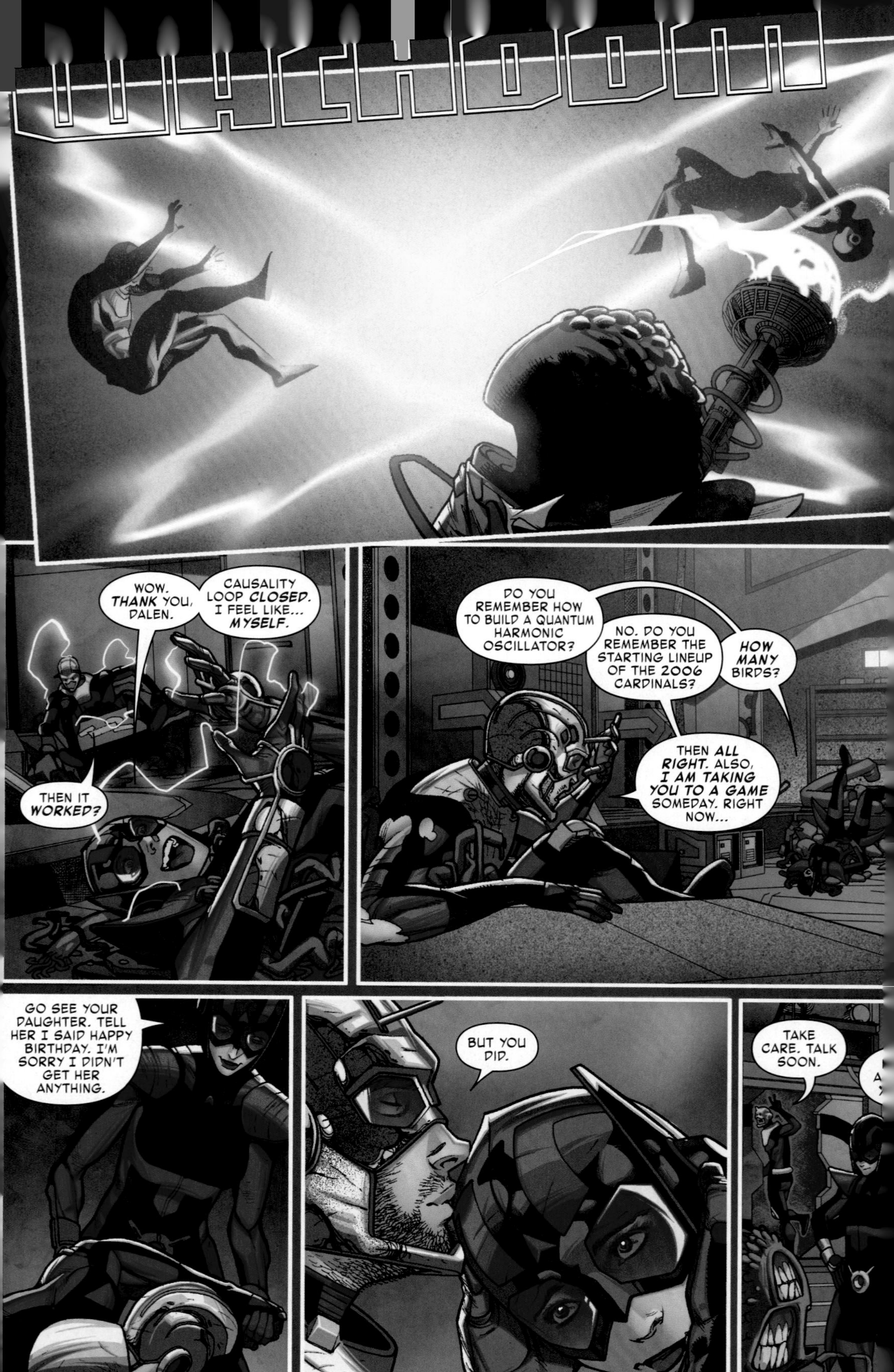
WOW. THANK YOU, DALEN.
CAUSALITY LOOP CLOSED. I FEEL LIKE... MYSELF.
THEN IT WORKED?
DO YOU REMEMBER HOW TO BUILD A QUANTUM HARMONIC OSCILLATOR?
NO. DO YOU REMEMBER THE STARTING LINEUP OF THE 2006 CARDINALS?
HOW MANY BIRDS?
THEN ALL RIGHT. ALSO, I AM TAKING YOU TO A GAME SOMEDAY. RIGHT NOW...
GO SEE YOUR DAUGHTER. TELL HER I SAID HAPPY BIRTHDAY. I'M SORRY I DIDN'T GET HER ANYTHING.
BUT YOU DID.
TAKE CARE. TALK SOON.

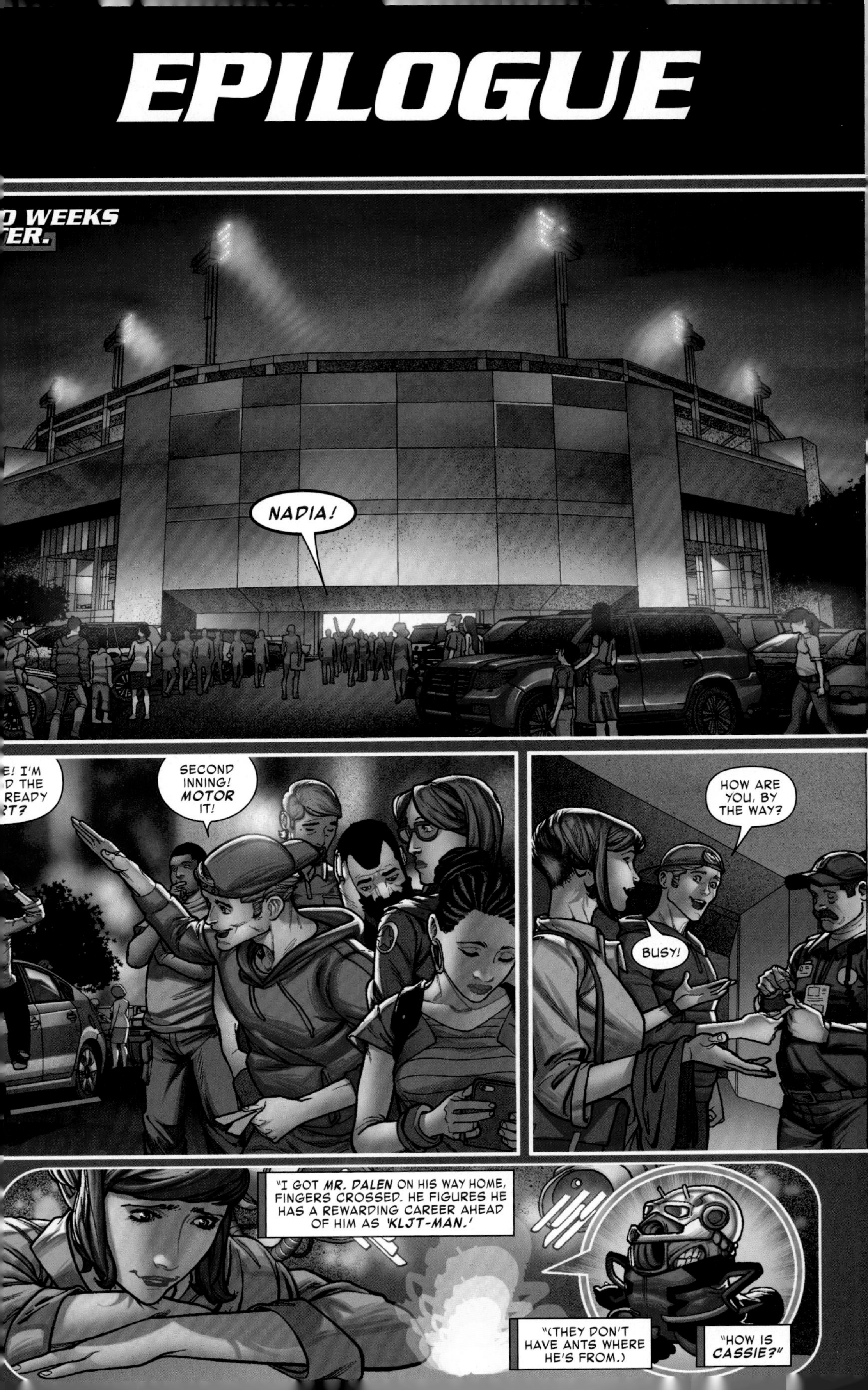
EPILOGUE
NADIA!
SECOND INNING! MOTOR IT!
HOW ARE YOU, BY THE WAY?
BUSY!
"I GOT MR. DALEN ON HIS WAY HOME, FINGERS CROSSED. HE FIGURES HE HAS A REWARDING CAREER AHEAD OF HIM AS 'KLJT-MAN.'
"(THEY DON'T HAVE ANTS WHERE HE'S FROM.)
"HOW IS CASSIE?"

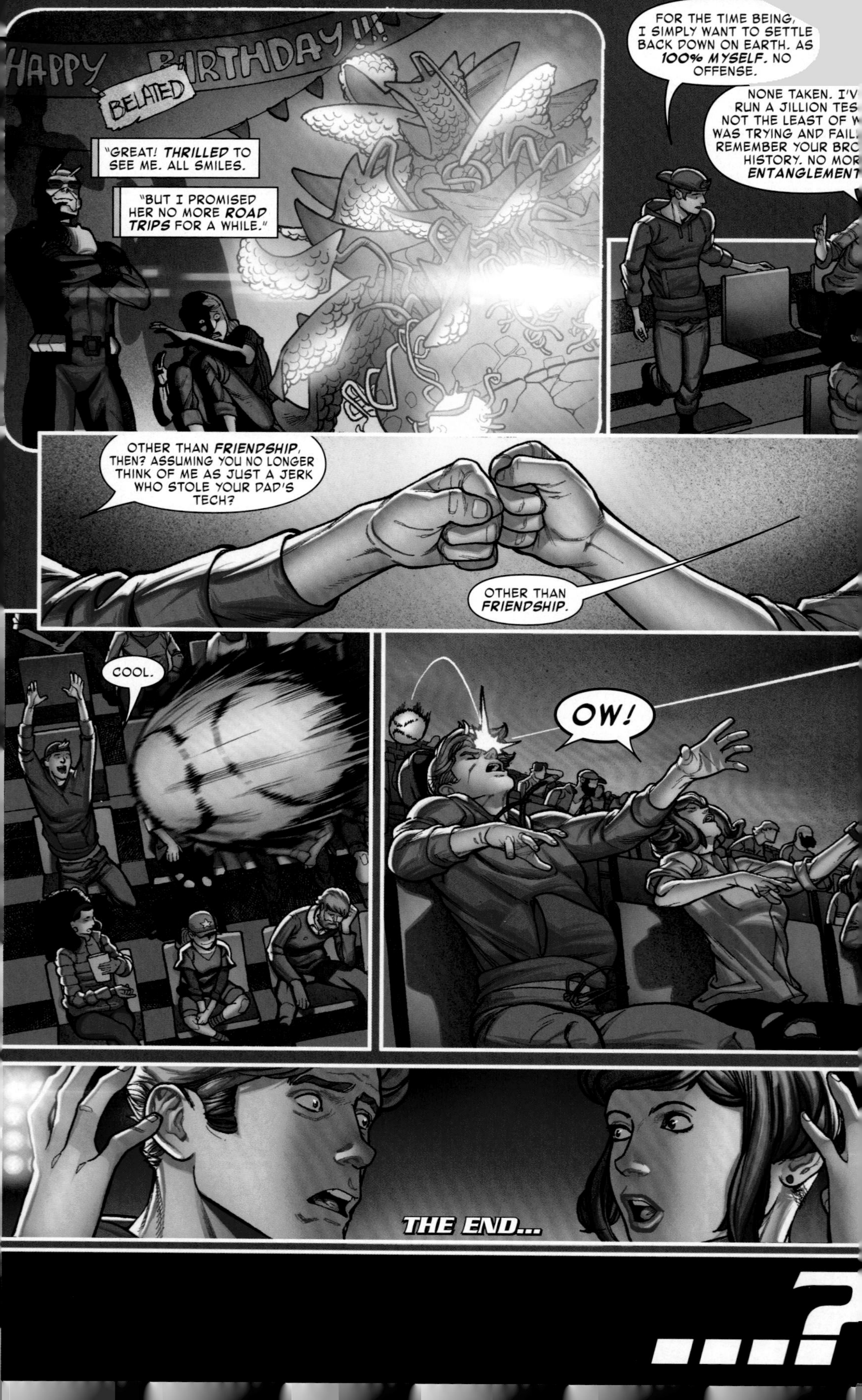

HAPPY BELATED BIRTHDAY!!!
"GREAT! THRILLED TO SEE ME. ALL SMILES.
"BUT I PROMISED HER NO MORE ROAD TRIPS FOR A WHILE."
FOR THE TIME BEING, I SIMPLY WANT TO SETTLE BACK DOWN ON EARTH. AS 100% MYSELF. NO OFFENSE.
NONE TAKEN. I'V RUN A JILLION TES NOT THE LEAST OF W WAS TRYING AND FAIL REMEMBER YOUR BRO HISTORY. NO MOR ENTANGLEMENT
OTHER THAN FRIENDSHIP, THEN? ASSUMING YOU NO LONGER THINK OF ME AS JUST A JERK WHO STOLE YOUR DAD'S TECH?
OTHER THAN FRIENDSHIP.
COOL.
OW!
THE END...
...?

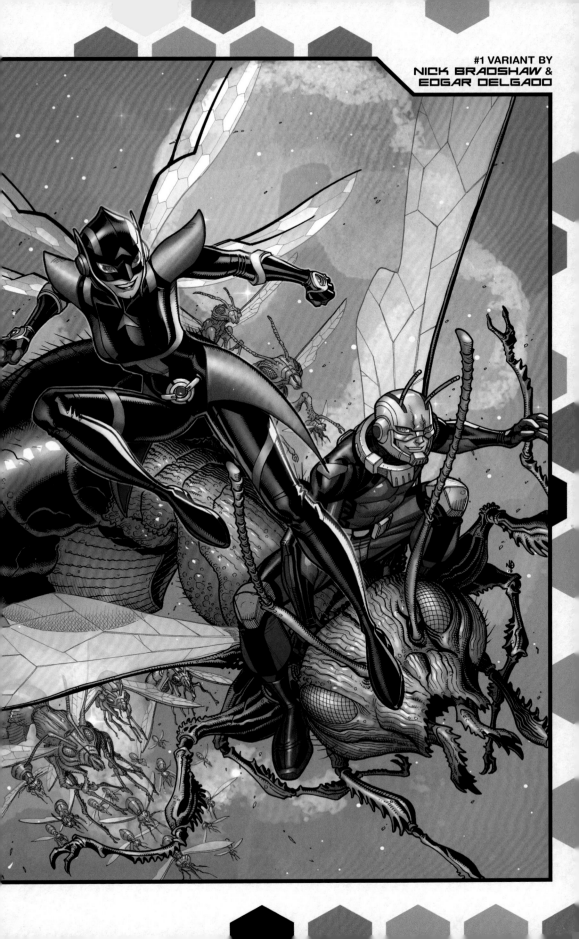

#1 VARIANT BY
NICK BRADSHAW &
EDGAR DELGADO

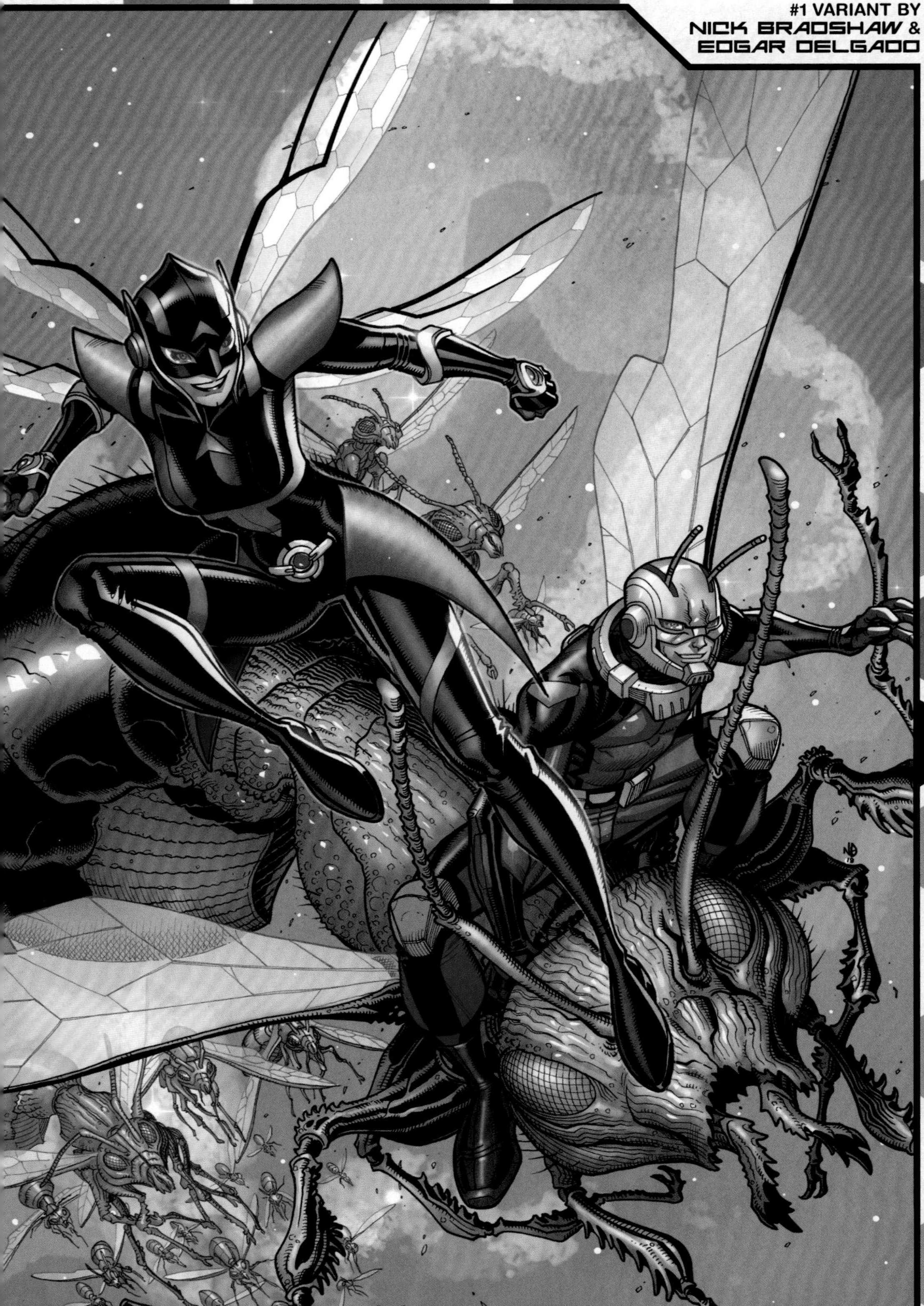

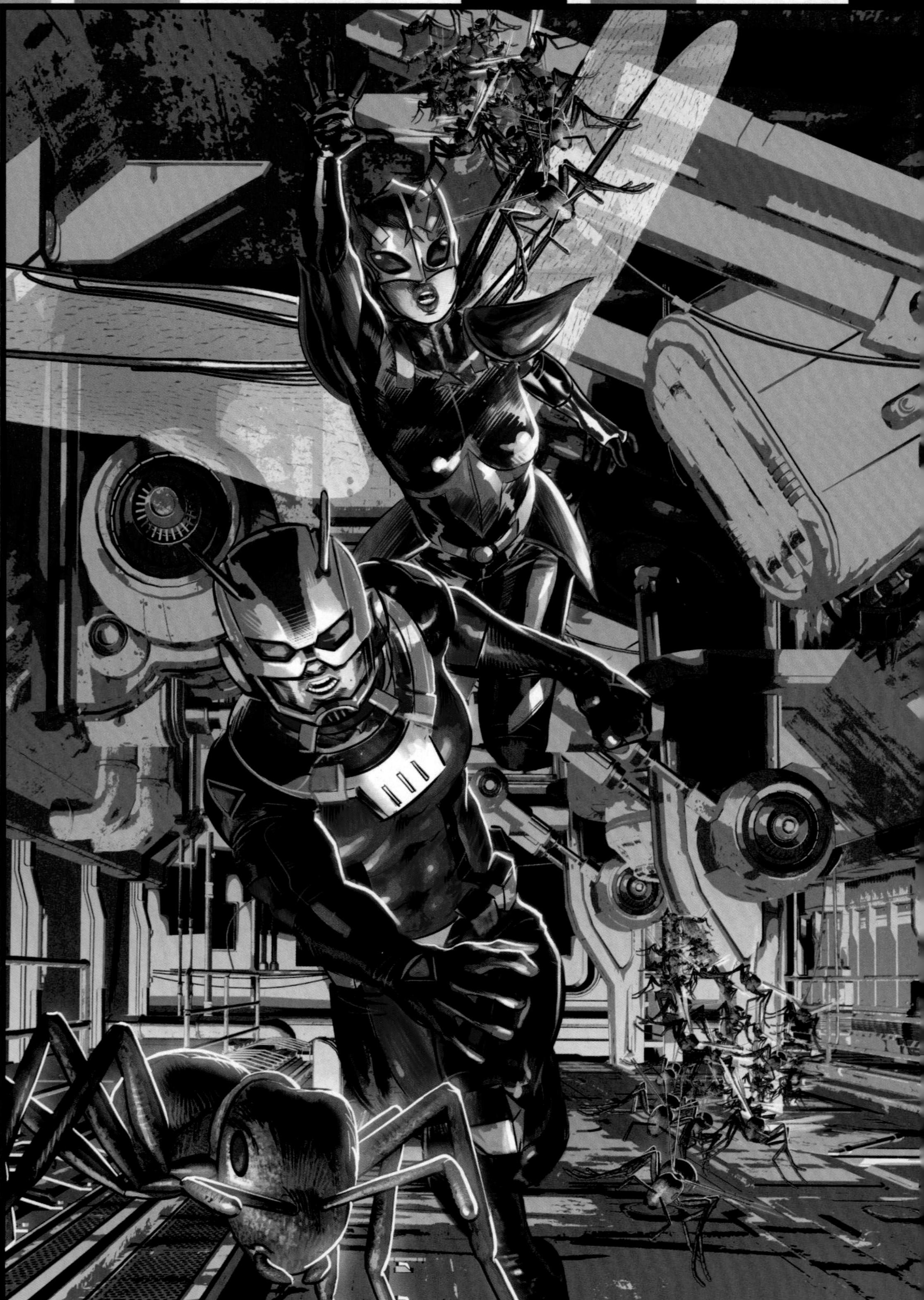

#1 VARIANT BY
MIKE DEODATO JR.
& RAIN BEREDO

#1 INTRODUCTION LETTER

**Oh no!
Looks like some errant Pym Particles got into the printer! Better get your Mighty Marvel Magnifying Glasses*, True Believers!**

***Regular magnifying glasses**

MICRO-FRIENDS!

Welcome to this new adventure! We assume you know Scott Lang, either from the many comics he's been in or...maybe...a big movie? With another one JUST MONTHS AWAY?!?! You may not know Nadia Pym, but you should! She's been on the Avengers over the last couple of years, but you have to check her out in Jeremy Whitley and Elsa Charretier's THE UNSTOPPABLE WASP! She's great and we're super excited for her to co-star here.

We here at Marvel would love to introduce you to a neophyte named Mark Waid. I'm sure he's written something, but I'm not familiar. Is he the guy who wrote that awesome AGE OF ULTRON A.I. Hank Pym one-shot? Couldn't be. Did he write those sweet AVENGERS issues that Nadia Pym was in? Can't be possible. He wasn't the guy who wrote DAREDEVIL and *Kingdom Come*, right? That's crazy talk. But I sure liked this issue.

Javier Garrón, on the other hand, is an accomplished and lovely man. Hailing from beautiful Barcelona, Javier has done some AMAZING SPIDER-MAN, SECRET WARRIORS, SECRET WARS and more! He was recently named one of our latest class of Marvel Young Guns and deservedly so. He has drawn some of the craziest things I've ever seen in upcoming issues.

And big thanks to Editor JORDAN D. WHITE, who did the hard editorial work and put this team together (including incredible cover artist David Nakayama, incredible colorist Israel Silva and our ever-faithful JOE CARAMAGNA, who lettered this while also lettering our 80-page AMAZING SPIDER-MAN #800)!

Mark, Javier and the rest of the team have so many astonishing plans for this book, and you're going to see a part of the Marvel Universe you've never seen before--THE MARVELOUS MICROVERSE!!! It helps that Mark, young and inexperienced in comics and the world in general as he is, is a huge physics nerd and has actually studied this sort of thing.

See you all in 30!
Nick

ANT-MAN
AND
WASP
1.
2.
3.
1.
2.

-5 COVER
ETCHES BY
AVID NAKAYAMA

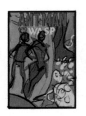

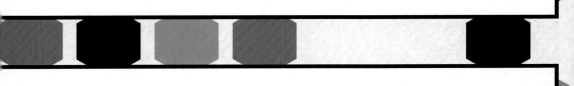

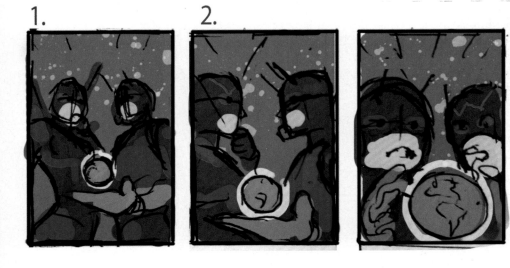

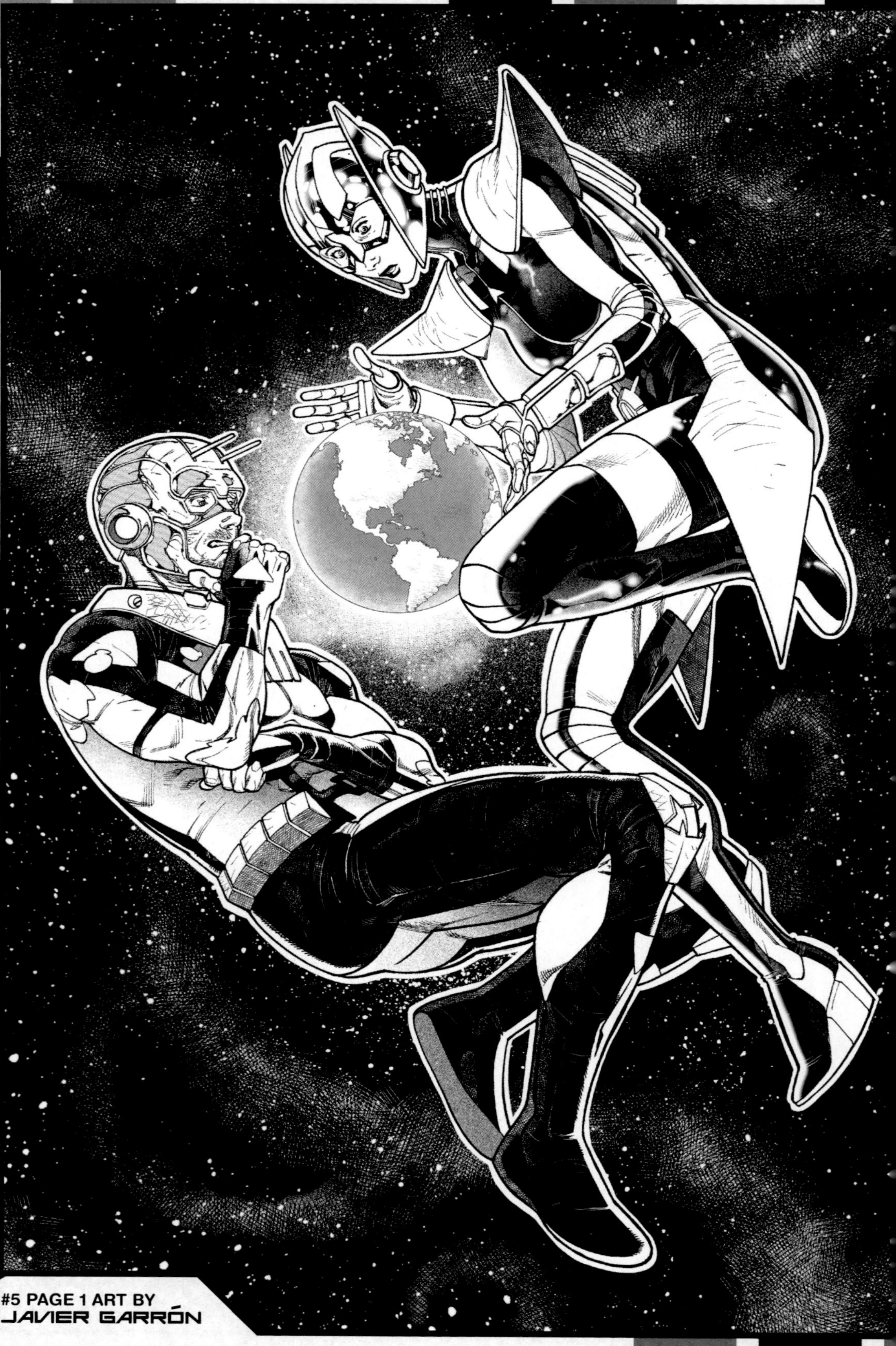

#5 PAGE 1 ART BY
JAVIER GARRÓN